Cornflakes with Whisky

Cornflakes with Whisky

*One career, two lives, one marriage — a
real story of community policing and of an
enduring relationship over four decades*

Les King

authorHOUSE®

AuthorHouse™ UK
1663 Liberty Drive
Bloomington, IN 47403 USA
www.authorhouse.co.uk
Phone: 0800.197.4150

Published by AuthorHouse 11/24/2015

ISBN: 978-1-4969-8699-3 (sc)
ISBN: 978-1-4969-8700-6 (e)

Print information available on the last page.

This book is printed on acid-free paper.

CONTENTS

DEDICATION

To Jud and all the long suffering partners of police officers
everywhere.

Jud,
You were there before the beginning, with me
throughout and still there long after this story ended –
with love and thanks for a long journey!

Les

FOREWORD

Based in the Midlands and particularly around the beautiful counties of Worcestershire, Herefordshire and Shropshire known as West Mercia this is a 'warts and all' story of community policing over four decades.

All cops who have served for some time could both tell and write some good stories.

In that respect this book is not unique. I hope that what is unique is that this story picks up the emotions, the characters and the true feelings that so often are not described when cops recount their experiences.

But, this is more. It is a story of two loves. The first is the love of a job that served me well for 33 years, spanning four decades, but, just as importantly it is a story of love and marriage that has survived even longer.

The job and the marriage were entwined inextricably because in the days when this story started they had to be – there was no choice.

Does this sound like survival? Well at times it probably was, for both of us. Do I regret any of it? No, not one bit. Does my wife Jud? Well, you had better ask her!

This is a story of being privileged. I feel privileged to have been allowed to experience the things I have seen and to have been allowed into the lives of the thousands of people I have met and dealt with. Some were bad, some were evil. Some were vulnerable and kind but all of them were fascinating.

To all the fantastic colleagues I have worked with, whether or not you are mentioned I thank you for great times and both the fond and sometimes tough memories we shared.

I am also privileged to have had the support, loyalty and love of my wife Jud and our two lovely daughters, Mandy and Caroline, who made it all possible.

I called this book 'Cornflakes with Whisky' and as you read on you will realise why in the early hours of the morning they provide a great antidote to hunger and stress.

This book is raw in parts. That is the way it was and the way it is. There is some crude language and some of it is from me. Sorry, but that is the way it happened and I hope it captures the moment.

As I recount some of the incidents from the 1970's onwards they feel anachronistic within the context of present day political correctness, but, they were regarded as correct at the time. They were also amusing then and I hope they will be now and that the reader will make allowances for the passage of time.

There are odd stories of people like the poacher who nailed his ear to a tree and the midnight milkman. There are also the more serious but personal accounts of some of the major murders and crimes that have rocked the midlands counties over the years.

Please note that names and details have been changed where I consider it necessary on grounds of confidentiality.

The views, accounts and indeed any errors recorded in this book are mine and mine alone and do not represent on behalf of either the police service generally or West Mercia Police specifically.

I hope you have a sense of humour and I hope you enjoy it.

Les King
2015

CHAPTER 1

SHARP INITIATION

Anybody reading this will know that when you are frightened about something but trying to look in control you develop a certain walk. Why? Because fear produces volatile gases up your backside which combined with a wet feeling in your underpants makes you walk with your legs tight together in mincing steps just in case something explodes and slips down your leg that is wet, warm and smelly.

I must have had this feeling and this walk when I was spotted by two off duty special constables who drove past when I was walking towards a local pub at Redditch during a fine spring afternoon in 1973.

It was my first week as a fledging young copper. I had paraded at 1.45pm and at 2pm was heading towards the town centre to face one of my first 'bottle' tests as a bobby. It was only a short 3 minute walk from Church Road where the 'nick' was but I had all the hallmarks of fright. Dry mouth, sweaty forehead and ass twitching half a crown and sixpence. I was to experience these feelings every day for the next 30 years!

The switchboard operator was fairly brief, 'You're on the town – there's a guy in the pub, he's playing up and the licensee wants him to leave, please deal. If you need assistance radio in.' I replied with a confidence that convinced the operator but not me that I was attending and in control.

As I entered the pub I remember trying to recall what they told me at the training school about the law and drunks failing to quit licensed premises. Sat at a table in the centre of the bar on his own and in stony silence was a man that I failed to observe was about twice the size of me. I was concentrating so hard on the law I also failed to take in that a broken flagon of cider and a load of broken optics indicated this man had picked up the flagon of cider and thrown it across the bar just missing the licensee. Things were not helped by virtue of the fact that the licensee was Italian and between the language barrier and his excitement I could not understand a bloody thing he was saying – all I knew was he was not happy and wanted this guy out of his pub!

Summoning up all of my 5'9' stature and feeling very vulnerable and conspicuous in my uniform I was aware that that the world and their wife were now in this pub to see what was going to happen next and whether or not I would 'bottle' it. 'Excuse me mate, the licensee wants you to leave, can you please go.' Stony silence was the reply. 'Listen, if you do not go I will have to arrest you.' 'Fuck off,' came the reply. I was relieved we were now developing a rapport!

'If you do not leave I will have to arrest you.' 'Fuck off,' he said, but this time with feeling.

Now I am not the sharpest tool in the box but I was fast getting the impression he was not going to play ball and my first arrest was imminent.

'I am now arresting you............' CRASH!!! the world exploded as this mountain of a bloke stood up and brought the card table he had been sitting behind crashing down onto my head and shoulders. Pain, shock, bewilderment and total panic now took over.

We both ended up on the floor, my radio and helmet went flying and we set to in a really good scrap. Never mind the law, this was survival. He was not the last bloke I was to meet in the Police whom I would fight and realise was a lot bigger and harder than I would ever be. I just hung on to him and shouted to the licensee words of two syllables understood in any language together with a plea to get me some help and quick. I was losing it fast, my muscles were aching and I felt sick.

Fortunately, the two off duty special constables who had seen me waddle into the pub a few minutes before decided that I looked like I needed a bit of help and had followed me.

The four of us had a really nice time rolling around the floor to the cheers of the locals for what seemed like eternity before eventually this mountain of a man was subdued and handcuffed.

Now, at times like this as you are trying to regain your composure, I find you worry about the daftest of things like, 'Where's my helmet and radio?' I found my radio very quickly, but I could not see my helmet and realising that it may be a discipline offence to go back to the nick without it I started searching frantically. One very helpful customer upon realising what I was looking for said, 'Officer, don't worry I will help you find it.' Suddenly my faith in 'joe public' was restored but instantly destroyed when he continued, 'What colour is it?' Now I realised he was taking the piss and somehow I just didn't see the funny side of it but I did retrieve the helmet and made my back to the station.

Chummy (everybody was called chummy) was charged with assault and failing to quit licensed premises. Fortunately the only bit of me that was seriously injured was my pride. It transpired that this guy was not a bad lad really. He had never been in trouble before and had recently suffered a tragic death in the family. Tensions had mounted and after going on a bender I was the first person to cross his path.

So, this was my inauguration into the foibles of operational policing at Redditch New Town. At the age of 19 years I was posted there after initial training and had never heard of the place.

I soon found out that this incident of violence was not to be an isolated occurrence in the Police and that during the next two years I was to become very familiar with the local Smallwood Hospital – as a patient!

I came from a little village near Bromyard in Herefordshire and it is fair to say that Redditch might as well have been on the other side of the world for all it had in common with Bromyard. However, I soon settled in and the highlight became the Classic cinema on Unicorn Hill where during a week of 2pm-10pm shifts you could see a whole film if you went in at staggered times!

I was on a shift of about 6 constables and our Sergeant was Geoff 'have a fag kid' Benbow. Geoff acquired this nickname because being blessed with a high level of interpersonal skills he was accustomed to calming down the most violent of prisoners with a chat and the offer of a fag. So persistent was Geoff that even those who didn't smoke succumbed in the face of his persuasion just to keep him happy! We were all young bobbies on the shift and Geoff who had been an experienced detective prior to being promoted to uniform Sergeant was like a 'dad' to us. A big, jovial man with a fantastic sense of humour and a big heart we learned to respect Geoff as our 'Sarge.' He was fiercely loyal towards us and nothing ever fazed him. Like all Sergeants in those days he was the 'gaffer' and seemed to know everything. Geoff allocated me a parent constable, Chris Chetwyn. Chris only had about 6 months service in the job, but six months was light years in terms of experience to me.

One of the first jobs I went to with Chris was a sudden death where he was to show me the ropes. This old chap had dropped down dead in one of the local factories. The doctor declined to issue a death certificate so it became a Coroners case where the Police investigate. Before we arrived at the factory the body had been removed to the local mortuary. We collected the man's elderly wife and took her to the mortuary to identify the body of her husband. Chris stressed to me the sensitivity of these procedures which must be done formally. Chris pulled back the sheet from the over the body and immediately the man's bald head was uncovered the woman started to cry hysterically. Not wishing to prolong her agony we accepted the identification as positive and arranged to get her a lift home.

Chris then explained to me that one of the jobs (in those days) was to strip the body of all clothing and possessions and ensure they were bagged and labelled as well as inspect the body for any suspicious marks. He whipped back the sheet completely whereupon we realised that not only was the body completely naked and clean but that it had been subject to a post mortem. Now, there was no way that a chap who had just dropped dead in a factory had been stripped, post-mortemed and cleaned in that time! Ohhhh… Shit! We had the wrong body identified! So, where was the real body? Chris and I hunted high and low through all the fridges – no body! A variety of shapes and sizes but not one that resembled the one we were after.

After a while we went to the station and confessed all to Geoff. Wrong body, wrong identification and lost the real body. Geoff took it all very calmly as he always did. 'Listen kid, I have been in this job years and one thing I do know is that stiffs don't bloody walk, now bugger off back to the morgue and don't come back until you've found it.'

We did. Eventually we found the real body in one of the metal carrying trolleys with enclosed sides! Phew! Next problem, how do you tell a woman who has been married 40 years of her life to the same husband that she has identified the wrong man?!

I thanked Chris for lending me the benefit of his experience.

It was not long before I had to attend my first post mortem. Whilst on a 2-10 shift I was walking back to the station which in those days was not far from the mortuary at the back of the Smallwoood hospital when I was told via the radio that I was to meet an undertaker at the mortuary who was bringing in a body. My job was to help unload the body into the mortuary, get the undertaker to formally identify the body to me and then stick a label on it with his name (the body's name that is, not the undertakers!) The following day I was to come on early attend the post mortem and identify the body to the pathologist and mortician.

As I walked towards Church Street along Church Green the hearse drove past me. Because it was a chilly evening I wondered why all the windows and tailgate of the hearse were open. A few seconds later I was met by the most god awful smell and it didn't take me long to realise why. This chap lived alone out in the country and had had been lain dead for several days in front of an electric fire. The body was putrefied! It stank like hell!

There was no sentiment because what was left didn't resemble much like a body anyway.

I put a hanky round my face, ran into the mortuary put a label on what I think was a toe and hoped it would still be in place in the morning. I tell you, I was in and out of that mortuary like a rat out of a drain. However, the next day was even greater fun.

Attending post mortems is a ritual you go through in the Force. The other ritual is being told you must have a full breakfast before you go. 'It will make you feel better they told me – settles the stomach!'

As I approached the outside of the mortuary next morning I could hear the sound of something like a drill whirring. 'Strange, doing a bit of DIY at this time,' I thought naively. As I walked in, bloody hell, I thought I was in an abattoir. Bodies everywhere and all cut open. I avoided looking around and tried to concentrate on finding the remains of my man with the label on his toe. Big mistake - that was the body the mortician was working on and the sound I had heard was the small circular saw he was using to take off the top of his head! 'Can you identify him?' he said, in all seriousness. The irony of asking me to identify a body that in the first place was putrefied and in the second place had just had the only bit removed I might have stood a chance at recognising seemed to pass him by. The only thing that I could identify was the smell! I quickly looked at the label said, 'Yes that's him, got to go, got a call on the radio,' and fled outside as fast as I could. The only thing I did achieve was keeping the breakfast down!

The next stage was passing a test to drive Police vehicles. I had a one day test which qualified me to drive unmarked police cars only, vehicles with no blue lights or Police markings. It was great not to have to walk the town all the time.

We were on nights and I was on general cover of Redditch New Town which in those days had a population of around 60,000. Major development was taking place both in the town centre and on the outskirts.

Just before mid-night we received a 999 call to attend Ipsley Court where there was a report of intruders. I made my way as fast as I could in my plain vehicle which was a CID Mini Clubman. Chris Chetwyn shouted up to say he would also attend. I made a discreet approach which means turn off headlights and drive quietly as you approach the area, park a short distance away and then walk to the location and check it out. Chris joined me, we walked round. No sign of intruders or a break-in so we decided to make our back to the nick for a cup of tea.

Ipsley Court was being built at the time as a large office block. It was a building site and ripe for disaster for some enterprising young Police driver. Determined to get back before Chris I started up the car, put the headlights on and swung it round in one fell swoop.

Suddenly I was confronted by a low brick wall which surrounded a bloody big hole containing soil and gravel where they intended to plant a large tree.

I braked fiercely, but my right boot which was covered in mud from walking round the site slipped off the brake straight onto the accelerator. The car lurched straight over the low wall into the hole and remained with its ass end sticking up and its front end buried in the hole. I discreetly called Chris back via the radio and wondered how I was going to get out of this. I had only been driving a few days and had now knackered up the CIDs pride and joy! Chris gave it a quick once over and seemed optimistic we could get it out of the hole and nobody would be any the wiser. 'The only problem is that the front offside wing is bent out but I reckon if I kick it in just the right place it will spring back in – there's no paint missing!' Chris did just that. The wing sprang back into position as sweet as a nut – for a split second. Then it sprang back out again and a million particles of paint floated over us. I looked at Chris and under the headlights of the Police car I could see one flake resting on his forehead. He said words which immortalised the situation, 'I think that's just about knackered it Les. Game's up'

We called the Sarge on the radio. Geoff arrived, lit up a fag, surveyed the situation and said to me, 'Think you've buggered that up kid.' By that he meant the accident had to be formally investigated and I was to be suspended from driving Police vehicles until the inquiry was over and a decision made. Back to walking! We lifted the car out of the hole and Geoff instructed me to drive it back to the station where it was abandoned. When the vehicle examiner looked at it at a few days later he wrote it off because the suspension and chassis were knackered. They could not do me for driving carelessly because the accident did not occur on a road. However, the report came back and said I was to be severely admonished. Geoff called me in and said, 'It says here I have got to give you formal advice and admonish you. I will just say this, consider yourself bollocked and take more care in future.' 'Thanks Sarge', I said, gratefully and picked up a set of panda car keys to start again.

If there is one thing I never ever got used to in the Police that never failed to surprise me is the conditions that some other people live in. I grew up in a fairly impoverished country house with no modern amenities, a pee pot under the bed and in winter, ice on the inside of the windows.

However, nothing would prepare me for some of the sights I would see in other people's homes.

A little while after I was back driving the plain vehicle I was sent to a call at a house on one of the older estates at Redditch where a notorious family lived. I was told that there were a number of kids in the family, all of which were in care but one had gone missing and I needed to carry out a home visit, conduct a search and if necessary take the kid back to social services. Armed with directions and a description I made my way. As I left the station I was given a few knowing grins by colleagues but didn't think much of it.

When I reached the house it was on a typical brick built post war council estate. The garden at the house was like a wilderness with grass several feet high that had never been cut littered with bits of metal and old bicycle parts.

I went via the most walked down area of grass to the front door and was about to knock when I realised that there was no door just a boarded up doorway with one wedge of wood missing just wide enough to step through.

'Surely no-one lives here?' I thought to myself. I stepped through into the hall and shouted, 'Is there anybody in?' No reply. Just off the hall to the left was a kitchen.

Other than the fact that it was just about the dirtiest room I had ever seen the one thing that struck me was that the sink was piled up with utensils and on the cooker was a frying pan about two inches deep that was overflowing with fat because it had never been cleaned. Obviously the house was inhabited.

The next thing that hit me was the smell. A horrible fousty smell combined with the smell of crap. Then I heard snoring coming from upstairs. I crept up the stairs which were bare boards and the snoring led me into the main bedroom where I could make out the body of what appeared to be an old man lay on a bed which contained just a moth eaten old mattress and a coat. As the floorboards creaked he stirred, opened up one eye and just stared at me without any surprise. Obviously he was used to Police visitors.

I adopted the usual authoritative inquiring Police voice and requested to know who he was.

He replied in words of two syllables, turned over and went back to sleep.

I decided to persist with my task and visit the bathroom and toilet which is very quickly where I ascertained the smell was coming from. The loo was completely full of shit, right to the top of the pan.

Now in my naive muckspreading country way having grown up with outside toilets where you had to dig a big hole to bury it at least once a month I have always been intrigued by the modern flush toilet and regarded it as rather a luxury. I thought that the least I could do was flush the loo even if they were too idle to do it themselves. So I did.

What I had not reckoned upon was a volcanic eruption that started with a gurgle and then overflowed liked a nuclear explosion showering shit left right and centre over the bathroom and pebble dashing everything in sight including me.

I ran down the stairs as fast as I could, my boots covered in muck. I made it outside and was never so relieved to smell fresh air. I radioed the result in, 'Thorough, search of house, no trace of child but bit of a shitty experience really!'

Eventually Police were stopped going to the address because of the fear for health and safety, but that was too late for me. Throughout my Police service I was to experience the effects of poverty and deprivation but surely there can never be reasons other than perhaps mental health for people to live in conditions like that? Unfortunately, as any Police Officer or member of public sector services who regularly visit homes will tell you these experiences are not isolated, even today.

Besides Chris who was appointed my mentor (he came from Staffordshire and was and always has been an ardent Stoke City supporter) there was a good shift of colleagues and all of us were young. In fact the oldest member only had 6 years service so that must have put a lot of responsibility on Geoff to supervise us.

There was Ken 'never hurry a' Murray who took everything in his stride and was ace on a snooker table. Alfie Elliot who was a cockney with a wicked sense of humour and in both name and features resembled Alf Garnett on the notorious TV programme 'Till Death Us Do Part'.

Then there was John Price. John came from Hereford and later was to be my best man. I always admired John because he was very keen and very ambitious and married to a Chief Inspector's daughter. However, whilst some people try to be one of the boys but really they are not, John was the opposite. He really was one of the boys but tried hard not to be. No matter how hard he tried to be good, either temptation or his thirst for good old fashioned positive policing would ensure John ended up in the proverbial. That's why I admired him!

Tony Langford also came from Hereford. A slim and good-looking sod with jet black hair. What really upsets me about Tony is that now 40 years later he is still a slim good looking sod with black hair! I hate him!

Tony was one of my drinking partners. Another one was Denville Wyke. Denville came from the wilds of Shropshire and was from farming stock – like me he was a true country boy and we became good friends.

Mick O'Donnell was another sound guy on the shift. Also young and good looking he was fit, athletic and could handle himself.

There was also Steve Jones from Much Wenlock in Shropshire. Another drinking partner Steve was also very keen and would book anything that moved.

Finally there was Jim Lucas. Jim along with Alfie Elliot was one of the 'daddies' on the shift with a few years service in. Always good for sound advice and totally reliable they both made good mentors.

Most of us were single in those days and free evenings were spent on the beer or partying until the early hours around the pubs in Redditch. A week of seven early turns (6am to 2pm) shifts was a whirl of up at 5 am and work till 2pm. Go to bed in the afternoon and then get up and go on the beer until the early hours. By the time the seventh shift came you didn't know whether it was morning, noon or bloody night. Many was the time during a winter evening when I would wake up at tea time, get dressed in uniform and start to make my way to work only to realise it really 6pm not 6am!

Another favourite pastime was snooker. After a 2pm to 10pm shift we would line up a few pints in the Police club and then play until the early hours of the morning. I never seemed as good as the other lads and usually played with a bent cue. As the others used to remark, 'A bent cue and the way Les plays, things even themselves out!'

Initially I lived in digs on a nice estate called Webheath. My landlady was very nice and made me welcome but my landlord Ray was rather gruff. After I had been there several months he suddenly said to me one morning, 'We are moving next week to a house on the other side of town, but you are not moving with us!' I took that as a hint that I needed to find alternative digs. Eventually I moved into fantastic lodgings at Studley just on the outskirts of Redditch but in Warwickshire where the food and company was fantastic. I remained there until I got married in 1975.

There were some real characters in the Police Station and most of them had rank. The two Inspectors were Ray Lloyd and Jim Cole.

Ray was a softly spoken Salopian with a twinkle in his eye, a big beaming smile and a face that never seem to age. His quiet and steady personality however belied a sharp wit and a shrewd character that meant whenever we were up to something we shouldn't be Ray would appear out the blue just in the nick of time to stop us! He always knew where we were and what we were up to.

Jim Cole was like me from Herefordshire with a broad accent to match. A very positive and up-front man Jim believed in leading from the front and would stand no messing from anyone. He used to say to us, 'If any of these yobbos want to fight you on the town give 'em some 'ammer!' Like many old style cops of that era he believed in summary justice.

The Sergeants were all of the same mould as well. They were positive, strong individuals who led by example with hard exteriors and hearts of gold.

Roy 'Basher' Burrett was one of those. Roy was an ex-guardsman and a large framed hard man who ruled his shift with a rod of iron believing in strict discipline until he knocked you into shape. He was known as 'basher' because he had a fearsome reputation amongst the local yobbish community as someone who you did not cross. Roy's personal philosophy was, 'If you've got to go to a fight make sure you enjoy yourself whilst you are there'.

He also suffered from a bad back which used to infuriate him in which case the first person who crossed his path would cop the fury of his temper. Heaven forbid if you dare come into the station early before the end of your shift. His favourite trick then was to send you back out and tell you not to return until you had booked someone when he would be waiting for you no matter how long it took. However, Roy was certainly not the iron fist in a velvet glove – he was the opposite. Very much a loving family man he cared for those around him and supported many officers through acts of welfare advice and help.

Whilst he imposed a tough regime on his shift he was the first to support them if ever they were in trouble or had been treated unfairly. Senior officers feared Roy knocking their doors because of his direct up-front personal approach. Nobody criticised his officers unless it went through him.

One of his pals was a fellow Sergeant, John Bradburn. John was another big hard man with hands the size of a frying pan who again led from the front. John was actually responsible for me getting married ….but more of that later!

Perhaps the greatest character of all was Sergeant Richard Thornton-Pett. Richard, known as 'Dick', a man of immense depth whose life and tales would merit a book on their own.

Richard was a highly intelligent, articulate man who was very well educated. He had served in the navy and seen and done most things in life. On nights he would allow us to smoke on the streets after 1 o' clock providing we were discreet. This was unusual because in other respects he was typical of the strict disciplinarian Sergeants who existed at that time and could be very harsh.

On one occasion Richard paraded us for duty on early turn and had forgotten to put his tie on. Because we were so in awe of him not one of us had the bottle to tell him. When he realised he gave us all a fierce bollocking for not telling him.

He also had an old Austin Maxi car which he called 'Bess' and which he daily abandoned on a tip of waste ground at the back of the police station each time he came to work. Uncared for and unwashed, full of fag packets it was his work horse but became almost as much of a character as himself.

Richard had a large family. When I knew him he lived at the Police Station at Astwood Bank just outside Redditch. Previous to that he had lived in one of the police houses next to the station which was then turned into the police kitchen. On nights I can recall him staring into the fire-place and with a faraway look in his eye reminiscing how much fun he had enjoyed in front of the fire-place!

He enjoyed making homemade wines and relishes. One afternoon whilst on a 2-10 shift I was sent to his home to tell him he was required in Court next day. Knowing that firstly he would not welcome being disturbed on a day off and secondly would not welcome going to Court next day I walked up the path to his house full of trepidation to be met with the smell of pickles and spices. He came to the door and I broke the news. 'Wait there and don't move', he bellowed at me. I froze not knowing what to expect. He returned with a jar of homemade marmalade which was overflowing with no top on it. 'Take this, eat it and enjoy it young man', he said. I drove back trying to balance this jar of marmalade as well as drive. I didn't particularly like marmalade but knew I must eat it because if I didn't somehow I felt he would know because Richard knew everything!

All of these men were characters of immense strength whose knowledge and ability to deal with any situation knew no bounds and of whom we all had tremendous respect. They epitomised leadership qualities by 'leading by example' and taking responsibility for their decisions and actions. They were always positive, firm and fair. I am sure they influenced all of us as constables and there was nothing we would not have done for them because they earned our respect the hard way.

On nights we were very often supervised by the night Inspector from Stourbridge who only visited very irregularly so there was plenty of time for practical jokes.

On one occasion on nights one of the shift members locked Jim Lucas in the toilet (or so he thought). After about half an hour he returned to unlock the door to find it was not Jim at all but the duty Inspector from Stourbridge who had crept into the station quietly to catch us out but had decided to have a crap on the way. 'Birchy' as he was known was not impressed at all. He just did not see the funny side of it. The problem was Geoff did. When Birchy went to remonstrate with Geoff about it, all Geoff could do was laugh whereupon Birchy turned on his heel and fled out of the station.

Unfortunately, life at Redditch had its hard times as well. A common denominator was violence and literally fighting for a living. As a New Town the population had soared but Police strength had remained static. We were lucky to put out 3 or 4 officers on an average nightshift and the workload was very busy. On a Friday and Saturday night it was routine for the 2pm to 10pm shift to stay on until about 1am on overtime to double up numbers. On a Saturday night in September 1974 we were on nights and Sgt John Bradburn's shift were on 2pm to 10pm. Around midnight all hell broke loose resulting in a lot of fighting between some of the local youths and the Police which started at the usual trouble spot of the 'hot dog' stand in Market Place. John Bradburn stood no messing and took the lead in ensuring order was resumed very quickly. John Bradburn and Roy Burrett were both Sergeants out of the same mould. Neither would start a fight unnecessarily but if someone wanted to fight they could willingly accommodate them!

On this particular night even when back at the nick the prisoners still wanted to fight and an almighty scrap took place in the parade/charge room area between us and the prisoners. The parade room was adjacent to the control room with a small hatch door that divided them. My mate Tony Langford was the duty officer in the control room and being a nosey bugger decided to put his head through the hatch to see what was happening. One of the prisoners decided at this precise moment that this was his opportunity and hit Tony smack in the face with a clenched fist.

Tony was sent reeling on his arse and became one of the few control room operators to be physically injured on duty!

In a nutshell the Police won the fight but more was to come. The following night was a Sunday when the pubs in those days shut at 10.30pm and was therefore regarded as a quiet night when we were down to minimum strength. The local troublemakers knew this and a number of them decided to set us up and get their own back following the previous night's fracas.

About 10.30pm we received a '999' call that a fight was taking place at the hot dog stand. I attended together with Geoff Benbow, Ken Morrey, Mick O'Donnell and Tony Langford.

When we arrived there were about 40 men and I mean men, not just youngsters present. There was a deathly hush and no fight. We asked what the trouble was but received no response. I was standing next to Geoff and when we realised there was no fight we started to turn around to leave. Suddenly a man stepped out from the crowd and shouted, 'Is that the bastard Sergeant?' It became apparent later that they had mistaken Geoff for John Bradburn who had led the arrest party the previous night and had been forced to take one or two of them on.

Geoff tried to calm the man down but he was not having any of it. He stripped off his jacket and moved threateningly towards Geoff. I remember my last naive and pathetic words, 'Do you want him arresting Sarge?'

Suddenly the whole bloody world exploded. What seemed like the majority of the crowd turned on us and beat seven bells of crap out of us. No time to radio for assistance (not that there was any more to be had anyway), no time to draw our truncheons, it was a complete ambush of about 40 to 5. We were heavily outnumbered and they were out for vengeance not caring what they did. All I remember is a sea of bodies and trying to make a grab at someone who was hitting out towards another officer. I was then hit hard in the face and dragged to the ground. Once on the ground I felt a series of kicking blows to my body and face and I struggled back on my feet. Once on my feet I tried to arrest and struggle with another man up against the hot dog stand who was fighting with colleagues. He hit me and I went back on the floor with several of them hanging on round my neck. At this point I remember thinking, 'Where the hell is Geoff, for

Christ sake come and give me a hand'. Then through the corner of my eye I could see Geoff who had two youths hanging on round his neck and a third hitting him. I realised he had his problems too!

I was dragged back onto the ground where I was again repeatedly kicked. I just concentrated now on survival in trying to protect my face and goolies. This was shitty, and I was scared as to how we were going to survive. It seemed to go on for eternity and I knew there was nothing we could do except take a battering. Eventually it ended and they ran off. I managed to get to my feet and surveyed what had happened. All I can recall is seeing Geoff who was bleeding from the lip and for once was not laughing! Then I saw Tony Langford who fresh from the previous night's smacking was now lying prostrate across the bonnet of a car having had another dink. He always seemed to be lying around! There were no arrests but at least we were all alive.

Anyone who has ever been in a situation like that will tell you that you exist on adrenalin. I felt no pain just fear. I felt fine but my face felt wet and I assumed it was because I had been spat on. It was when someone asked me what the hell had happened to me that I realised I was bleeding profusely from my left eyebrow and that my face was swelling up fast. Now I felt sick!

Tony and I both ended up in Smallwood Hospital casualty department that night on adjoining trolleys and were carefully attended to by the local nurses who gave us dressings, tea and sympathy. I had a few stitches in my eyebrow and plenty of painkillers.

There was no time to go sick. Reinforcements were called out of bed and we drove round trying to identify anyone involved. We went off duty at 6am and returned a few hours later to assist the CID in identifying the culprits.

As if that wasn't bad enough the Crown Court trial that followed was worse. Several months later a hardcore minority of the major offenders appeared before Birmingham Crown Court charged with affray and assault. This was only the second time in my career I had given evidence in Court and we were warned that we would be required for at least a week.

In the Police they talk about the Crown Court crap. It's where butterflies and adrenalin manifest themselves in the urge to defecate at regular intervals whilst squeezing your head in a trap one cubicle before giving evidence. There were plenty of times that week when Tony Langford and I shared adjoining cubicles whilst dreading the experience of going into the witness box.

Eventually towards the end of the week I was finally called into the witness box. Any copper will tell you that most would rather face a good fight on the street any day than be mauled by a barrister in the witness box. Normally you get two barristers, one for the prosecution and one for the defence. On this occasion because of the number of defendants there were at least six for the defence. They kept bobbing up and down like bloody topsy asking question after question trying to trip me up over my evidence in an attempt to vindicate their client. Problem was when you were answering the question you couldn't work out which defendant they were representing until they gave you a self-satisfied smirk when they had scored a point. However, in a way it was easy. It was just a case of recalling the truth of what happened and sticking to the facts.

I have to say because we were young fresh-faced officers the court appeared receptive to our evidence and the truth of what we saying just shone out despite the attempts by the various counsel to malign it.

On the Friday the trial was to continue but we were sent home because our evidence was completed. I breathed a sigh of relief and headed home to Bromyard for a well earned restful weekend.

Unfortunately, no sooner had I arrived at my parents' house than the local Bromyard bobby arrived and told me that I was required back in Crown Court on the Monday because there was to be a retrial! Why? Apparently one of the detectives in the case had allegedly been seen by a member of the defence in a pub over lunch talking to one of the jurors. The whole bloody thing had to be done again.

The following week we went through the same ritual with a new jury but this time the process was speeded up somewhat.

Eventually it was completed. The defendants were found guilty and sentenced to various terms of imprisonment. It was over! Overall the experience of giving evidence was probably worse than the beating.

There were two aspects that followed this incident which act as appropriate philosophical postscripts. The first involved counselling and the second marriage.

Within a month of being beaten up I was summoned to the office of a Chief Inspector who was a prim and proper character, always immaculately dressed with dark black hair that was always greased across his head. He had sharp features, a bellowing loud voice and staring eyes that used to frighten the hell out of us. When I entered his office I was full of trepidation and expecting a telling-off over something I had done wrong.

I remained whilst he said to me, 'Following your beating young man, how do you feel about walking the streets at night on your own now?' I immediately smelt a rat and replied, 'I am paid to do a job sir and I will continue to do it, no matter what.'

The Chief Inspector smiled and said, 'Good lad, because I was going to say, if the heat is too hot in the kitchen piss off out. This is a man's job and it takes a man to do it. Now sod off back out on the streets.' (Days of equal ops language was not yet born!)

This then was my back to work counselling and welfare session over! Eventually I settled £250 criminal injuries compensation money and with the proceeds my fiancée Jud and I later got married in 1975.

Meanwhile, the Chief Inspector's words were not totally worthless because the reality is you had to cope and my fighting days were not over. Within one month of the hot dog incident we ended up back at the hot dog stand fighting again.

This time a young amateur boxer was warned to move off the street to prevent an obstruction and refused to go. John Price said to him, 'If you don't move I will arrest you.' His reply was curt and to the point. 'If you try and arrest me copper you will end up in hospital.'

Well, to cut a long story short, John did arrest him and did end up in hospital! It went something like this:

John said, 'I am now arresting you for obstruction…………..' The boxer was holding a hotdog in one hand and a hot drink in the other. In one swift and furiously fast movement the boxer opened his hands and the drink and hotdog fell towards the floor. Before they had reached the floor the boxer struck John twice in the face with two of the fastest combination punches I have ever seen. The only thing that was slow was the way John fell to the ground in a crumpled heap.

I looked around; fortunately I was there with two other colleagues. One of them was my mate Denville Wyke. We both went in to arrest him. However, using his boxing sense he backed up into a corner between the hot dog stand and a wire fence where we could only approach him one at a time. As we went in he hit Denville knocking him backwards. Two of us were left to grapple with him and a fierce fight ensued for several minutes resulting in one hell of a struggle which we, the Police were starting to lose fast. After what seemed ages the boxer suddenly said, 'OK let's stop this before someone gets really hurt. I have loads left in me and I am really enjoying this but step back, let me go and I will walk straight into the back of that Police van.'

This seemed like a reasonable deal and because we were both knackered my colleague and I stepped back whereupon the boxer stepped straight into the Police van and was taken to the Police station. Phewww! What a relief.

The boxer went to Court, was convicted of assault Police. John and Denville were sore but got better!

One of the most common incidents the Police get called to is domestic violence in the home. They were referred to as 'domestics' in my day and one thing you knew was that you got no thanks from anyone and were always on a no win with a domestic. The ploy was get out of the house as fast as you could and only intervene if it was really necessary.

Within the context of how these incidents are dealt with today we provided a very poor service to the victims in those days, most of whom were women. But there are domestics and domestics as the two examples below will show.

One winter's night I was called to a house on the New Town at Redditch where there was the usual report of raised voices in a house reported by a neighbour. When I arrived a woman answered the door who was crying and obviously very upset. Inside the house a few things were tipped over and a young man with a bad attitude was stood in the living room shouting loudly and telling the world, me and the woman to f*** off. I also noticed glass smashed in the front door and assumed it had been kicked in.

The woman did not appear injured but wanted the man to leave. I led him to the front door where he started to struggle. By this time I had been joined by Ken Morrey, Geoff Benbow (Sarge) and a dog handler. Ken and I took hold of one arm each and led the man down the path backwards. He was wiry and strong but not big in stature so it was no problem. However, about halfway down the path towards the Police car he really started to kick out at which point Geoff and the dog-handler who were both pretty big blokes decided to push me and Ken out of the way and take over. Geoff elbowed me out of the way in an effort to grab the man's arm, expecting me to grab one of his legs. However, as I moved backwards I tripped over a kerb and fell backwards into a flower bed of roses which was a very sharp awakening! I started to pull myself up and could now see the man was really kicking out and twisting in all directions. He must have seen me rising out of the roses because suddenly he directed a well aimed kick right on my nose which threw me back almost unconscious into the roses again. I had lost interest now so decided to stay in the roses until my two macho colleagues had subdued the man. Eventually he was put in the Police car and taken to the station and I went to the Smallwood Hospital for treatment. They told me my nose was not broken but would be sore for a long time.

All I know is I am sure it was broken because ever since then my party piece is that I can spread the bugger right over my face and I couldn't do that before!

The postscript to this is that I had to serve the summons on this man for assault on Police and damage to the door. This was several weeks after the incident. By this time the couple had made up and when I went to the house he was now living there. The door was still smashed and when served the summons he was in bed with the woman and both of them told me to go forth and multiply.

Another domestic I attended was on the Batchley Estate with Chris Chetwyn. Big bloke in the house, built like a bull and raging like one. A middle aged woman with two young girls was in the living room. She was absolutely distraught, crying frantically and I could see a bald patch on the one side of her head where presumably this 'man' had ripped the hair out of her head. The girls were cowering behind the settee and looking frightened to death. This was the sort of domestic that required immediate action.

There was no point in trying to reason with the bloke who was still raging and was adamant we would not be arresting him. It was obvious we were in for a scrap. He taunted us to try to arrest him and backed into a corner of the kitchen by the draining board. Chris and I went in to grab him. He was strong and angry and we grappled for ages till my arms began to ache and I wondered how much longer I could hang on. We were able to hold him but no way could we get him out of the house and into a vehicle on our own.

He suddenly saw his opportunity to grab a knife on the draining board and went for it. Fortunately Chris who was also a big guy was able to stop him and push him back.

After what seemed eternity reinforcements arrived and we were able to arrest chummy and take him out of the way for a while.

I do not remember what happened afterwards. This was one of dozens of similar incidents and they all had the familiar cycle of Police called, arrest, woman too frightened to make complaint, complaint withdrawn, no action, reconciliation followed by further incidents. A revolving door of bullying and cruelty in which the Police felt powerless to act and in which we were given no thanks for intervening and incidents which at that time did not form part of Police detections and were not regarded as real Police work.

I am pleased to say that Police and other agencies response has now much improved compared to those days with dedicated units set up to investigate and support victims of domestic violence. However, this sort of violence will always go on and I will never forget seeing the fear in children's faces and the ongoing agony that women and families go through because of bullying partners most of whom are men in which alcohol and the inability to control anger combined with the need to dominate and hold power over women are the main factors.

Most serious violent or sexual offences that happen occur in the home and most are unreported! A sobering thought.

I spent two and half years at Redditch and learnt a lot. I was lucky to work amongst an excellent team of people and to work with leaders who were truly leaders. Many of my ideals and values and much of my outlook on life were shaped during those years. I learnt about life and I learnt a lot about people but much had gone on before and much was to follow.

CHAPTER 2

THE BEGINNING

I cannot say that I was destined to be a Police Officer. I was brought up in the Herefordshire town of Bromyard.

Dad was a motor mechanic by trade but later worked for a company who erected corn silos and drying machines. Mum worked in the fields during the summer picking up potatoes, peas and fruit. My first years were spent living in a two down one up lodge on the edge of Saltmarsh Castle, near Bromyard which is now a caravan site.

When I was six my grandfather died and we went to live with my grandmother in a cottage at Collington which is mid-way between Bromyard and Tenbury. I remained there until I was 16 years old and left to join the Police.

I went to local schools at Bredenbury and Bromyard Secondary Modern which then became a comprehensive.

I liked school but for all the wrong reasons. I was fairly bright and could cope with the lessons where I was in top sets for most things. I loved English and hated Maths.

School for me was a place to go for social frivolity and to enjoy. Whilst I was quite studious up until the age of about 14 after that I lost the plot. I developed a passion for the fairer sex, enjoyed doing anything for a dare (like placing a condom on the headmaster's door, but drawing a line at making sure it wasn't used!). I enjoyed fighting because I was good at it and hated bullies so would take them on. I also skived a lot and spent a lot of time in pubs and cafes when I should have been in school.

I was caned and slippered regularly and whilst I do not feel it did me a lot of good I don't think it harmed me either.

I had lots of friends and generally got on well with people because my parents taught me to be outgoing and friendly. I spent most of my time working at home helping my Dad maintain the gardens and orchard which consisted of about an acre of land. I also did lots of fruit picking and September was always spent picking damsons.

I rode my bicycle everywhere and as I got older I used to go to the local discos at Edwyn Ralph and Saltmarshe village halls where 10 bob (50 pence) would be enough to get me in and buy a packet of fags and a pint of beer which had to last all evening.

I recall one evening though where either I had more money or had a lot bought for me because I ended up totally drunk. I tried to ride my bike home but ended up in the ditch several times and eventually had to walk home where next morning I had a huge bollocking from mum because of the state of my clothes.

Unhooking people's gates, putting dirty postcards on people's front doors, smuggling cider into the school disco were typical of the sort of tricks we did but never usually anything that was malicious or caused damage.

I had a number of good friends at school. One of those was called Ted who was a farmer's son and who lived a few miles from me in a small village near Bromyard.

Ted and I looked alike except he had a way with the girls and a cheekiness I had not yet learned. He used to say if you can make a girl laugh they will always go out with you. Well it certainly seemed to work for him. Whilst I worked fairly hard at school up until the age of about 14 after that it all went to rats! Ted and I would spend our time skiving with some of the girls from the local grammar school and taking them up to Bromyard Downs or to any of the local pubs who were prepared to serve us.

Sometimes it was difficult because we were still in school uniform and we used to have to pool the money to get a round in.

In those days one of the pubs had a sign carved outside the front door which read something like, 'Welcome, come on in and rest for a while, make yourself at home and enjoy our refreshment.'

I was a little taken aback therefore when on one occasion Ted and I went there with two girls at lunchtime and after asking for a drink the barman looked at us up and down (suppose the school uniforms gave the game away really) and said, 'You must be joking, piss off.'

I was about to ask him how he reconciled his rude behaviour with the welcoming sign outside but a look from the barman and a smack in the ribs from Ted made me reconsider and we all made a tactical withdrawal.

On another occasion Ted and I jumped straight off the school bus one morning before we arrived at school and walked into Bromyard for a morning skive.

We went to Alf Wragg's coffee shop in the High Street where we ordered double portions of baked beans on toast and then started playing on the one arm bandit and the juke box.

We were just settling down to the beans when Ted's Dad, suddenly arrived in the Cafe where he had just happened to stop on his way through Bromyard. He grabbed hold of Ted by the ear and dragged him out of the cafe ignoring me completely. I knew the game would be up but was left with a dilemma. Should I finish up the double portions of baked beans on toast which we had lovingly paid for out of hard earned pocket money or should I go straight to school. Well, what would you do? Yes, I finished up the beans and then decided I might as well go to school.

Eating all those beans not only gave me terrible indigestion and the farts but it also gave me time to think up this bloody wonderful, creative story to cover up the fact that I had been skiving.

I decided that when I got to school I would say this. I overslept and missed the school bus. My Dad drove me to Bromyard but the car broke down and I helped him fix it. I had to walk the rest of the way to Bromyard and by the time I got there I decided I needed something to eat before I went to school because I was so cold and hungry. I went to Alf Wragg's Cafe and low and behold I bumped into Ted.

All I needed to do now was dirty my hands and get them oily so it looked more believable. On the way to school to I bumped into another mate called Dougie Newman who was riding his bike. I am not sure if he was skiving as well but at least I was able to wipe my hands on his bike chain. So, the plan was now complete. I was convinced I had a fantastic watertight excuse that would stand up to scrutiny because I knew they would not be able to contact my Dad to check out about the car.

As I walked up the Old Road at Bromyard towards school I was as happy as a dog with two dicks!

All of a sudden I was brought back to reality when a car pulled up beside me. The driver leaned over and I could see it was the Deputy Head Teacher Mr. Ray. We called him 'StingRay.'

StingRay told me to get in the car which I did. I was waiting for the grand inquisition but he ignored me and said nothing. I decided to tell him my story which I outlined in graphic detail being keen to point out my oily hands. Again StingRay said nothing. I thought, 'I've cracked this, he's swallowed it.'

We got back to school and I started to walk off to the classroom. StingRay said to me,

'Get into my office King and bend over.'

Whereupon, without further ado or explanation he caned me six times bringing tears to my eyes.

In my grand plan of course I had forgotten one vital part. The fact that Ted might have told StingRay the truth about what we did or that the school may have checked with the bus driver!

I have to say that I was very annoyed by this. Firstly that I had overlooked this very important point but secondly that StingRay could have given me some credit for this very elaborate and creative story I had concocted and could have reduced the caning to at least four stokes given my lateral thinking ability.

For a while after that I decided to go unilateral and skive on my own. I fancied this really attractive girl from the grammar school which was about one mile from our school. Her name was Ann and I was friends with her brother Brian so I passed a message to meet her mid-day in the churchyard at Bromyard next to the grammar school. Not the most romantic of assignations but I was fast running out of options in Bromyard as far as pubs and cafes were concerned and I had never heard of anyone being barred from a churchyard!

However, I needed a cast iron alibi to get out of school so I made an appointment at the dentists in the High Street for a check up.

I had the check up and was trying to escape through the door when the dentist called me back and told me I had a problem with a 'baby tooth' that had not fallen out naturally, was blocking another tooth coming through and must be removed. I tried to make an excuse but he was adamant I needed it doing then and there.

He removed the tooth and I immediately ran to the Churchyard where there was no Ann. Now I am not sure whether she stood me up or just got tired of waiting but here I was, missing a tooth, frozen mouth full of blood and no date!

The rider to this saga was that the second tooth never ever grew through so I was left with gap in my front teeth all my life in the name of bloody lust!

Ann did turn up for the next date though and didn't seem to be put off by the fact I was toothless!

Another great friend of mine was Steve who lived in the same village on a smallholding farm and was part of a large family.

Steve and I decided to go fishing one night, or rather poaching on a local farm. It was all very crude. We had to cut the rods out of tree branches, attach some string and dig up some worms. We also took some bread for bait as well because we didn't have much of clue what we were doing.

We waited for ages and I caught a smashing Rainbow Trout. The only thing was having caught it; I didn't have a clue what to do with it. I was also worried to take it home because of the questions that would be asked so I gave it to Steve to take home.

A few weeks later I got the courage to tell Dad what I had been doing whereupon he gave me the rough edge of his tongue for not bringing the fish home!

I was quite interested in mechanical things and in an old cow shed at home we had an Ariel 350cc NG motorbike. The bike had been Dad's but had long gone into disrepair.

Dad and I decided to do it up so I could ride it round the fields adjoining the house.

After getting it going Dad rode it round the fields with me sitting on the rear as pillion passenger.

Then, it was my time to have a go on my own. I got on and rode it down to the bottom of the field. What I had failed to take account of was that there was a herd of cows in the field who were now starting to get pissed off with this mechanical contraption invading their space. I was only going slowly; after all it was my maiden voyage! The cows seemed to sense my insecurity and started chasing after the bike. My reaction was to open the throttle to get away from them to the other end of the field. I did this and then realising I had left the cows behind I did a wide arc to circle back towards the house. Unfortunately the bloody throttle stuck and I started to panic. I went across the field into a large dip, a bit like a bunker on a golf course. Well, I tell you I came out of that bunker like bloody Evil Knievel, straight through a barbed fence and into the back of a chicken house. The bike slid sideways and I was flung off ending up on my arse in the field.

Dad checked me and the bike over and when he had stopped laughing got me to get back on and do it all again!

I didn't seem to have much luck with motorbikes. Another mate I had was a lad called Bill who was also a farmer's son and lived the other side of Bromyard from where I lived. Bill was slightly older than me and had a Scooter. One night we met at Edwyn Ralph village hall which is about 2 miles outside Bromyard. There was a disco taking place with a bar. We had a couple of drinks and then decided to make our way to Saltmarsh Village hall where another disco was on. This was about 3 miles away so I nipped on the back of Bills scooter and he gave me a lift to Saltmarsh. We stopped for a couple of hours and then decided to go back to Edwyn Ralph for the end of the evening before the bar closed.

Again I got on the back of Bill. Now, this was in the days before helmets became compulsory so Bill had one on but I didn't.

We rode along the small country lane between the two villages and the main road and it was a route I rode my bike along regularly so I knew it well.

Bill was hammering along quite fast and all went well until we started approaching a part of the road called 'Brown's Hill' which is a sharp right hand bend followed by a sharp descent. I could tell Bill was going too fast to negotiate the bend or the hill. I tried to shout to him but between the noise of the bike and his helmet he obviously could not hear. I tried tugging his jacket but again he took no notice.

Now, I used to work with a bobby in the Police they nick named 'Exocet.' Why? Because he was a pain in the ass and although you could see him coming there was bugger all you could do about it! Well here I was on the back of Bill hurtling towards what I knew was going to be disaster but there was bugger all I could do about it.

We just about negotiated the bend but as we entered the descent Bill lost it completely. The bike slid sideways across the road and we fell off into the road. I remember sliding backwards down the hill with Bill just in front of me. Then I could see sparks following me down the hill which I realised was the bike which was catching me up fast.

I screamed at Bill and instinctively threw myself sideways to the right into the hedgerow and ditch. I saw the bike go past me but could not see Bill. I lay in the hedge for a while and everything was deathly quiet. I was able to move and felt OK. I shouted out to Bill and was relieved when he shouted back something that was like, 'Bloody hell, that was close.'

We both managed to stand and waited silently for ages making sure all our bits were still in place.

We found the bike in the middle of the road and amazingly, although a bit dented, it started up and we decided to still go to Edwyn Ralph for the last drink and dance of the evening.

When we got to the Disco there is no doubt I was in shock so I consumed a couple of double rum and blackcurrants to celebrate being alive. We remained there for about an hour and I wondered why people kept staring at me.

Eventually, we left and I then cycled home. When I got home and the effects of the rum and blackcurrants had started to wear off I suddenly felt a cold draught round my buttocks. I then realised that the complete arse had disappeared out of my trousers and my flesh was exposed to the elements. Also, I had on a new jacket (well, second-hand new jacket) and the elbows were torn.

I went to bed and knew there would be questions asked in the morning. When Mum asked what had happened next morning I told her I had fallen off my push-bike coming down Brown's Hill which was partly true.....I suppose? 'You must have been going very fast,' she said!

Years later I told her the truth when I knew she couldn't catch me!

My greatest influencers were my parents. I got my devilment from both, particularly my Dad who was up for anything. He was a proud man, conscientious, hard working, a skilled mechanic and tough as nails. He enjoyed a drink and treated 10 pints as an aperitif. As he got older he suffered from arthritis which disabled him. Despite having to walk with two sticks he would still stand in the garden with a hoe in the one hand and a walking stick in the other determined to work whatever the pain it caused him.

Whilst in his 70's he fell off a ladder picking damsons and broke his hip. Mum stuck him in a wheelbarrow and pushed him up to the house so she could get help. Dad was more concerned they were losing daylight for picking damsons!

My enduring memories of Dad were when he lit up a fag. He was always going to do one of two things, either start a piece of work or go to the toilet. We had an outside toilet where once a month we had to dig a big hole and bury the contents out of the bucket into the garden. The vegetables were great! Dad never liked doing that and would usually heave and be sick so it was left to me and mum to finish the job off. But, you always knew when Dad was on the toilet because wafts of smoke would come over the top of the door accompanied by the odd grunt and a shuffle of the News of the World which was read and then used for bum fodder. The traditional form of environmental recycling!

It was Dad who taught me that sometimes in life you have to stand up for yourself and fight. I went through a period where I was bullied by a lad who lived in the same village. He used to call me names and when I got off the school bus he would throw my cap over the hedge or hold the bus door so I could not get off the bus.

I told Dad and he said I needed to stand up to him and learn to fight. He took me out into the garden and taught me to box. After a few minutes I got the hang of it and hit him once, hard in the stomach where he doubled up. When he recovered he told me to do the same to anyone who ever bullied me never come home whingeing to him again about being bullied.

The next time the bus incident happened instead of walking quietly away I called to the lad and told him to take his jacket off and we would fight to see who was best. We scrapped hard for about 20 minutes. He was older, wiry and strong but I had the weight. We boxed, wrestled and cussed and if I am honest then no-one won, we just gave up when we were both completely knackered. Nothing much was said but from that moment on I gained his respect and no further bullying ever took place.

I later took up boxing at Edwyn Ralph youth club where we were taught by a local farmer who was actually a very good boxer. Everything went well until one night when I was matched with a young lad who had just come out of the army and lived in Bromyard. He was small and I wrongly assumed this would be a walkover. Basically I only lasted two rounds and for much of it I only saw stars! He knocked seven bells out of me and I suddenly realised there were a lot of tougher and harder people around than me. It was a salutary lesson!

My Mum was a diamond. A gentle, loving and truly wonderful lady who saw the best in everything and everybody. Every cloud had a silver lining for mum.

However, she was no fool. She had the most beautiful handwriting and loved both reading and writing poetry some of which she had published. Mum always instilled me to treat others as I would want to be treated myself and whilst the terms of equality or diversity would have never entered the language she used she bestowed the virtues of treating everyone fairly no matter who they were or what they had done. If ever I said anything rude about someone who may be disabled or looked different in anyway then I would have the wrath of Mum's tongue.

Whilst I did not always like the way Dad treated Mum she took it in her stride and gave as good as she got but in more subtle ways.

My grandmother who we lived with was called Mary King and she had inherited the house from my granddad when he died. She always made it clear that she wanted my dad to stay at the house but not me or my mum. The first words I heard my grandmother say when we arrived at the house were to my Father. She said, 'Well, I don't mind you being here John but what about her (my mother) and that bloody thing (me).'

Nothing like feeling wanted!

During the early years she made a lot of mischief between my Dad and Mum which on reflection I think was to split them up. It never worked and Dad quickly realised what my Gran was up to. However, both Mum and Dad kept their head down because Gran promised them that when she died we would inherit the house and surrounding land.

The night my Gran died was the night before I was about to take my O'levels at age of 16. By then my Gran had mellowed somewhat and towards the end I think she realised that my Mum had done her best to take care of us all and deserved her respect.

It was therefore a shock when, that night we sat down with a copy of Gran's last Will and Testament to find that she had left the house and land to the Church of England but that my Dad could live in it during his lifetime.

I didn't really care but my Mum and Dad were devastated after all they had put up with for many years. It made Dad ill and for years he could not even talk about it and would not consider contesting it. So, that was that.

Many years later after my Dad died I sold the property on behalf of my Mum and handed over a cheque to the local Church who allowed Mum £6,000 to pay the rent on a flat at Bromyard.

The only postscript on this for me was the fact that my Gran originally told my parents that if she could name me 'Leslie' when I was born I would eventually inherit the estate. Well, she did and I didn't! I have always hated the name Leslie and always change it to Les on every opportunity!

One of the best and most lasting things that happened to me before I left school was meeting my future wife Judy Milner. Jud was a year younger than me and we started going out together when she was 14 and I was 15.

Jud lived in a neighbouring village called Upper Sapey with her Mum and Dad. Jud was the youngest of six children but her brothers and sisters had all grown up and left home.

Always immaculately dressed in smart school uniform with long dark hair, dark complexion, brown eyes, great legs and a fantastic figure Jud mesmerised me from day one and was to be my lifelong partner.

Jud's Dad and Mum quickly accepted me and I got on well with them. Jud's Dad, Ivan was a retired builder who spent all his spare time in the garden. His wife Aggie (Agnes) was the full time housewife who had devoted her life to her family and loved to have a chat. Sometimes we would talk for hours and I was always made to feel welcome.

Ivan started to call Jud 'Queenie' because of going out with a King.

These were fantastic days and life was good but I knew I needed to find something to do when I left school.

I always had my heart set on following Dad into the mechanical trade and working at the garage where my Dad worked. However, the boss of the firm Harold Edwards was killed in a tragic car accident near Bromyard, the firm folded and Dad was made redundant so that reduced my only option to nil.

In early 1970 I went into the Library at Bromyard and whilst looking in the careers section found a book on Police Cadets. My cousin Tony Tribe was in the Police in London so I had a vague interest and decided to pursue it.

I applied for the Police Cadets in West Mercia Police who were due to take on their second intake in September 1970.

I was invited to take an entrance exam at Bromyard Police Station which was supervised by Constables Pete Warrington and John Haines.

Half-way through the exam they got called out to deal with some pigs that were wandering on the road which gave me loads of opportunity to look through a dictionary and correct my spellings.

When they came back Pete set me the maths test which I was less impressed with.

He gave me a little extra time and after looking at my first draft suggested I might like to revisit a couple of the answers.

I passed the exams which I am sure was in no small part due the chance I was given by John and Pete. I have reflected many times in my life that everybody needs a leg up sometimes and their help changed the course of my life. How competitive life is these days and how difficult it is for kids to get on the first rung. It's no wonder some give up along the way.

Eventually I went for an interview at Droitwich Police Training School which was an old Army barracks where I was interviewed by a panel of three men including Barry Florentine who was eventually to become Deputy Chief Constable of West Mercia Constabulary.

I was told my hair was too long by their standards, told I would need to learn to swim and asked what I thought about the situation surrounding the Vietnam War? I told them it was bad, which was as much as I could muster at the time! Somehow I felt they were looking for a little more!

I left feeling totally disillusioned and out of my depth convinced that I had better start looking for another job. Whatever they appeared to be looking for I was on another planet.

I had virtually put it out of mind when about a month later a letter came through telling me I had been accepted as a Police Cadet and was to report at the Droitwich Training Camp on the 7th September 1970.

I was over the moon, very surprised but the main thing I remember about the letter was telling me to bring several pairs of black or dark blue socks and plenty of shoe cleaning kit!

I was still only 16 years old, had never been away from home before and was now heading towards 12 months of residential disciplined training. So, there was a mixture of pride, fear and intrigue. My Mum and Dad were very pleased but Dad told me I had better start getting fit straight away to cope with the physical side so he got me a job on a farm over the summer months to get me in shape.

So, I spent the summer bale hauling, fruit picking and generally labouring. It was tough. I did lots of overtime and started to learn what hard work was really all about. In addition to that Dad found me plenty to do at home such as cutting hedges, digging gardens, mowing grass with a scythe and generally keeping the place tidy.

When the 7th September 1970 came round I was feeling fit but very apprehensive.

Dad dropped me off at Bromyard to catch a bus to Worcester and then onward to Droitwich. As I left Dad said to me, 'Listen kid, don't let anybody ever shit on you. If it gets too bad come on home, we will work things out.'

Over the next 12 months I thought of Dad's words many times. There were loads of times when I felt like jacking it in but because I knew Dad was behind me and would support me whatever I did, I decided to give it all and not let him or Mum down. However, it would be more difficult than I ever envisaged.

CHAPTER 3

A SERIOUS AWAKENING –
BULLS**T AND BLACK SOCKS

As the Midland Red Bus stopped outside the Droitwich Camp on the A38 I felt serious twangs of homesickness and trepidation. It was Monday 7th September 1970.

I was a country kid and even though this town of Droitwich was only about 25 miles from home it felt like the end of the world.

As I crossed the road carrying a small case neatly prepared by Mum I saw a bus coming from the opposite direction and fingered the change in my pocket ready to get on and return home.

However, I resisted the temptation and reported to the reception.

I was allocated to a dormitory and the first thing that struck me was how formal it all was. This was strict discipline, no mucking about like at school and instructors that meant business.

I shared a dormitory with four other lads. There was Gerry Newton from Wellington, Shropshire. Pat Newman and Eddy Gallagher from Hereford and a lad called Hayden Bailey. I am not sure where Hayden was from but I know he already had a brother in the Police. We were later joined by Del Lawrence who was also from Hereford.

Gerry was a smashing lad, easy to get along with and probably my best mate.

Pat was a skinhead with all the trendy gear. He was a good looking lad and popular with the ladies. Eddy was a real character, a good friend and loved sport. Both Eddy and Pat had known each other before they joined the Force and had played sport together. When they played any form of team game together especially basket ball they were absolutely magic. Eventually they had to be split up because if both were on the same team the opposite side stood no chance. They would just run rings round the rest of us.

Hayden was quiet, studious and very conscientious. He would carry on working and cleaning his boots long after the rest of us had passed our 'bugger it' threshold.

Del was a real comedian, a laugh a minute with a fantastic sense of humour and quick wit. This was made funnier by virtue of the fact that he was tall, thin and gangly with a shock of blonde hair that hung into his eyes so he was funny to look at as well.

One of the first things we were told was to report to the stores and get measured up for uniforms and PE kit. We reported on time to be told to go away because we were too early. We all went back to the classroom where we were given a bollocking for not remaining at the stores and sent back again. I did think at the time it was part of some sophisticated intelligence game but quickly realised that it was just a cock up of left hand not knowing what right hand was doing. I remember thinking the Police must be more efficient than this. After all they are dealing with murders and serious crimes. Later on when I went out to a Division and witnessed operational policing that dream was shattered as well. Policing has and always will be surviving by the skin of your teeth and making it up as you go along. That is the way it is.

From day one the bar was set as to what life as a Police Cadet would consist of.

Early morning rise, parade on duty, drill and marching, inspection, classroom studies on law and Police procedure, vocational academic studies with Bromsgrove College, bulling boots, pressing uniforms, cleaning dormitories, making beds and loads of physical sports including negotiating an assault course. The rules were bullshit and must wear black socks.

We were constantly on the go from first thing in the morning to last thing at night. There was only one standard and that was the highest possible standard which I found out the very first week.

Every Friday before we went home for the weekend we had a room, kit and wardrobe inspection. Everything had to be immaculate. Just like being in the army you had to ensure all of your kit was laid out on the bed in exact order with your wardrobe door open. The bed had to be boxed. That meant it was stripped and you had to fold the sheets and pillowcases in a certain order and measured exactly to the same length with the bed cover wrapped around it. We had to stand to attention by our beds waiting for approval before we could go home. That first week the Chief Inspector found a cob-web in the bottom of my wardrobe and I thought the bloody world had come to an end. Following a king-size bollocking I had to go and find a dustpan and brush and clean the entire inside of my wardrobe and then have it re-inspected. I almost missed the bus home and was devastated at this level of attention to detail.

Also, in the first week I had three haircuts and still it was not short enough for them. I knew I was in trouble when Pat Martin who had a skinhead cut was made to have his cut even shorter! I stood no bloody chance.

We had a drill sergeant called Ken Timmis who you always referred to as 'Sir'. We started off hating Timmis but ended up having great respect for him. Timmis was an ex- military man and demanded the highest standards of turnout and precision when carrying out drill. He was a stickler for detail and demanded immaculate uniform turnout with bulled boots, pressed uniforms and even your cap had to be brushed in a circular motion to the right. Any deviation from this regime would result in twenty press ups on the parade ground followed by 'jankers' which consisted of picking up stones off a piece of waste ground during recreation time.

However, most of us preferred picking up the stones because the press ups meant you knackered your boots and had to completely re-do them that evening with spit and polish until the marks were removed ready for inspection next morning.

We spent hours and hours bulling boots and pressing uniforms.

We also spent hours drilling as a squad until our marching and co-ordination was so perfect we could do it silently by numbers.

When we weren't drilling or cleaning rooms and kit then there was plenty of enforced physical activities. These consisted of 5 mile cross country or road runs with heavy boots on to strengthen your legs. Also, circuit training, gym work, rugby training, cricket, football, basket ball, hockey, swimming, canoeing and the dreaded assault course.

On top of this we had Police studies which consisted of learning law and Police definitions and had to retake any O'levels we had not obtained at school. I took English language, Economics and Sociology.

In addition to this every few weeks each dormitory took a turn at doing Duty Squad. This involved a number of duties such as waking the duty officer up first thing with a cup of tea, helping the kitchen staff to prepare meals, doing washing-up for the entire camp and carrying out evening duties such as staffing a shop in the recreation area which sold essential goods.

What this really meant was you were on your feet doing duty squad and carrying out your normal duties from about 6am till 11pm at night when lights went out.

If you weren't doing squad you were allowed out one night per week which was on a Wednesday. Prior to going out you were inspected to make sure you wore nothing less than smart casual clothes, which, combined with the short hair cuts did rather give the game away to the locals who we were in addition to looking a bit of a pillock compared to the contemporary dress of the early 1970's. At age 16/17yrs I think it was all part of a plot to keep us out of the pubs, which worked to some extent!

I had some trouble coping initially with being away from home. I was a country boy with a deep Herefordshire accent amongst a load of fashionable 'townies'. I had the mick taken out of me because of my accent and because I did not have a clue about latest music, sport or fashion. I was missing Jud because we could now only meet at weekends with one letter in the week and one telephone call. Jud was not on the phone at home so on a

Wednesday night she used to wait for me to ring her in a kiosk just up from her home.

I also hated the physical side of doing sport and exercise. Whilst I was reasonably fit I was not as fit as the majority who were also very good at most sports. I was built for comfort not speed, had two left feet and lacked co-ordination for most other activities.

I felt very inferior and if you were not good at sport then you were really made to feel like that.

On one occasion whilst doing a gate vault over a scrambling net on the assault course I fell off from top to bottom and lay on the ground seriously winded wondering if I had broken anything. One of the instructors came over, and told me to get up and stop hanging about!

Fortunately, nothing was broken and I resumed back on the net to complete it. Think it's what they call tough love without the love!

On many occasions I felt very lonely, homesick and my esteem was through the floor. I would lie in bed at night crying to myself quietly so the others could not hear me.

Things came to a head one night over the most trivial of things. My Mum who was not well had been trying to earn some pin money by working in the fields picking up potatoes and fruit and with some of her hard earned money had bought me a pair of slippers for my birthday. They were the old fashioned type with a check top and made by Pirelli. I didn't think much about it so I took them to the camp and boy did I get the piss ripped out of me.

The lads were racing them round the room going vroom, vroom after Pirelli tyres.

I took it in good part for a while but then got upset. When they asked what was wrong I told them about how my Mum had bought them with some hard earned money and how worried I was because she was not well. The lads were sympathetic and backed off.

I lay in bed that night and decided I had to either give up or make a fight of it. I decided that the one thing I did enjoy was anything we did around the academic side particularly the subjects on law and Police procedures. Also, that the physical side would not matter a lot once we joined the Regular Police so what the hell did it matter anyway.

I became determined that I would do my best with the academic work, get top marks and sod the sport. I would live with it. It was my turning point. After that I put all my efforts into the academic subjects, the drill and looking smart. I started getting top marks in most subjects, the accent became less of an issue and I started to win my spurs with the rest of the group.

It was to be a useful lesson for me. In every job you ever do in the Police at whatever rank whenever you start you are tested and have to win your spurs with the people you work with. It's called the 'bottle test'.

I still hated a lot of the things we did, particularly canoeing. I could hardly swim and had a fear of water so doing an Eskimo roll under water was not my idea of fun, much less capsizing in the River Severn at Worcester and floating down the river hanging onto the end of my canoe being called a 'wanker' by a passerby.

The one PE instructor we all had time and respect for was Terry Mann. Although Terry knew that I and a few others hated the physical side he still had patience with us and any criticism was always balanced with his fantastic sense of humour. His favourite saying when putting us through torturous circuit training was, 'Lads, it's all a case of mind over matter as you feel the pain. Remember I don't mind and you don't matter!'

On one occasion we were playing football and I missed a sitter of a goal. Being embarrassed I shouted out 'Bollocks.' Instead of taking me aside and disciplining me for my inappropriate outburst Terry retorted, 'What did you say you had between your ears King?' 'Point taken Sir,' I said.

I learned from Terry that the key to dealing with people was to treat everyone the same, with respect and humility and with a sense of humour. No one took advantage of Terry because he earned rather than demanded respect. I never heard anyone say a bad word against him and he was popular with everyone who ever met him.

After a few weeks the rigid discipline started to become less of a chore. Many would say you become brainwashed. I disagree. What happens is that you learn the art of self discipline. You learn to take care of yourself and to take a pride in what you do and how you look. You develop confidence and are proud to walk down the street with short hair looking different because you know how to look smart and walk with authority.

Most of all you learn to adopt the highest standards and achieve things that you never dreamed you would or could do. Even if you fail you know you have tried and as long as you have personally put in maximum effort that is all that matters. Eventually you start working as a team, building on your strengths and helping each other with weaknesses.

You learn to take care of yourself, to laugh at yourself and in my case to toughen up a bit and take things less personally.

Many people criticise disciplined training. The majority are those who have never experienced it. Sometimes there are casualties and the environment is one of bullying and sadism. That is wrong and should never be condoned. But, where discipline is carried out as it was with us in a controlled and supportive environment it is the making of most who experience it. Probably not for everybody but many of today's youth would benefit from this type of experience where you have to be disciplined first before you learn self discipline and self-respect.

Although life was busy and to me quite hard we did have some fun.

In the dormitory at night after lights had gone out we would lie in bed telling jokes and generally taking the piss. One of the favourite jokes was to wait until someone fell asleep and then go over, shake them awake and say something stupid like, 'Do you want to buy a battleship?' A few minutes later they would reciprocate the favour by waking you up and say, 'What colour is it?' This would go on through the night until it broke out into a pillow fight or both fell asleep.

Gerry Newton used to bring in old records of Derek 'Blaster' Bates who was a renowned explosives demolition expert and was an even better story teller. Blaster originated from Cheshire and his tales of blowing up chimneys across Northern England are legendary. We would lie in bed laughing at these records until we ached.

On one occasion we practised a séance using a glass and letters of the alphabet which we spread out on the polished floor of the dormitory.

We got in touch with a woman spirit who spelt out that she was from Wychbold which is a small village on the main A38 in Worcestershire between Droitwich and Bromsgrove. She told us she had been bombed out of home during the war and evacuated to the country. Some prat then asked if she was an evil spirit to which the glass went to 'Yes.'

Somebody else then said, 'Do you mean us harm?' Again the glass moved to 'yes.'

At this point we started shitting ourselves. Someone in the group said we must break up the glass, burn all the bits of paper and pray. Well we did that but Eddy and Pat were still not sure that was enough so they insisted on painting some black crosses on the windows with boot polish and putting up crosses on the window to keep out the evil spirit.

Sounds daft now but at the time we were serious. What I am convinced about is that no-one in the room was moving the glass or buggering about. The story the woman gave was not something that was in the minds of 16 year old boys and from that day to this I have always had a healthy respect for things of the supernatural. I personally believe there are lots of things we know nothing about and some things are best left alone.

On our one night out in the week there was nothing to do in Droitwich except go to the local disco in the Winter Gardens or visit the pubs. The problem with the pubs was firstly every bugger knew who we were with short hair and having to wear smart clothes to go out and secondly the instructors used to visit the pubs to check for Cadets drinking under age. However, one night we decided to brave it and a bunch of us went out to the Dovey pub which was on one of the estates rather than in the town centre.

One of the crowd we were with encouraged us to sample the delights of draft Guinness. I don't think I drank a lot but by the time we left the pub at closing time I was completely pissed. So pissed that I wandered up somebody's driveway on the way home mistakenly thinking it was the road and lost the others who went ahead without me.

Somehow I must have made it back to camp before the 11pm deadline but God knows how? I got to bed but was sick and heaving up all night. It was too far to go to the toilet so I used the communal dustbin which by morning stank like hell. Fortunately, I was not alone.

In the morning I was still sick, before during and after breakfast. I only managed to drink a cup of milk and brought that straight back up. I was now dreading the muster parade but the one thing I knew was that I could not go sick. The staff would immediately realise it was just a hangover and either I would be kicked out or be doing jankers for the rest of my life. I managed to get out on parade, desperately hoping I would not throw up in the middle of the drill square and stood to attention waiting for Ken Timmis to shout out his instructions.

At the training school we always had a squad of experienced bobbies who were on a backward bobbies 'refresher' course usually for a couple of weeks at a time.

They were renowned for taking the piss out of the instructors and each other and this particular morning was no exception.

Ken Timmis would shout out to each squad, 'Are you present and correct?' The officer standing at the right front of each squad (called the right marker) would then step forward, salute and say, 'Yes,' or report if anyone was absent.

Timmis started off, 'Are you present and correct A squad?' Yes Sir,' was the reply.

Are you present and correct B squad? 'Yes Sir,' was the reply.

Are you present and correct C squad? 'Yes Sir,' was the reply.

Are you present and correct Police Refresher Course? The right hand marker stepped forward and without faltering said, 'One sick, one in Court and one gone fishing sir!'

Although everyone knew the reference to gone fishing meant he was given the day off for Force Sport the way he said it meant everyone pissed themselves laughing including poor old Timmis who by now had tears rolling down his cheeks but trying to keep a straight face!

Then we started marching and a miraculous thing happened. A combination of the discipline required to march combined with the cold air meant my hangover lifted completely and by the time we went inside I was as right as ninepence! I survived to fight another day and drink another night!

Eventually the 12 months passed and it came time to practice for the passing out parade and ceremonies.

Not content with a marching round the drill square this had to be a complete example of all the things we had practised during the year including the physical sports and the dreaded assault course.

Because I did not excel at the sport side I ended up in a team where we had to compete with the opposing squad and of all things carry a telegraph pole across the assault course. Yes, a bloody telegraph pole! Now I don't know which 'Wally' thought that one up but I tell you I wish I had known at the time. We practised for days and days until the team work came together to perfection.

Alongside that we had to carry out silent precision marching. This means you drill and carry out complicated moves as a squad with no verbal instruction. You do it largely by memory and counting between moves. Very difficult, but when you get it right it looks very impressive.

We also had to do a display on judo and self defence which wasn't too bad but a really funny thing happened during practice. One of the things we had to demonstrate was what to do if someone held a gun to your back wearing the full judo kit. The idea is that if the gun is held up against your back you turn round quickly, chop the arm of the opponent and the gun away and then disarm them using other tactics. We were using a starting pistol which was loaded with a blank and we had to time it so the person holding the gun fired the discharge a split second after the person in front had turned and knocked it out of the way.

The two lads who were to demonstrate this were 'Lenny' Lendrum and Jim Crum. Jim had the gun and Lenny was the one being held up. Lenny turned quickly to knock the gun away but Jim fired the gun just too quickly which resulted in the gun being discharged right up against Lenny's Judo kit jacket. It was a few seconds later when we realised that the jacket was on fire and Lenny who was still in it was sprinting a marathon round the parade ground trying to put the flames out! We thought it was hilarious but somehow he didn't share the joke of being knocked to the ground and having the shit pummelled out of him to put the fire out. No health and safety in those days!

Along came the eve of the passing out parade and it is fair to say we practised everything to perfection and knew our turnout and uniform must be immaculate.

I was pretty good at pressing uniforms and Del Lawrence was great at bulling boots. So, we decided I would press his uniform and shirt whist he would bull my boots which usually took hours. By the time I came back from pressing the uniforms Del had finished both his boots and mine and at the time I remember thinking, how does he do it so quickly? Well, next day I was to find out!

We rose early. It was a beautiful summer's day and I have to say it was one of the proudest days of my life. Jud and my Mum and Dad came and we did our bit on the assault course with me shitting myself.

After that it came to the Judo demonstration (which this time went off perfectly) and then the drill square marching followed by inspection. The drill went really well and it is fair to say that there is a tremendous feeling of achievement in working so closely as a team which is what policing is all about.

Then it was the formal inspection by the Lord Lieutenant of the County, the Commandant of the Training School, the Deputy Chief Constable and Timmis himself.

We stood waiting and I looked down to have a quick last look at my boots. I was horrified. The toe caps had turned white! I shifted my eyes left and right and could see that everybody else's boots were OK except Del's and his were white as well.

Blast! I instantly knew what had happened. Del was in the habit of putting floor polish on boots to finish them off and give them a final shine. The problem was it was not a known quantity in rain or shine! In view of that the previous evening I had told Del not to use floor polish on my boots and he had promised not to. Well obviously the bugger had and now my feet having been soaked with sweat on a warm summer's day had soaked through and caused them to go white. I could cheerfully have killed him.

Any way, we got away with it. The inspection did not seem to notice and everything went according to plan.

We passed out with flying colours and Jud wore her best hat. In fact her only hat! She looked a treat and we were both proud of each other.

Time came to leave the cloistered environment of the training school and move onto a real divisional Police Station as a Cadet until we were 19 years old and could join the regular force.

I was posted to Leominster which is a market town in Herefordshire only about 12 miles from my parents' home.

It was here I was to find out what Policing was really about and to realise I had made the right choice after all.

CHAPTER 4

'HEARTBEAT' COUNTRY AT LEOMINSTER

In September 1971 I arrived at Leominster which is a quiet and rather lovely rural market town in deepest North Herefordshire. In policing terms this now reminds me of the fictional policing series 'Heartbeat,' featured on television about rural policing in North Yorkshire during the 1960's.

The bad news was I had to live in digs even though I was only a few miles from home. The good news was that they were next door to a pub and my landlady worked in the local fish and chip shop which was a few yards up the road.

My landlady was called Carrie and a very lovely lady she was too. From the word go she made me and my fellow Cadet lodger Mick Clarke feel at home. Carrie's husband Fred worked at a local bakery and they had an extremely attractive daughter who had jet black hair and a fantastic figure. Unfortunately, or fortunately, whichever way you look at it, she was happily married and only called in to see her mum and dad occasionally but when she did it was a real sight for sore eyes. On one occasion in the summer she was wearing a pair of hot pants and Mick and I were both there to relish the sight having almost fallen out of the bedroom window to get a better view.

Although I slept in the same bedroom as Mick we were rarely there together because we were on opposite shifts and had different days off.

The Police Station was situated in those days in Burgess Street, a short walk from the town centre. It was run by a Chief Inspector called Dick Blythe and Inspector Ron Keyse.

There were three Sergeants, three to four Constables on each shift and three CID officers including a Detective Sergeant.

There were only about two or three Police cars and the Beat bobbies based on the outlying patches still used motorcycles. PYE pocket phone radios had only recently been introduced but we had a telex machine and a switchboard as well so it was all very modern!

The duties of the Cadet seem to evolve mainly around making tea, domestic chores, cleaning police vehicles and manning the switchboard.

The tea making and cleaning cars were monotonous but the job I hated worst was manning the switchboard which we did whenever there was no telephone operator.

It operated on flick switches and I was forever crossing the calls, cutting someone off, losing the calls or generally making a complete balls-up of the whole situation. I got the rough end of Blythe's tongue on more than one occasion.

What amazed me most was that at the age of 17 years I was left at times on my own in complete charge of the Station dealing with all incoming telephone calls, 999 calls, radio transmissions, personal callers and the telex machine. It frightened me and if only the public of Leominster had known how little I knew it would have bloody frightened them as well.

On one occasion my old Deputy Head Teacher 'Stingray' from the Queen Elizabeth School, Bromyard, who had regularly disciplined me came into the Police Station to report something. He looked at me with bemusement and asked if there was anybody sensible he could speak to. I told him it was me or nobody and that I was in charge. He reluctantly gave me the information and he left the Police Station looking distinctly insecure. I bet he didn't sleep soundly in his bed for a long time!

Life was fairly mundane for a while and consisted of lots of office work and cleaning but all the time I was watching and learning. The first most interesting thing I had to do was to clean the blood and gore off a shotgun that had been used by a chap to blow his head off out in the country somewhere. I wanted to go to the scene but they wouldn't let me. Once the gun had been examined they wanted to return it to the deceased's wife and I had the job of bringing it back to pristine condition.

One of the characters at the nick was a constable called Tony Bull. Tony was a big man with a big stomach who always rode a little scooter to work in full uniform with his Police helmet on (this was before the days of wearing regulatory helmets). I have to say his helmet looked like a tom tit on a shovel. Tony would regale us with boring tales of woe and made Victor Meldrew look like a happy chappie!

One of the funniest messages I recorded was a report of 'Cows straying on the A49 at Dinmore Hill. Result – 8.09 am PC Bull attending!' I think things like that are so funny.

One of the greatest pleasures of Policing is the characters you meet along the way both inside and outside the job. One of those characters was Tom, the local milkman. Tom had a small dairy just below the Police Station in Burgess Street which is now a cafe. People said Tom was in his eighties. I am not sure but he certainly looked old and winter or summer you would see Tom shuffling along the streets of Leominster pushing a small metal trolley with a few pints of milk making his deliveries. He seemed to work only at night and was always about in the early hours of the morning and later he became known as 'the midnight milkman.' He looked dishevelled, always wearing an overcoat and hunched over. Always a man of few words Tom was totally reliable and never seemed to miss his round which he carried out completely on his own on foot.

To me he was a man of mystery and no-one seemed to know much about Tom. The one amazing thing was that apparently he was very well read. In the wee hours in the dim light of his dairy Tom would sit having a well-earned cup of tea reading works of literature in small print with no glasses or reading aids.

I was always surprised he was never robbed but in those days during the middle of the night at Leominster the only people on the streets would be police officers, milkman and an early morning postman. I also think he was a man who had tremendous respect in the town and was so much a part of the town hardly anyone would have dared upset Tom. I wish I had found out more about Tom and got to know him better.

There was another well-known local family in the town who were notorious for their ability to fight. One of them I will call Mark. Mark was one of those likeable rogues who when drunk and wanting to fight was particularly obnoxious. However, in the cool light of day when sober he could be one of the nicest guys you could meet.

Tale has it that Mark in a drunken row with one of the local cops at Leominster Mark lost his temper and hit the officer knocking him unconscious. Being immediately sorry for what he had done he picked him up, put him over his shoulder and carried him to the Police Station where he brought him into the Police Station, laid him on the front counter and then apologised profusely for what he had done.

I first met Mark one night when he was brought in for fighting. He was really aggressive and I helped others put him in the cell. Mark looked through the hatch at all of us and said, 'You're all a bunch of fucking pigs,' then looking at me in my distinctive Cadet uniform he said, 'And you are just a fucking piglet.' I had to smile.

Next morning I stayed on late after nights and gave Mark his breakfast in the cells. He had calmed down by then. He asked me how old I was and when I was due to join the 'regular' Police. I told him in a few months and he wished me the best of luck in my future career. Nice one Mark and none so strange as folk!

Just before Christmas of 1971 I went with one of the Sergeants, Pete Preece to a sudden death. This was the first real death I had ever been to and I was both intrigued but also full of trepidation as to what we had to do.

The term sudden death means that a death has occurred and either the death is suspicious or for various reasons the doctor attending cannot issue a certificate as to the cause of death, usually because it is unexpected and they have not treated the person recently.

In this case it was an elderly man who appeared to have suffered a heart attack and had died in his own home, which was a small semi-detached house on the edge of town. When we arrived the doctor was still present and explained that although it appeared natural causes, for the reasons explained above he could not issue a certificate and therefore we would need to deal with the case on behalf of the Coroner who would no doubt issue a certificate once a post mortem had been carried out.

Whilst technically this appeared quite straightforward I was more interested in the practical implications this had for the man's widow who was sitting in the lounge, very distraught looking at her husband who was lying dead in front of the fire-place surrounded by all the decorations and usual trimmings of Christmas including numerous cards on the mantelpiece. I quickly gathered they were both elderly, had been married for eternity, were obviously very close but had no-one in the family immediately available to support them. The man had been quite fit and his death was completely unexpected.

What really got to me was the similarity between them and my own parents. A loyal and loving elderly couple who led a simple life together and were quietly looking forward to spending Christmas together as they had for more years than they could probably remember. The woman was very sweet, once she regained her composure she was more interested in our welfare and the etiquette of playing host rather than her own very sad dilemma she now faced alone.

We called the undertakers, had the body removed and completed the multi-page sudden death report (well at least the Sergeant did). We made sure the lady was in the care of neighbours and necessary next of kin had been informed and then we carried on.

I went home that night, went to bed and cried my eyes out reflecting on the poor lady's plight and the similarity between the couple and my own parents and how lucky I was at Christmas to have mine alive and relatively OK.

That was the first sudden death I ever attended. There were to be literally hundreds more and one has to toughen up, which I did. However, you must never toughen up so much that you do not feel for the people involved. Once you do that you lose the ability to empathise. Whilst always routine to the Police the death you are dealing with is probably the biggest thing in the relative's life. They are real people with real feelings and deserve the respect and kindness of the professionals dealing with it. What you must not do is lose control yourself. It's a fine line and one that you never perfect exactly because each time is different and each time you learn something about how fragile human life is and how much we take it for granted.

Life was not all bad news though. I worked with a very experienced and to me an 'old' cop called Bill Wallis. Bill was nearing the end of his service and was one of the most wily chaps I ever worked with. I learnt a lot from Bill about how to deal with people and speak to the public. Bill was old school and although the days of the Police cape had long gone he still wore his with pride. Bill knew where every cup of tea was to be had on the town and could talk the hind leg off a donkey.

He used to say that if you want to get information from the punters about what is going on and who is doing what you need to make them feel you are confiding in them and give them information. I never once heard Bill tell anyone anything they could not have got through the local newspapers but Bill always ensured they thought it was privileged information and in return people would confide in him.

I spent many hours walking with Bill around the streets of Leominster on nights having debates about women and life. On early turn we would go to the Royal Oak Hotel and have a freebie breakfast which was one of many stops Bill had developed.

One of the patrol vehicles was a Morris Oxford which was a huge tank of a car. Every time I went out with Bill I could smell this horrible smell which was worse if the heater was on. Bill could not smell it at all and told me I was talking rubbish.

I began to think I was until one of the other lads smelt it too. Eventually it got so bad they took the car into the Police workshops and they found a dead mouse behind the heater box. I took great pleasure in telling Bill!

By now I was thoroughly enjoying myself and realised that Policing was about dealing with people which I loved. I was learning so much about dealing with incidents, making decisions, putting the law into operation and completing reports. I made it my business to learn everything I could from the officers I was working with including how to make safe shortcuts, essential in every job.

In March 1972 this was interrupted when they sent me on a compulsory one month's Outward Bound course to Aberdovey in Wales.

I knew this was not going to be my cup of tea and from the tales of those who had already been I knew it was a long month of walking, camping, rock climbing, canoeing and lots of other physical activity. I was the only one who went from our area and on a cold damp dismal March morning I caught a train from Hereford.

When we arrived at Aberdovey the staff from the centre put us in a land rover and drove us to the Outward Bound Sea School. We were told to immediately change into swimming trunks and pumps and to parade by the flag pole to be given our joining instructions by the Commandant of the place. Yes, a Commandant and yes he was like that!

We paraded in the cold, shivering and apprehensive. The Commandant then got a hose pipe and sprayed us with cold water continually whilst he gave us our joining instructions. He told us that it was his intention to ensure that for the next month we were going to be cold, wet and thoroughly uncomfortable so that when we eventually went home we would appreciate the creature comforts of home.

Well, I tell you he never said a truer bloody word.

We slept in bunks and on the first morning we were woken at about 5.30am by one of the instructors who was shouting, 'Good morning, it's a beautiful morning, the sun is shining the birds are singing, now get out of bed for a special treat.

What he really meant was, it was the middle of March, it was freezing cold outside, pitch black and he wanted us to put on pumps and swimming trunks and run down straight to the outside swimming pool. The first task was to break the ice in the pool and then swim one length of the pool and get out. If you couldn't swim then you had to walk across two widths and dip your head under before you got out.

The special treat the instructor spoke about was a cold shower afterwards! The amazing thing is the cold shower felt like boiling jets of hot water compared to the coldness of the pool.

the other lads was having a crap in the same stream just over the hillock. When I pointed this out to Ben he was not impressed!

Another favourite pastime was rock climbing. Having experienced rock climbing I have to say that I consider it is the most challenging and gruelling of all sports I have ever tried and I take my hat off to all those who participate.

You see in most sports you can give up when you are knackered. Try doing that when you're several hundred feet up in the air. There is only one way to go!

What I am about to relate was probably one of the most scary moments of my life and one in which I consider I grew from a boy into a man and will never ever forget because at one point I was convinced I was going to die.

Near the village of Tywyn on the west coast of Wales on the south bank of River Dysynni there is a piece of rock known as Craig-yr-Aderyn or 'Bird Rock,' so called because it is home to a number of species of birds including the Great Cormorant.

On a misty morning in March we were in the back of a lorry travelling towards Bird Rock which we were told was the destination for a day's rock climbing.

As we drove towards we could see it looming out of the sky, 800 feet above sea level, a massive and formidable looking rock. The previous day we had practised on some sea cliffs about 60 feet high but this was different.

We asked the instructor on board if we were expected to climb near the bottom ridges or the top and how high we would be. He told us we would be climbing from the top at a height of at least 500 feet.

Full of trepidation we parked up and walked to the top via a path that only goats and outward bound students used!

As we looked down from the top I can remember seeing cars passing on the road below which looked the size of match boxes. I could not believe what we had to do.

The instructor told us that the challenge was to abseil down 120 feet onto a ledge and then climb back up. Our colleagues would manage the rope and we would take turns.

I have to say that one or two of the lads refused and were visibly upset. I felt I could not fail because to do so would mean going back without the coveted outward bound badge and I was not sure what this would mean for my career. So, when it came to my turn I decided to have a go. I abseiled down onto the ledge with no problem. In fact I found the descent exhilarating. I then commenced the ascent. When I was about half way I hit a problem. A big piece of slab in the rock with hardly any toe or hand holds that I could reach easily. I only have legs that are 29 inches long and try as hard as I could there was no way I could safely find a good foothold. I tried shouting but there was no response.

I decided to take a chance on a slim foothold and take the weight of my body with my hands. As I pushed upwards I slipped off the rock and fell immediately at a fast rate.

Now, whether the guy at the top was having a crafty fag or just not paying attention I do not know, but I do know that I fell the full length of the abseil rope before it suddenly snagged. At that point I was now hanging several hundred feet up in the air on a rope and was shitting myself. I looked down and thought, this is it, and I have had it. I prayed for a miracle.

I could hear shouting from above and see that the instructors were worried. However, they weren't as bloody worried as I was because I just could not see how I was going to get out of this mess unless I could be winched up. The instructor tried to get me to resume the climb but could quickly see I was in no fit state to do anything.

Eventually he climbed down himself. He tied me to him and then brought me down across the rock onto some shale where we began a gradual descent that took eternity.

When we reached the bottom I was numb, shaking and could not move for ages.

I learnt a number of things on that climb: to face my greatest fears, to have faith in the instructors that were leading us and never ever to go bloody rock climbing again!

Despite that I have a fond spot for Bird Rock, a bit of a love hate relationship. An affinity to both the Rock and the area. So much so that in recent years I have returned with Jud and my family to look at the mighty presence of Bird Rock. On one occasion when no-one was looking I kicked it, swore at it and had a pee up against it. Then I went into one of the local villages and bought a watercolour of Bird Rock which hangs proudly in my home as a reminder of the day when I grew from a boy into a man.

One of the other favourite pastimes at Aberdovey was the assault course and gymnasium – not!

The gymnasium was an old hut with a brick floor and broken windows. The assault course consisted of a rope, a scrambling net and immediately below it a grot pot. The grot pot was a big hole filled with something that stank which was rumoured to be pig shit! I am not sure it was but it certainly resembled the very worst nightmare you might ever have.

The point of all this and the farce of it all was that we carried out circuit training in the 'gym', whereupon if you made a mistake you were ordered to run down the bank, climb over the scrambling net and jump into the grot pot. Then you ran back up the hill and resumed circuit training exercises on the floor of the gym. It mattered not whether you made a mistake and had to jump in the grot pot because by the end of the session the floor was swimming in whatever crap was in the grot pot and you were covered anyway.

Not sure what health and safety would make of that today!

Up until the third week I had religiously done my washing each day. When I could see light at the end of the tunnel and we could escape at the end of the week I gave up and threw all my dirty washing into a black bin liner under my bunk. The problem was that some of clothing had been soiled by the grot pot.

I recall that on the way back on the train I attracted some funny glances due to the smell but I didn't care as long as I was going home having completed another endurance test.

By the time I got the bag home and dumped it in the hall at home it virtually walked across the floor on its own!

I resumed back at Leominster knowing that from the December I was due to join up the regular Police as a constable. I carried on determined to learn everything I could.

However, there was still more physical punishment to come which involved attending an External Leadership Course based at the old Police Station at Bishops Castle, Shropshire which had been converted into living accommodation. This involved more hill walking, canoeing and camping across both the Long Myndd at Church Stretton and the Elan Valley in Wales. More tramping across desolate hills with heavy packs and more bloody blisters. I hated it but the instructors were good and I saw it through.

One of the instructors was a great big guy, a sergeant called Tony Allen who was ex SAS. He had a tiny little head sitting on shoulders that were as wide as a five barred gate. He used to carry a 40lb pack on his back as if it were a lunch box. He had a wicked sense of humour and would walk us on a diversion lasting miles just see something interesting like a rock formation. Somehow he didn't have a lot of patience for my blisters or anyone else's for that matter. No pain, no gain was his motto and one has to say that over the years whenever I have felt like giving in to a job, the memories of yomping over those hills in pain and keeping going when you were thoroughly exhausted did remind me that we all have hidden reserves and the only time to give in is when you physically collapse and cannot go on any further.

Towards the end of my stint at Leominster I was on nights working with Constable John Leedham in a panda car when we came across a local well known villain who was attempting to jemmy open the cash container in a telephone kiosk. The villain dropped the jemmy and then ran down an alley way. I got out of the Police car and chased after him down the alley where I managed to catch him and hold onto him until John arrived. I hadn't got a clue what I was doing, whether or not I had power to detain him or what the hell I was to do with him afterwards. However, I adopted the principle Bill Wallis had told me which is if in doubt, act positive and do what you think is right because it is better to be disciplined for doing the job than not doing it. I have always found that good advice and providing you act in good faith you cannot go far wrong but always make a decision. Fortunately John did know what he was doing and was very pleased to arrest the guy who was known and suspected to be actively carrying out similar crimes in the area.

We recovered the jemmy and took both jemmy and chummy to the nick.

He denied any knowledge of the jemmy or the offence but from memory I think fingerprints and forensic tied him in with the jemmy and the jemmy with being used to prise open the cash container.

However, he pleaded not guilty and eventually I had to give evidence in my first ever case at Hereford Crown Court where he was convicted and I had mention in dispatches (a commendation) for my efforts which really meant just being in the right place at the right time.

Eventually the time came for me to join the regular Police as a constable which I was eligible to do on my 19th birthday in December 1972.

However, it was not just a natural stepping stone. It involved going for a formal interview with a full review of the two years work as a Cadet.

The day came and I bulled my boots and pressed my uniform to perfection. I just had one problem. I had tried to improve the appearance of my cap by bending it which had resulted in it being very pointed at the front. In fact I had made a bit of a hash of it and whilst it was passable for duty wear it was not going to pass the scrutiny of the Deputy Chief Constable who was holding the interviews.

A colleague Cadet of mine leant me his cap to wear for the day which had a slashed peak but I thought it looked quite trendy and was loads better than mine. A slashed peak is what most drill squad sergeants did in those days which was to undo the stitching on the peak of the cap and bend it forwards so that the peak rested down over the eyes towards the bridge of the nose giving a very smart but evil appearance.

I went for the interview feeling much more confident wearing my colleague's cap. I marched in, stood to attention and saluted the group of three which included the Chair of the group, Alex Rennie, Deputy Chief Constable, a man who has a notorious reputation for hard discipline.

Rennie ignored me for a couple of minutes because he was looking down reading my report. In his broad Aberdonian accent he said to me: 'Ah Cadet King, you haven't had a bad couple of years with us laddie'........... and then he looked up and saw my cap! His face contorted and went red. 'What the hell have you done to that cap King?'

I was about to reply to the effect that it was not my cap and that I had borrowed it from a friend because mine was misshapen. However, I had already learned enough to realise that opened up a whole load of other questions to which the answers were ones that might drop me even further in the crap. So, even though I had this distinct feeling of wanting to relieve myself immediately I decided to brazen it out. I said, 'I haven't done anything to it sir, it was like it when issued.'

Rennie looked me up and down and then blasted me with his voice saying, 'You expect me to believe that, you little short arse, you come here today with your granddads boots on all bulled up expecting me to promote you. Well let me tell you, if ever I find you damaging Police property again I shall kick your backside out of the job, do you understand?'

It suddenly dawned on me what he was saying, 'Do you mean I am accepted Sir?'

'Yes,' said Rennie, 'Now get out before I change my mind!'

I saluted, turned round and virtually ran out of the room. As I left I could hear Rennie laughing, I guess that I was the sport for the day. I didn't care because I was now in the job as a regular cop

Not the best interview I was to have in my career but not the last time I was to meet Alex Rennie and do battle over an interview but more of that later.

CHAPTER 5

FULLY FLEDGED COP – RYTON TO REDDITCH

The theme of caps seemed to remain. On a bright winter's day in early 1973 I drove my little Morris 1000 car to the police training school at Ryton on Dunsmore, which is just on the outskirts of Coventry.

The Training school was typical of ex military buildings and consisted of big billets sprawled out in rows next to the Chrysler car factory.

I got my case and headed towards the reception full of intrigue and apprehension. I saw the opportunity of a short-cut across the grass and had just stepped onto the grass when I noticed two things. One was a sign saying, 'Keep off the Grass.' The second thing was a booming loud voice shouting, 'Get off the bloody grass.'

I looked round and could see a large lump of a Sergeant in full uniform walking towards me with a 'pace stick' under his arm and a bright red sash round his torso. The other thing that struck me was his cap with the peak slashed right down to his little piggy eyes and a bright red face looking very angry in my direction. I realised immediately that this was the infamous drill sergeant who ruled the training school with a rod of iron and a climate of fear.

I immediately stepped off the grass, apologised and ran towards reception, not daring to look back. It did occur to me to question the irony of having a bollocking from my Chief Constable for wearing a flat cap with a slashed peak when the man responsible for discipline at the District Police

Training school wore his with pride! However, I did not think there was much point in questioning this at the time. Somehow, I don't think the irony would have been appreciated.

As I got to know the drill sergeant at Ryton I realised he was not a patch on Ken Timmis who had been our drill sergeant at Droitwich. This one was bullish and ruled by fear whereas Ken Timmis ruled by being firm, fair and gaining respect through insistence of only the highest standards.

As an example of this I can tell you that I honestly did not need to bull my boots or press my uniforms for the entire 13 weeks I was at Ryton (except for the passing out parade) due to the impeccable standards insisted upon by Ken Timmis before we were despatched out of Force and left Droitwich with our Cadet uniforms converted to Constables insignia.

On one occasion we were on the drill square at Ryton when some poor lady came walking across the square to report that she had just seen a load of cows straying in the road just up from the training centre. Now, what could be more normal than spotting a load of cows on the road and then within two hundred yards you are confronted by about 200 cops parading round a drill square. She must have thought it was like 'a gift from God.' Playing the good citizen she had decided to report it immediately.

Unfortunately she had not appreciated the etiquette that a drill square is sacrosanct and no-one sets foot on it unless you have the permission of the drill sergeant.

As she walked across the square and tried to speak the Sergeant roared at her, 'Get off my square woman, what the hell do you think you are doing?'

At that point the poor woman burst into tears and the rest of us were stood to attention, frightened to move and completely nonplussed wondering what the hell to do.

Fortunately, one of the Inspectors heard the commotion, came out, consoled the woman, despatched some of us to go and round the cows up and gave the Sergeant a bollocking. At that point 200 pairs of shoulders starting rolling with laughter!

Our Instructor for the 13 weeks was Sergeant Frank Carsley from my own force West Mercia. Frank was a lovely man. He was old and portly with a shock of grey hair that continually fell into his eyes as he laughed and Frank did a lot of laughing.

Fairly quiet and unassuming he was referred to as 'Dad' by his colleague instructors because of his avuncular nature and good humour.

Frank's style suited mine. I could listen to him all day reciting law and that was fortunate because most days that was what we did.

On some occasions we would have student instructors come to lecture to us and be assessed by Frank as to their ability. On these occasions the commandant of the training school who was a Chief Superintendent would slip in the rear entrance of the classroom and plonk himself on a chair at the back in order to observe and try to be as unobtrusive as possible.

Now, we had a chair that was broken and unwittingly left it at the rear of the classroom out of the way, or so we thought. The Student Instructor starts lecturing. A few minutes later in walks the Commandant and plonks himself down on the broken chair whereupon it collapses and he goes 'arse over tit' onto the floor. This was not helped by virtue of the fact that at the point we looked round following the crack of the chair as it broke all we could see were size 12 boots flying backwards. We pissed ourselves laughing but unfortunately the commandant did not see the funny side of it and tried to blame us all for setting it up. Now I would like to say we did but honestly we didn't! The student instructor was failed; largely on the grounds he couldn't keep a straight face either.

The accommodation was good at Ryton and the food wasn't bad either. We each had separate bedrooms which was luxury compared to the dormitory arrangements at Droitwich. The only problem was lack of toilets. The buildings themselves were long billets with a toilet at either end which was a long way to walk in the middle of the night.

Hence, some of us learned to pee in the sink. What was funny was lying in bed after a night on the beer and one by one hearing the taps running in each of the bedrooms like a chorus of waterfalls!

I quickly established a routine at Ryton and made my mind up to work as hard as I could and get top marks building on my previous knowledge. I teamed up with another recruit called Dave Onions who had not been a Cadet but we got along well. Each night after tea we went back to the classroom where we would spend at least two hours re-reading and reflecting on the day's knowledge we had learned and then pre-reading the next day lectures and learning definitions of law which I can still recite today.

We only had one rule and that was to be in the bar by 9 o' clock to have a few pints. I have to say for 13 weeks we never failed on any night to either work or drink!

I developed a real thirst (pun intended) for learning law and procedures and was able to use my operational experience at Leominster to contextualise the theory so it all became real to me.

As I look back now, I enjoyed the three months at Ryton as much as I have ever enjoyed anything in my life. It was like an extended holiday where I was learning interesting things, mixing with great friends and colleagues and enjoying the social life. Sport and exercise were kept to a minimum which suited me.

Discipline was still tough though. I had a friend who shall rename nameless. He was very greedy. Greedy, because he was caught with two policewomen in his bedroom by the drill sergeant and sent back to Force for the remainder of the course.

What happened was that this friend was innocently entertaining the two policewomen to afternoon tea in his bedroom – as you do! Unfortunately, there was a rule that members of the opposite sex were not to visit each other's residence blocks.

Friend sees the drill sergeant approaching the male block walking with a purpose and decides to be safe and hide the girls. He puts one under the bed and the other in the wardrobe. However, he had forgotten one thing. All the bedrooms were at ground level. It was a warm day and the outside window was open. The drill sergeant had apparently heard the women's voices and decided to investigate.

Everything went to rat shit when the sergeant instead of walking through the entrance door to the block decided to walk straight in through the open window into the bedroom. As he stepped onto the bed it collapsed and the woman underneath screamed. That led to the second one in the wardrobe deciding to come out to see what the hell was going on. The rest is history and my friend was sent back to Force and admonished but kept in the job. He had an excellent career and eventually made it to Superintendent so it obviously did not affect him unduly!

One of the things we had to do at Ryton was learn to give evidence in Court at a mock hearing. The irony was that the night before this was due to happen I was summoned to Hereford Crown Court to give evidence in the real trial of the man we had arrested trying to break into the telephone kiosk so it was a baptism of fire! The case went well and despite a fierce cross examination my evidence stood up well and he was found guilty.

That filled me full of confidence and was to stand me in good stead for the future.

We had three lots of major exams at monthly intervals which you had to pass otherwise you would find yourself back coursed.

I did well at each stage getting marks of 90% plus in all exams. Also on the course in the same class as myself was a policewoman from Loughborough in Leicestershire (unfortunately her name escapes me). We were neck and neck in all the exams and I realised she was a formidable adversary.

When the final results came of the three months work we were in the bar at a function when Frank Carsley approached me, his white hair flopped down over his forehead and a pint in his hand. He informed me that I was runner up on the whole intake of students and would be getting the 'Welfare Book Prize.' He also told me that the policewoman from Leicestershire had beaten me by less than one percent. I was over the moon both for me and the policewoman but especially for Frank who had achieved both the top and runner-up student in his class. What a result for him!

The day of the passing out parade dawned which was preceded by a formal evening black tie dinner. Because I was runner up on the course and going to receive an award it was my duty to escort the Commandant's wife into dinner and remain by her side until after the festivities were completed. I also had to make a formal toast. The policewoman had to escort the Commandment and do the same.

So, my bloody prize for winning an award was to accompany a much older woman into dinner. To make formal small talk all evening with someone I had absolutely nothing in common with and worry myself all evening because I had to make a formal toast. All this and I was confronted by my mates taking the piss and enjoying themselves on the other tables. Anyway, all went well and the minute the dinner was over I excused myself and escaped to be with my mates.

Next day was the passing out parade which was attended by my Mum, Dad and Jud who had an excuse for another new hat!

My prize was a book on the Laws of Evidence awarded by Stanley Bailey Deputy Chief Constable of Staffordshire and Stoke on Trent (later to become Sir Stanley Bailey and Chief Constable of Northumbria). It was a very proud moment for me and my family.

As he gave me the prize Mr Bailey said, 'Best of luck young man and always give it everything you have got.' There have been many times in my life when I have reflected on those words and I have always tried to live up to them believing duty comes before everything as far as work is concerned. Only family should come first.

I was particularly impressed by the significance of his words when many years later I read about Sir Stanley Bailey and realised that he originated from a very impoverished life and as a young man in 1945 had actually spent three days in custody for refusing to go down the mines as a 'Bevin Boy' preferring to join a fighting unit in the forces. Two years later he was given a second chance and joined the Police and went to the top.

In many ways I was sad to leave Ryton but was posted to Redditch and looked forward to being a real cop on the streets. Eighteen months later and I was back at Ryton on another probationary constable 'continuation course.' This time I worked extra hard at the legal exams and was pleased when I came top of the course.

This book began with my first experiences as a young Police Officer at Redditch where my Cadet and initial training had prepared me well to translate law and procedures into practice, to write reports and to give evidence in Court.

At the end of my two and a half years at Redditch Jud and I decided to get married and I applied for a Police house. My probationary period as a Police Officer was now up and I had very good reports.

Eventually I was offered a Police house and local beat station at Barnt Green which is in the Lickey Hills just outside Birmingham. I readily accepted, but little did I know what I had let myself in for!

CHAPTER 6

BEING A REAL BEAT BOBBY 'GRAVY AND GRENADES'

On the 24th May 1975 Jud and I got married on the proceeds of the criminal injuries compensation I had earned getting beaten up in a fight at Redditch. We married at Upper Sapey Church in Worcestershire and had the reception at the Lion Pub at Clifton on Teme.

John Price my Police colleague from Redditch was best man and Geoff 'have a fag' Benbow was one of the guests with his lovely wife Sadie.

Jud and I were still very young. Jud was 20 and I was 21 but that was the way things were in those days.

We spent 3 days honeymoon in Aberystwyth, West Wales and then moved into our new home which was one of two Police houses situated at Bittell Road, Barnt Green, just south of Birmingham.

It was a modern house with good facilities right on the side of the main road which connected Birmingham to Alvechurch. The only problem was the garden. It was a massive plot which was completely overgrown and had gone wild. Jud could not even hang the washing out because the grass was too high.

The beat itself was an interesting patch. It consisted of the village of Barnt Green which is very prosperous stockbroker belt just at the foot of the Lickey Hills. Barnt Green was notorious in policing circles as having a reputation for high-class burglaries. Some of the houses in the new developments were occupied by jumped up sales executives made company directors who treated you as if you were something the cat dragged in. However, further out of the village lived some of the ladies and gents who had always had money and at least knew how to treat people properly and which side their bread was buttered as far as the local Police were concerned.

In complete contrast to that my other bit of the patch was Cofton Hackett and Rednal which form the boundary with Birmingham and covered amongst other things the East Works at the Longbridge car factory, two late night drinking clubs called the Chalet and Cofton Club, the amusement arcades that surrounded the old tram terminus at Rednal and of course the facilities of the Lickey Hills.

The car factory was at the time under the thumb of the unions and ruled by the infamous Trade Union convenor and shop steward Derek Robinson, better known as Red Robbo. Whenever they were on strike, which was very often in those days hundreds of workers would spill out onto the massive Cofton Park which was opposite the factory. The factory was a village in its own right and as a cop whenever you went to investigate an incident you had to be very low key otherwise a strike would be called or you would be made very unpopular.

Just up the road from the East works was a huge storage area and car transporters for British Leyland where the company would report literally thousands of pounds worth of equipment stolen from the stored cars each month such as Range Rover wheels and radios. I was always a little dubious that it was an inside job which was finally confirmed on one occasion in the snow when they reported that someone had cut through the wire fence from an adjoining field and stolen a load of wheels off the stored cars. Problem was that the only footprints in the snow were on the inside of the fence and the snow had been there for days! Suspicion was that the property was being hidden on the transporters and going out of the gates by a dishonest driver. However, time and motion studies and union objections meant the company could not impose even occasional spot-checks on the transporters when they left so we were left with a problem.

Somewhere between the stockbroker aspect of Barnt Green and the tourism and industry of Cofton Hackett and Rednal lay the tranquillity and peacefulness of Blackwell and Burcot, two lovely villages not far from the market town of Bromsgrove.

Although Blackwell and its surrounding hamlets had its own beat bobby in the shape of PC Jock Reid I was often expected to cover that patch when Jock was off and vice versa.

Blackwell was very rural and had its own share of work in the form of sheep worrying, poaching, firearms and shotguns applications, a local post office that tended to be targeted by Birmingham villains for robberies and a children's home run by Birmingham Social Services where the kids were forever either running away or being involved in violence with the staff.

All-in-all these three 'patches' brought a great deal of business and versatility to what was described as rural policing.

Whilst I had acquired a lot of experience at Redditch it did not totally prepare me for all the challenges I was to face. For a start there was only one Sergeant who was based at Rubery which was our section station. Rubery is the last village outpost of Worcestershire before Birmingham. In fact the Birmingham boundary is literally a stone's throw from the Police Station. It has one long main street called New Road which always gave me the impression of being one of those towns you see on TV Western films.

The section sergeant was Roger Cleveland, a big tall man and an ex guardsman who was always whistling and did his best to keep us in order. However, when Roger was not working then we had to call on the sub-divisional Sergeants at Bromsgrove who were never keen to come out to the northern outposts of our sections in case the Brummies got them! This meant that you worked most of the time on your own and made your own decisions. Whilst the work did not come in as thick and fast as it did working shifts at Redditch, there was no-one to share the workload and no-matter how busy you were it was down to you.

Also, it was discretional working hours and basically covering 24 hours in which you attempted to work just 8 hours but sometimes it could be long days that stretched from first thing in the morning till last thing at night.

Our home was also the Police station, which meant the public calling at all hours and a telephone that never stopped ringing. We were woken many times during the night and sometimes it was just routine inquiries from 24 hour staffed Police Stations in Birmingham wanting you to check whether somebody had produced their driving documents! They could not believe that this was a small rural Police station where often it was Jud as the unpaid wife and slave who was answering the phone when I was not there.

Our only salvation was that it was a dual Police Station with a Police colleague and their family based next door who shared the work and took turns on being on call and answering the phone.

When we went shopping and I was on call we used to have to ring Bromsgrove and let them know where we were going and how long we would be whether or not you had completed your shift for that day.

The workload was amazing. In the first two weeks I dealt with 14 road accidents. In addition there were continual high-class burglaries which would necessitate taking statements describing numerous items of exclusive and expensive valuables and antiques. The other thing was every other bugger who lived in Barnt Green and Rednal seemed to work in Birmingham where many would park on double yellow lines, ignoring the fixed penalties and I would end up having to serve summons or carry out inquiries to establish who was driving the car on behalf of the Police in the West Midlands area. Then they would plead not guilty, take it to the wire and I would end up attending the Victoria Law Courts in Birmingham where I would have to give evidence and then the case would be proved in their absence. They would end up with a much heavier fine than the fixed penalty but they didn't give a hoot because usually their company would pay and they had succeeded in causing as much hassle as possible!

At night there would be numerous fights at the Cofton and Chalet night clubs and sometimes they resulted in people being stabbed or seriously beaten up. The offenders were usually known to the victims who would refuse to name them and get their summary justice the following week. When a fight broke out it was the Police at Longbridge we relied upon for assistance because there would only be one or two officers working at Rubery and by the time reinforcements arrived from Bromsgrove it was all over.

Then there were lost kids on the Lickey Hills, abandoned stolen cars, thefts of and from cars, naked couples copulating in bushes and in cars down the lanes, numerous reports of indecent exposure (flashers), sheep worrying, theft of livestock, parking problems outside the East Works factory, lost and found property, stray bloody dogs and domestic disputes! Oh yes the domestics.

Even the salubrious stockbroker belt villages of the rich and famous have their domestics but instead of chucking the telly out of the window they break the onyx tables or scratch the BMW and the Porsche. I will give you an example.

Jud and I had only been married a matter of weeks and were living under the sort of pressure I have described above. We were still learning to live together and jockeying for position as you do at that stage of married life. We were also learning to negotiate and compromise and at the age of just over 20 years we were coping with being at beck and call 24 hours, phones ringing all hours, people knocking at doors and having the responsibility of dealing with whatever turned up. Jud had moved from her parents' home and had to give up her job working in 'Elts' shoe shop in Worcester. She was now confined to the house, in a strange environment somewhere she had never heard of, with no friends and me working from dawn to dusk with no guarantee of when the day would end.

With this is mind, one night about 11 o'clock, whilst off duty we were having a full pitched domestic row about the amount of hours I was working, lack of privacy and Jud generally feeling like an unpaid slave for the Police and feeling like she was in prison herself.

Jud was at the top of the stairs in her nightie just getting ready for bed. I was at the foot of the stairs in the hallway just by the front door and we were both having a very forthright shouting match with Jud telling me where to stick my Police Station, panda car, telephone and torch! Suddenly the door bell went. I opened the door and was confronted by a middle aged couple I will call Mr and Mrs Sourton who lived on the outskirts of the village. Mrs Sourton was in floods of tears and Mr. Sourton was shouting at her. They were both extremely emotional and it was obvious they were having a domestic similar to the one I was having in the house! I recognised the couple because I had been called to their house numerous times to attend disputes which were only ever temporarily reconciled.

Through the crying and shouting I managed to establish that Mrs Sourton was alleging Mr. Sourton had tried to poison her dog and Mr. Sourton was alleging Mrs Sourton had tried to stab him.

I was just establishing that firstly the dog was still alive and secondly that Mr. Sourton had no injuries when Jud, who was not best pleased to have own domestic interrupted yet again by the public of Barnt Green started shouting down the stairs, 'For goodness sake, don't people think we ever need any peace, tell them to go away and come to bed now.'

I said something back, like, 'Sod off to bed and let me deal with this, it's my bloody job, if you don't like it then tough'

I always remember my Dad telling me that whenever Mum got close to throwing the clock at him he used to shout out to her, 'Time flies and waits for no man!' Something told me that I was now very close to having a clock or the nearest implement thrown at me so I dived out of the front door to and spoke to Mr and Mrs Sourton on the front lawn.

By now they were looking rather bemused that having come to me for advice and support and they were virtually in need of sheltering me from Jud's wrath if she came down the stairs and had not realised that Police Officers have their domestics to!

I decided to take the bull by the horns and capture the moment. I asked them how long they had been married to which they replied 25 years. I then proceeded to tell them that I had been married about 25 weeks and that as they could see things were not going too well and therefore whatever possessed them to think that I at the wise old age of 21 could sort out 25 years of married acrimony. However, since they had asked I went on to tell them that I did not think their marriage stood a chance of survival. I told Mr. Sourton to sleep in his car on the front of my Police Station all night and Mrs Sourton to go home. That in the morning they should both see a solicitor and seek a divorce and I was not prepared to deal with any further domestic incidents involving either of them until they sorted something out formally. I then told them I would like to be excused because I wished to resume my own domestic and hopefully resolve it better than they done over the last 25 years.

Both of them were left speechless but complied with my request and eventually got divorced. Things were quiet thereafter, in their house anyway!

Eventually, Jud got a job working in Woolworths at Redditch which meant she had her own life outside of working for West Mercia Police. In addition the Force put some switches on the house phones so that they could be turned off when we were off duty. The only problem then was that you had no idea if friends or family were trying to ring you but it was better than continually having life disrupted answering flipping stupid questions to Joe Public 24/7. We actually embarked upon a social life but it did not stop the knock on the door from personal callers who couldn't get a reply on the phone.

Whilst it was hard, this was the life a beat bobby was all about where home and work merge together and where you are usually gardening in your uniform and then discussing the most intimate of problems in the middle of the night in your pyjamas.

Stray dogs crapping on your best carpet, motorists who were lost walking straight into your kitchen to ask the way and gravy with grenades, yes really!

I was out working 10am till 6pm on a Sunday. Jud was at home cooking lunch and stirring the gravy when there was a knock at the door. Jud turned the cooker rings down and answered the door. Standing there was a guy holding a grenade in his hand who in one breath told Jud he had just found the grenade by the side of the canal at Hopwood and decided he better hand it in. Also, he couldn't stop because he was in a hurry. He plonked the grenade in Jud's hand and then walked away.

Jud was unsure what to do with the grenade but knew it was time to switch the cooker off. So, she took the grenade in the kitchen, turned the cooker off and then decided to deposit the grenade outside by the front door. She then rang through to Police control room to let them know what had happened and ask me to return because firstly somebody had handed in a bloody grenade and secondly dinner was ready.

The radio call went something like this:

Control Room: 'Bravo Kilo 20, PC King Barnt Green from YK over'

Me: 'Bravo Kilo 20, go ahead over'

Control Room: 'Can you return to your base please and see your wife as soon as possible because someone has just handed in a grenade, over. Also, your lunch is ready and you are late!'

Me: 'Roger and Wilco. Can you tell her I am on my way but in the interim period pull the pin out of the grenade and if she is still there when I get back I will deal with it'

Control Room: 'Yes Wilco, will ring her now' Roger and M2 YK out.

Deathly hush!

Shit, now the above last comment was a joke but it suddenly dawned on me that the controller may have thought I was serious; after all they employed a lot of civilian staff and suppose it was some naive bugger on their first day?

I did then think that no-one could be that daft and if Jud received a call to say pull the pin out surely she would realise it was a joke?

Anyway, I decided to take a chance and not embarrass myself by pleading with the control not to pass the message. When I got home the grenade was still on the front step, Jud was stirring the gravy and it was apparent no-one had said anything about pulling the pin out!

I picked up the grenade and took it down the garden, buried it under some sandbags, where the next door neighbours kids couldn't get at it and called Bomb Disposal at Hereford. What I learnt was this. Because the grenade was now at a Police Station it was no longer a priority to collect it. I tried to explain that this was also our home and I wanted to mow the bloody lawn but it was to no avail. Two weeks later they came and collected it.

They took one look at it and tossed it in the back of a land rover telling me, 'It's OK mate it's a dud.'

The gravy was good though!

Another example of the life of a policeman's wife not being a happy one was on a winter's afternoon about 4pm. I was about to start work when I answered a knock on the front door to be confronted by a man who was in an extremely distressed state. He was holding both arms together which were covered in blood with large lacerations around both wrists. He was crying, shaking and could hardly speak but I ascertained that he had driven to the Police station in an Austin Allegro car which was now parked on the front of the station. He told me that he had tried to slash his wrists with a razor blade in an attempt to kill himself. He had then collapsed in the car but his wrists must have bound together and in the cold weather the blood congealed which stopped the flow. He woke up some time later feeling very sorry for himself and decided to seek help.

I immediately called an ambulance which came and took him to hospital. I then knew I had to recover the car to Rubery Police Station in order for it to be examined and preserved in case he should die or it was found to be foul play and not as he suggested. On going to the car I found the front driver's seat and carpets covered in blood and large pieces of flesh where he had hacked his wrists.

Jud bless her got a dustpan, brush and some cloths and cleaned it up sufficiently so I could drive it into Rubery. No thoughts about health and safety, AIDS or hygiene preservation in those days. Pair of rubber gloves and away you go!

Not long after we moved in there was a local fete at Barnt Green 1st School. Jud donned a lovely bright yellow dress and decided that even though I was working she would go and get to know the locals. As she was leaving I was trying to get the Panda car started and fiddling around with the engine covered in oil. Jud tried to help me and then we decided that it must be a flat battery and she would have to give the panda car a push whilst I drove it. Jud gave me a good push down the road and it started a treat. I pulled up to thank Jud but could see she was still running after me shaking her fists. I looked back, opened the window and could see that the front of her dress was now covered in oil! I drove off fast and skipped attending the fete.

We decided to embark upon our first decorating experience and to wallpaper what was a very large combined lounge, dining room. Jud knew about decorating but I didn't. We had bought some typical 1970's big flowery wallpaper for three of the walls and some dark brown chocolate emulsion for the fireplace wall. Jud told me before we started paper hanging that because it was matching paper that we needed to use a plumb line to make sure the paper was hung straight. I thought that because it was a modern house with straight walls that this was unnecessary as long as we took care so chose to ignore her advice at my peril. Halfway across the main wall and focal point of the room I realised things had gone seriously wrong. These massive bloody great flowers were now not matching by about 1'. I was left with a serious dilemma, either plough on and leave it looking an absolute mess or rip it all off, buy some paper and start again.

Jud was very quick of course to remind me I told you so and in the middle of hanging a piece of wallpaper we were having a heated debate when there was knock at the door. I was actually on leave and we had pinned a note to the front door politely asking the public not to disturb us but to call at the Police house next door or to call the Rubery Police Station. I could see through the window an elderly lady, very smartly dressed who was reading the notice but still knocking hell out the door. Jud decided she would answer it in her own inimitable style. The lady wanted to report that there was a stray dog running around in the village and that the Police should go immediately and capture it. Jud tried to explain that I was off duty and requested that the lady go next door and report it to my neighbour or his wife or alternatively we would ring Rubery Police Station.

This woman was having none of it and demanded that Jud fetch the policeman now whether or not I was off duty. At that point Jud told the lady where to go who responded that she was a local magistrate and would make a complaint about Jud and failing to act. Jud told the woman that she was neither paid by or accountable to the Police only as an unpaid wife and that the woman could do what the hell she wanted. Jud slammed the door and the woman went off in a huff. I am not sure what happened to either the woman or the dog but no further complaints were received about either.

I ended up going up the Northfield, buying several new rolls of wallpaper, ripping the old lot off and repapering. A lesson was learned!

A lot of our life seemed to evolve around stray dogs. People would find them, we would temporarily have to take care of them in the house or the office, Jud would start to fall in love with them, I would then quickly have to take them to the RSPCA at Barnes Hill, Northfield and if they were not claimed or re-homed after 7 days then it was inevitable that they had to be put down.

I saw some awful sights in the Police as most Police officers do, the sort of things that make your stomach churn. However, one of the few times I was ever sick to the point of vomiting was through a stray dog. In fact, this was not to be the last time a dog made me sick.

Somebody brought in a big fat Labrador. I put him in the back of the Police mini-van and tied his leash to the fuel pipe that crossed over from filler cap to fuel tank in the back of the van. I used to let them roam free in the back of the van until I realised that if you braked fiercely the dog would slide from back to front of the van or they would sneak up behind you whilst driving and start licking your ear out which was very disconcerting in heavy traffic.

I got the Labrador to the RSPCA and was just letting him out of the van when he was sick all over the floor of the van. What really revolted me was the point where before I could get him out of the van he started gobbling it up. The sight and smell in a confined space made me feel very ill. At the point where one of the kennel maids came out I was spewing up in the drive and the dog, which had now finished his own meal was looking at me pathetically. The kennel maid was very good, cleaning up both mine and the dogs sick but the look on her face said it all!

On another occasion I was in bed having a lie in on a day off when a young couple came to the door with a stray dog they had found. The dog was a lovely mongrel cross who looked very thin and dishevelled. Due to the fact I was on a day off and did not want to spend half of it either arranging for the dog to be picked up or take it to the RSPCA I tried to convince them to take it to another Police Station at Rubery or Bromsgrove. They were on their way to go on holiday, knew the law and were having none of it.

Due to the fact I was undressed and talking from my bedroom window my powers of negotiation were limited so I decided to take the dog in.

I donned my dressing gown, went outside, got their details and placed the dog in the little police office next to the main house.

After carrying out my ablutions and having some breakfast I went out to the office intending to take the dog in the panda van to Rubery Police Station where they could take it on to the RSPCA. As I entered the office I could see that the dog had messed all over the floor, had got up on the desk and had scattered my papers onto the floor which were now in the mess. I tried to get hold of the dog which kept running round the office until I slipped arse over tit into the dog crap on the floor. By this time the smell was getting to me, so I opened the window and shouted at the dog in sheer frustration. The dog leapt onto the windowsill and straight through the window, across the lawn and into the main road where it kept running up and down. I realised I could not catch it and was running out of ideas what the hell to do with it even if I did.

I decided to consolidate my position and clear up the mess hoping either the dog would come back or bugger off and never be seen again. My day off was not going well at all!

Two lovely old ladies lived next to us called Mrs Lintot and Mrs. Bishop who were sisters. I was busy cleaning up the mess and reciting a few well known choice phrases when they both came to the office door and asked me if I had seen the little dog that was running up and down the road causing chaos with early morning traffic. I closed the office door quickly and denied all knowledge. What dog? What a shame? Oh dear, perhaps we had better try and catch it then!

Eventually between the three of us we managed to entice the dog and round her up. Mrs Lintot and Bishop then decided to keep the dog because he was, 'So, sweet.' No one claimed the dog and it remained with the two sisters who cared for and treasured the dog for many years. They called her 'Lady.' I have no doubt that Lady lengthened the lives of the two elderly ladies for many years and had one of the luckiest escapes ever from a police station.

CHAPTER 7

LIFE WAS NOT A PARTY!

Married life was still very hard though and the hours long and tough to cope with.

One night I was travelling back from Rubery having just booked off at mid-night. I was driving the panda van down Kendal End Road at Barnt Green when I saw a car parked up in a lay-by just opposite the Barnt Green Inn outside some very big detached houses. I pulled up alongside the car and could see two youths inside the car one of whom I recognised as being a notorious burglar from Birmingham who prided himself on being the fastest at burgling any house in South Birmingham. He was distinctive because of his face which was covered in spots and pock marks. The car immediately sped off toward the direction of Hopwood. I chased after it and after about half a mile they suddenly braked liked hell and slewed the car across the road into Bittell Farm Road. The car was blocking the road completely and I had to swerve into the ditch to avoid hitting it. The two youths got out and literally jumped over a hedge into a field nearby. I did the same, fell into a load of mud but could not see or hear a bloody thing. I realised now that I had no radio, no torch (which were all in the van) and needed help. I climbed back over the hedge called for assistance on the Police van radio both for a dog handler and assistance to get my van out of the ditch and the car (which I presumed was stolen) out of the road.

Eventually, Tony Partridge a dog handler from Rubery attended and the dog picked up a track across the field. Tony told me to stay approximately 20 to 30 yards behind the dog and not show any light so as not to disturb the dog or make the youths aware we were on their track. I followed Tony and the dog for a while but it was not long before they left me behind. I was frightened to use my torch and my personal radio did not work. I wandered round this sodding field for hours and could not even find a way out. I fell over in the mud again, was soaking wet and now getting concerned that I might be lost out there until it got light. I had no idea in which direction I was heading or even how to get back.

Eventually, I could see the lights of a house in front of me. I climbed fences, hedges and barbed wire until I made it across a track to where the house was. I banged on the door which was answered by a nice couple who most surprised to find a uniform Police Officer on their door step in the middle of the night, completely lost, torn to shreds and covered in shit looking like a little lost boy!

I used their phone to telephone Bromsgrove Police Station who came and picked me up and were most amused at my predicament. The officers who came out told me the two youths had been found walking up a nearby road and had been arrested on suspicion of theft of the car. I went to Bromsgrove Police Station and helped out with the interviews. The only consolation I had was that they were in denial about everything until they saw me and realised they were covered in the same mud that I was and that I was able to identify them.

I got home about 7.30am and Jud was just getting ready for work. I had now been working best part of 16 hours, was wet, tired and had not eaten since the previous tea time. I had not rang Jud to say I was still working because the first few hours I was incommunicado and by the time I arrived at Bromsgrove it was the wee hours and I did not want to disturb her.

Unfortunately, what I did not realise was that Jud had rung Bromsgrove in the middle of the night and some berk on the Police switchboard had told her I had booked off at mid-night and didn't know where I was. Jud was not impressed and assumed that either I had been involved in an accident on the way home or I had spent the night with other female company. As soon as I got home the relief from Jud came out but she accused me of carrying on with some woman and rolling around in a field to cover my tracks!

What followed was a heated argument which resulted in Jud rushing out of the house to go to work and slamming the door behind her. I decided I would go to bed so I locked the door behind her and then spotted she had left the car keys behind in the kitchen. Jud realised very quickly, came back and started to knock the door to gain my attention. I decided to play daft (not hard for me) and pretended I could not hear her. Jud then started hammering on the wooden frame of the door to attract my attention whereupon her fist slipped and went straight through the glass panel where she cut her wrist.

By the time I got to the back door Jud was standing there covered in blood, crying and surrounded by glass. It was like a scene out of a bloody soap opera.

Eventually we got it sorted and both apologised. Jud for making incorrect assumptions and me for playing silly beggars!

On another occasion we decided to attend the local Police Ball at Bromsgrove. The tickets cost us a few quid we could hardly spare, Jud had her hair done and made a dress.

I was just going up for a bath and change when there was a knock at the front door. A man was standing there who said that he had just run over a big white mountain dog in Bittell Road just above the Police Station. He told me it was blocking part of the road and because it was dark he was concerned that it needed to be moved as soon as possible.

Big white mountain dogs are not that common and I immediately guessed who it was owned by, which was a family who lived just outside of the village.

I was still in uniform so I told Jud it would only take a few minutes to sort the dog out and to keep the bath water warm. I jumped into my Police Mini Van and drove the few yards up the road. Sure enough, lying across the one side of the road was one big white mountain dog. A massive thing. I had a quick look at it and realised it was still alive but looked severely injured. I called the control room to get a vet to the scene as soon as possible and then drove to the house of the family who I guessed owned the dog.

I quickly established that their dog was missing. A teenage lad from the family agreed to come back with me to the scene where the dog was lying. I parked up on the opposite side of the road and put on the blue light. The young lad, I will call him Barry, kept leaning over the dog into the road and I warned him to stand back on the pavement because traffic was building up, it was dark and the streetlights were poor. I decided I had better turn the van around so it would protect the scene and put some Police Slow signs out. I walked across the road and was getting the signs out of the van when I suddenly heard two thuds, followed a screech of brakes and then a loud scream.

I looked round and could see that a car had driven up the road and had collided into the young lad who was now lying in the centre of the road and shaking vigorously. The car had stopped and the driver was standing by the side of it looking very shocked because he had also run over the dog and wondered what the hell had happened.

I now had a very serious situation to deal with and immediately realised the implications of what had happened both for the young lad, the driver of the car and me having not put out warning signs and protecting the scene of the accident from the outset.

After calling for an ambulance I tried radioing for a Sergeant to attend the scene from Bromsgrove but because of the Police Ball there was minimum cover and the only one on duty for the division was not available to attend.

I called for a colleague from Rubery to assist but again there was no response.

I decided I had to get on with dealing with the incident and went about protecting the scene and cordoning off the road as well as seeing what first aid I could render to Barry.

By that time both the Ambulance and the vet had arrived. The ambulance took Barry to Selly Oak hospital and the vet put the dog down which then required specialist removal.

In addition to this I tried to get immediate measurements of the accident scene and draw a rough plan whilst the car and dog were in situ.

I then had to interview the driver of the car and breathalyse him as well as get a message passed to the family of Barry both about their son being injured and the dog being put down.

Friends of the driver of the car had now arrived at the scene and it was obvious he was very shocked. I decided to take him back to the Police Station to speak to him and breathalyse him.

I have a lasting memory of him and his friends sat on the settee in my lounge drinking tea with Jud bringing in a tray of biscuits dressed up to the nines in a beautiful long dress with her hair in curlers but realising that any ambition to attend the Police ball was now well and truly gone.

After dealing with the driver who had not committed any offences I drove to Selly Oak Hospital to check on the condition of Barry and to speak to his parents. We had a curt conversation about how the accident had happened and they inferred they held me responsible. I informed them that I would hand my evidence over to a supervising officer the next day and that they would need to make any formal complaint to that officer.

I inquired about the condition of Gavin and ascertained that he had sustained serious but not life threatening injuries but was expected to be in hospital for some time.

I returned back to my Police Station where I completed my notes and updated the control room log via the telephone as to the result to date.

By the time I got to bed it was the early hours of morning and I had been on duty since 8am the previous day, approximately 18 hours earlier. Even though I was tired out I could not sleep because of the responsibility that I felt for the accident and the uncertainty I felt over Barry's condition and what would happen if the parents made a complaint or sued the Force for my neglect.

I probably had no more than two or three hours sleep and even though I was supposed to be on a day off the next day I started work early to make sure I handed over all particulars of the accident to the Sergeant who was to deal with it. I had also arranged for a specialist accident investigator to attend the scene – common practice where any accident involved very serious injuries or where the Police may be culpable.

I met the Investigator at the scene and assisted him to make a thorough examination and scale plan of the scene.

Eventually, Barry was released from hospital but I believe he had some long term injuries to his leg. I had no further contact with the family and no formal complaint was made. I am not sure if any civil claim was made against the Force and if it was then I was not informed. I did not receive any official reprimand or discipline but to me I learnt a lesson as follows.

During the rest of my service as a constable and later when I obtained rank the first thing I would do when I attended the scene of a collision was to put out warning signs before even attempting to tend to the injured. When I became a Sergeant many constables had a sharp bollocking if I attended an accident and found no signs displayed.

Yes I learnt a lesson and the circumstances could have been far more tragic and almost were. Policing is like that, sometimes you do not get a second chance.

The second lesson I learnt was never make social plans because they are likely to be disrupted.

About a month later I promised Jud another night out. Same dress, new tickets and new hairdo. I was working 8am till 4pm and under a three line whip from Jud to be home in plenty of time to go out. Not like last time.........!

Just before 4pm I was called on the radio to attend a report of a burglary in progress at a house in Warren Lane, which is right at the top of the Lickey Hills and a well known tourist spot. When I arrived I found the occupants had detained a young man who they had found in the act of burgling their house when they returned home. He was only a teenager about 15 or 16 years old and quite a pleasant quiet young man who looked nothing like the stereotypical burglar. I arrested him and took him to Bromsgrove Police Station. I was hoping to hand him over to CID to carry on with the case so I could go off duty and take Jud out. However, shortly after arriving at the Police Station the young man started talking and it transpired he had an accomplice who was a man who had befriended him and had been present at the burglary at Warren Lane but had run off and left the youngster to take the rap.

We managed to get enough information to suggest that this man and the boy had been living at a flat in Birmingham, that the man was wanted and it was likely they had been committing burglaries all over the West Midlands area.

The CID officers went off to Birmingham to look for the man and I was left to interview the young boy. I ascertained that he originated from the London area and had gone missing from a residential drama school where he was studying to become an actor and had starred in several TV and theatre productions. He seemed very naive, had no previous convictions and seemed to have been completely led astray by his adult accomplice. Because his parents were not immediately available it meant that I needed to get a Social Worker before I could formally interview the youth. This took some time to arrange and the interview took several hours due to the complexity of events which spanned a life of crime over several weeks. There were no tape recordings in those days and the interview was recorded contemporaneously in a statement form by hand. It was a strange story and a rather unusual alliance which I do not think we ever bottomed out completely.

Eventually the man was arrested which resulted in further interviews and inquiries with other Police Forces. The case was handed over to CID because it required further extensive inquiries over a number of weeks. Both the young boy and the man were remanded in custody but I am not sure what the eventual result was.

What I do know is, that I did not get home again until the early hours and another 'social do' went down the pan much to Jud's disgust. This was getting to be a habit and it did not end there!

Jud had a good friend from her home village at Sapey Common called Jenny Witt. Within a short time of the above incidents being very fresh in Jud's mind Jenny invited us to her wedding. The wedding was due to take place on a customary Saturday. On the Friday night I was down to work

6pm to 2am which was usual half night cover over the weekend. As I left for work I can recall Jud telling me that I must be home on time and if we missed going to the wedding next day I would be under pain of death!

Everything was quiet and going quite well until about 1.45am. Just before I booked off I decided to drive down Warren Lane at the top of the Lickey Hills (yes, the same spot where the last incident with the burglars took place). Warren Lane was infamous for having cars broken into or stolen or stolen cars abandoned. This usually occurred on Friday and Saturday nights when the Cofton Night club was open which was situated right at the bottom of Warren Lane and attracted a lot of miscreants from the neighbouring outskirts of Birmingham.

I drove to the lane feeling it was the right thing to do before I went off duty but praying I would not see anything suspicious. As I drove to the bottom of the lane the headlights picked up the figure of a young man who was standing next to a line of cars and moved away very quickly when he saw the headlights. I stopped the Police van and jumped out. The youth stopped and tried to act as if nothing had happened. I shone my torch towards the direction of the car where he had been standing and could see that someone had broken the front offside window.

I tried to question the man as to his identity and what he was doing there but he was both partly drunk and being obstructive. I told him I was arresting him on suspicion of attempted theft whereupon he struggled and would not get in the Police van. I used my radio to call for assistance and was joined by PC Bob Middleton from Rubery. Bob was a lovely man. A typical old school cop who was a big man but usually a gentle giant. I say usually because Bob had a shock of bright red hair, big red cheeks and if he chose to a temper to match. On this occasion Bob spoke to the youth very nicely, explained that I had arrested him and that he was required to get into the Police van whereupon he would be escorted to Bromsgrove Police Station and then we would all be happy ever after. The youth was having none of it and remained obstructive, refusing to get in the van and denying he had done anything. Bob repeated his request politely on two or three occasions and then the red rag started flying.

Bob suddenly grabbed hold of the youth, and told him in no uncertain terms that if he did not get into the van in 10 seconds flat he would be getting into the van in pieces or words to that effect! There was something about Bob's demeanour that looked like he meant business and his size alongside his demeanour meant the youth decided Bob was not joking and got into the van.

We drove him to Bromsgrove Police station and left him in custody for the CID to deal with him in the morning. However, by the time I got home it was gone past 4am which was acknowledged by a grunt from Jud when I got into bed. I knew whatever happened I had to be up early to get to the wedding.

Next morning I was wide awake, got up early and made it to the wedding in time. Unfortunately, by lunchtime, a nice meal and few drinks I was nodding off all afternoon and had a few digs in the ribs from Jud!

For the next four and half years our life consisted of these types of incidents where private, personal, family and professional life merges into one. That was the job and to a large extent still is. It is a vocation and in those days family life and commitments always came second.

CHAPTER 8

VARIETY WAS THE SPICE OF LIFE

Thefts from cars were prolific particularly in the beauty spot areas of the Lickey Hills and from the car parks of the Cofton and Chalet night clubs on a Friday and Saturday night.

One of my main allies in combating this was a senior officer from the special constabulary called Cecil Goddard who was a farmer and lived on my patch. Cecil used to join me doing observations (obs) on the target areas late at night. On a cold night it was a case of dressing up in plain clothes and taking a bottle of whisky and milk to sip during the wee hours to keep the cold at bay. A favourite trick of some officers was to put on a pair of women's tights under your trousers to keep legs and nether regions warm. I never did this and if I did I am not admitting to it, OK?

One particular night myself and Cecil were hiding in a tree opposite the Chalet night club at the bottom of Rosehill watching the car park where there had been a spate of thefts from cars over a period of several weekends.

Approximately 2 am just before the club closed we saw an old Rover car driving around the car park with three occupants all looking very suspicious. Suddenly, the car stopped and one of the rear seat passengers got out and shone a light into several of the cars on the car park. Cecil and I made our way quietly across the road to the car park whereupon we heard the sound of smashing glass and realised one of the cars was being broken into.

We then ran across to where the Rover car was. The male driver ran off up the car park and was hotly pursued by Cecil. The other male had now got into the back of the Rover car and I was determined to grab hold of him because he was the one who had been sussing out the cars with the torch. I could vaguely see that the front passenger was a young girl who was sat just minding her own business.

As I approached the Rover the male tried to get out of the other side door. I lunged across the rear seat at him and tried to pin him across the rear seat. He was struggling hard and almost breaking away. I held him round the neck whereupon he reached through the rear door, scooped up some gravel in his hand and then rubbed it into may face and eyes. I shouted to the bouncers who were stood nearby who I was and to get help. They refused and told me to leave him alone. I could not afford to let go of the male to reach my radio so was snookered.

I kept hanging on until an elderly man who was waiting in a car for someone to come out of the club came across. He went and phoned for the Police and then went to see where Cecil had got to. Eventually Cecil returned with the other male and Police reinforcements from Longbridge turned up.

We took the prisoners including the girl to Bromsgrove Police station. It transpired that the Rover was stolen on false plates, that they had been stealing and breaking into cars across the West Midlands area but that the girl was just being used as a decoy and had only recently joined the two males as a recently acquired girlfriend who was quite respectable, worked in a bank and until that night was largely oblivious to what was happening.

On another occasion I was off duty in the evening and went up to the Barnt Green Inn for a drink which was a very nice posh pub about 500 yards up the road from my Police station and home.

As I was about to walk through the front entrance I could see two men standing by a car who appeared to be waiting for me to go in. I was suspicious so walked straight in through the door but then doubled back to watch from the entrance without being seen. The two men suddenly smashed the window of a car parked next to the one they had been standing by. They quickly reached in, snatched some items from the car and then jumped into the other car and started to drive off. It was over in a flash. I ran across the car park but stood no chance of catching them. However, I did manage to get the number of their car which I wrote down and then went over to the car which had been broken into which was a sports car of some description. I went back into the pub and phoned colleagues at Rubery. The car I had chased after was registered to someone in Northfield, Birmingham but surprisingly was not reported stolen.

Eventually, the owner of the sports car came out of the pub with his girlfriend and discovered that an expensive sheepskin jacket had been stolen. I found out he was also an off-duty Police officer from West Midlands. I told him I would deal with the crime when I was back on duty and left it at that.

The next day I was working so I went with a detective colleague called Mick Benting to Northfield to establish who owned the car I had seen. The house occupier claimed no knowledge of the car or name of the owner and it was looking like a cold trail of a car that had changed hands several times and was not going to be easily traced.

On the way back home it was late evening and I decided to drive onto the car park of the Barnt Green Inn to see who was about. Low and behold the same car I had seen drive off the previous night was parked on the car park with no-one in sight. They had obviously been oblivious to me chasing after them the previous night and word had not reached them that the Police were trying to trace the car.

I immediately rang Micky Benting who came down in a plain car. We hid the Police car and sat in wait to see what happened.

After a few minutes two men left the pub and walked in the direction of the car I had seen. Then, it got even better. They decided to try and break into another car parked next to theirs. Mick and I leapt out of our car and detained them. They were two big blokes and started struggling. We bent them over the boot of the car and managed to hold onto them until assistance arrived. We then arrested them for theft and took them and their car to Bromsgrove Police Station. When I searched their car I was met by a bonus.

Inside I found stocking masks, balaclavas' and some wooden coshes. The next day we were visited by the Robbery Squad from Birmingham and it transpired that the two men who were a father and son were planning attacks on insurance cash collectors across south Birmingham. They were convicted of a range of offences including the theft from the cars at Barnt Green and overall, typical of most good pieces of Police work it came together through a combination of good luck, coincidence and being in the right place at the right time. A good dose of inquisition also plays a part!

Life was not always about crime. Death in Police work is never far away and every so often you get the radio call to attend a 'sudden' death. Most are pretty routine and unusual, some are funny in a black humour sort of way and some are unusual. This one was unusual.

I was called to a big mansion house on the outskirts of Barnt Green village in a very rural area.

It transpired that the gardener/handyman had found his employer who was an elderly lady collapsed and dead in the bedroom of the house having suffered a haemorrhage She lived alone, was a very shy individual and although she had been ill for a few days had not called anyone. The handyman was concerned because the previous day he had realised she was ill and had taken her a meal which he had left outside the bedroom door at her request. He offered to call the Doctor but she would not let him. When he returned the next day he realised something was wrong because the meal lay untouched outside the door. He went into the bedroom and found her dead. He was beside himself with guilt for not having taken more positive action the previous day.

I tried to console him and then started the routine of getting a doctor to certify death, make sure there was nothing suspicious, call an undertaker, notify relatives and secure all valuables and the property.

My Sergeant Roger Cleveland attended and we inspected the body and assisted the undertaker to remove it. It was not a pleasant sight and the poor lady had bled profusely.

We called the Police Officer who acted as Coroner's Officer whose nickname was Brock.

Brock was assisting us search the house for valuables when suddenly he shouted out in surprise. He was searching a wall cupboard and found what appeared to be a live grenade and a load of firearms.

The handyman told us that he was not surprised, because the lady's father had been a high ranking officer in the war and had often said that he kept some memorabilia!

Another day in the life of a Constable on the beat.......

Mental Health is also a common issue for a Police Officer. Both their own and dealing with the foibles of others' illness!

On the outskirts of one of the villages lived two ladies, both unrelated. One had a problem with her husband and mental illness and the other one with alcohol.

The lady who had a problem with her husband and mental illness lived in a detached house and regularly used to call me to attend the house where I would find her with her husband in a distressed state. She would claim that someone used to regularly crawl through her bedroom window at night, tie her to the bed and then whip her with chains. The window she referred to was too small to crawl through and she had no marks. Her poor husband was usually present and at his wits end. I was aware she had a long history of mental illness and was being treated by her GP. Eventually she claimed that her husband was responsible for the beatings. All I could do was attend, console the lady and her husband and keep the GP updated.

One afternoon a colleague received a call from the local GP to say that this lady was at the surgery, lying in front of his car and he couldn't go home! When the officer suggested to him that possibly this lady needed formal sectioning and help the GP was dismissive of this suggestion and stated that she was receiving the best treatment she could. The police attended the surgery and detained the lady under the Mental Health Act. As per procedures they took her to Bromsgrove Police Station as a place of safety under the provisions of the Mental Health Act.

Specialist doctors and a social worker then attended to carry out an assessment as to whether or not the person should be formally detained and treated as a mental health patient in secure accommodation. The lady was assessed but they decided she was not at the threshold that required formal treatment. She was released and taken back home, whereupon she picked up a carving knife and stabbed her husband in the back causing serious but not life threatening injuries. She was arrested and this time eventually detained for mental health treatment. Hindsight is an exact science!

The other lady lived alone in a large detached bungalow. She was an attractive, well spoken, elegant elderly lady who still had a twinkle in her eye and someone whom I would imagine had broken a few hearts in her prime years. I knew the lady vaguely because I think the house had been burgled or something stolen from the property.

Late one Sunday afternoon I responded to a 999 call to attend the address because she had reported disturbing a male intruder in the bedroom of the house who had run off. Because I was patrolling near to the scene and was there within a few minutes I decided to make a quick search of the area and call out a dog-handler and additional Police patrols straight away. After about half an hour there was no sign of anyone on foot or looking suspicious in a car so I decided to go and see the lady to get the full story. (Bear in mind I had now mobilised most of the North Worcestershire Police Force who were out searching).

The lady concerned was still very upset and smelt strongly of alcohol. She was drinking when I arrived but due to the shock she was in I was not unduly surprised. I had trouble establishing from her what had happened but after a few minutes she told me between sobs that she had gone to lie down on the bed for a mid afternoon sleep when she was woken by a noise. When she opened her eyes she could see a tall man leaning over on the bed. She screamed and he immediately ran off. She chased him out of the house and he disappeared up the road. Nothing was missing, he did not say anything and she immediately called for the Police. I was mystified because she told me all doors and windows had been locked and there was no sign of a forced entry?

I asked if she knew the man and she seemed unsure. I asked her to describe him and she went into intimate detail about his height, colour of hair, build, facial features and the fact that he had a black handlebar moustache. When I asked if there was anything unusual about him she said, 'Yes, his clothes.' I asked her to elaborate and she told me that he had been dressed in full World War II RAF Flying Officer's uniform and how attractive he looked!

I now started to cotton on that in the midst of a semi drunken stupor this lady had dreamt of a conquest or possibly one that got away during her years in the war. I am not sure whether she was chasing him to catch him and crying because he got away or genuinely confused. Either way, there was no intruder so I had to call off every man and his dog from making the search.

After a while she started to realise that it was dream and was most apologetic at having wasted so much time.

From speaking to a neighbour I gathered a fuller picture that the lady did tend to drink a lot and did get very confused after her afternoon nap!

There was a night when I was extremely lucky to escape with my life and a night neither Jud nor I will ever forget and yet it all started to so simply.

About 7 o' clock one autumn evening just as it was drawing dark I was called to Plymouth Road, Barnt Green where there was a report of a tree fallen down. When I arrived sure enough there was a tree down and it was a big one. I called the Council to remove it and waited for them to attend. Whilst there I could feel the wind was getting up and it was obvious that a bad storm was on its way. I stood talking to some of the residents in the road and then realised that my Police Mini Van was parked right under a large tree which was swaying like hell in the wind. I decided to move the van further down the road. I was just pulling away when suddenly I felt the van shake and realised the tree had come down and as I was driving away some of the branches had struck the rear of the van. I accelerated away and then got to see that it had just missed the van but would have buried it had the van still been in the same place with me in it! It was a massive tree and that was just about the beginning of one of the busiest nights of my life. Report after report after report of trees down across roads kept coming in. Eventually, I was trapped between fallen trees in various roads and could not get any further or return home. The council were only able to respond to those trees down on major routes or where there was an accident or potential for further injury.

Jud was at home with the phone constantly ringing for hours taking reports of trees down. When she managed to get through to Bromsgrove, then she would give them a list of trees down and they would then call me via radio to try and check and make sure no-one was trapped but eventually I was just forced to park up somewhere safe and wait until the Council had moved a tree so that I could get through.

Whilst no one was killed there were numerous accidents and people injured which resulted in an aftermath of accident reports.

When I eventually got home Jud was still sat on a chair with the phone in her lap exhausted. It was not till the early hours of the morning that we got to bed.

However much there was variety, it was routine, but the more serious incidents were always just around the corner and parts of my early career touched briefly upon a number of what are now cases of national notoriety.

CHAPTER 9

MURDER AND MAYHEM

Birmingham Pub Bombings

At approximately 8.30pm on the evening of the 21st November 1974 two bombs exploded in the centre of Birmingham in two of the city centre pubs known as the Mulberry Bush and the Tavern in the Town. A total of 21 people were killed and 162 were injured.

That evening I was on duty patrolling in Redditch. I was driving a police panda car and trying to drive off the forecourt of Bordesley Garage on the Birmingham Road at Redditch having just refuelled. I was astounded by the continuous stream of traffic heading out of Birmingham in the direction of Redditch. It was a short while later when I realised that it was people driving out of Birmingham in sheer panic to get out of the City after the bombs had exploded.

Very soon afterwards it became apparent that this was a terrorist attack and word spread that it was the responsibility of the IRA. Emotions started running at fever pitch across Birmingham against the Irish with many wanting to take vigilante action against anyone who was Irish, in retaliation. Six men were subsequently very quickly arrested and charged and the case became known as the infamous Birmingham Six. In 1975 they were convicted for taking part in the atrocities but 16 years later these convictions were overturned because the verdicts were considered unsafe following what many refer to as one of the gravest miscarriages of justice that has occurred in this country.

During the early part of the proceedings against the men, one of the Stipendiary Magistrates who heard the initial hearings lived just on the Worcestershire boundary and it was feared there may be a threat to his life by the IRA. It was decided therefore that his house must be placed under 24 hour protection.

I was on a week of nights so each night it was my turn with a dog-handler to patrol the grounds of the house all night and ensure that no harm came to this vulnerable member of the judiciary or his family. However, it did occur to me that standing between this poor old stipe magistrate and the mighty forces of the IRA stood me, a dog handler and a dog, the dog being the most useful of the three of us. No firearms team, no authorised firearms officer and no standby crew in those days. The most we could have done was to have shouted up on the radio for help, released the dog and bloody run or hide!

However, we were provided with a caravan in the front garden where we could make a brew, play cards and while away the hours which went on for eternity but with the ever present threat that if the IRA did turn up we were done for.

I would like to say I played a major role in the bombings operation other than this but sadly not. However, I served with colleagues who had been working in Birmingham the night the bombs went off and went into the pubs where the explosions occurred. They were met with one of mainland Britain's worst terrorist atrocities that had ever occurred and with absolute carnage and devastation that shattered many lives and from which they will never recover. The impact of that night affected everyone in the West Midlands area and created fear amongst communities for many years.

Not long after the above atrocity came an incident that was to have national notoriety for several years and one of the most difficult and controversial cases that West Mercia Police were ever involved in that spread nationwide.

The Black Panther

During the early hours of the 14th January 1975 a young heiress called Lesley Whittle was kidnapped from her home at Highley, in Shropshire by a man called Donald Neilson, more commonly known as the Black

Panther. This notorious case was to create a nationwide hunt that went on for 12 months until Neilson was arrested in December of 1975 by two uniformed officers in Mansfield Nottingham following a routine stop check which almost resulted in their own deaths after he held them captive with a shotgun! Unfortunately, during the interim period Lesley Whittle was found dead in an old mineshaft at Kidsgrove in Staffordshire. Neilson was also linked to a number of other post raids and shootings that had occurred across the country including the shooting of a man at the nearby Dudley Freightliner depot at Dudley.

The kidnap and subsequent killing of Lesley Whittle resulted in nationwide publicity and the hunt was led by one of West Mercia's most experienced and capable detectives Detective Chief Superintendent Bob Booth.

This inquiry impacted upon every officer and every aspect of work throughout the Force. Due to sightings received the Black Panther was portrayed as a loner character, possibly of no fixed abode who was wearing a cloth cap and probably sleeping out and keeping on the move. This resulted in hundreds of sightings of both individuals and likely properties where he could be sleeping out which had to be checked. Every time you stopped someone you had to be mindful this could be the Black Panther and a dangerous man. For several months we lived and breathed the 'Black Panther.'

During the early stages of the inquiry it became apparent that the Black Panther was using a stolen Morris 1300 car which was on false plates. Every officer and traffic warden was asked to check their notebooks and records for sightings of the car on either the stolen plate TTV 454 H or its original plate FDH 878 H.

Two things happened locally as a result of this. Firstly a traffic warden at Redditch had noted the original plate in her notebook parked on a short-stay car park on the morning of 12 November 1974 which was before the kidnap of Lesley Whittle but less than 24 hours after the murder of a postmaster at Langley in the Black Country only 15 miles away.

This resulted in numerous inquiries within the town centre of Redditch to establish whether or not the Black Panther had been 'casing' out another potential raid to carry out or had been depositing money in a bank or building society. Furthermore, this coincided with a later further sighting by a taxi driver who reported seeing the stolen Morris 1300 on the new development estate of Redditch.

I was one of 50 officers despatched to carry out extensive house to house inquiries across two major estates of Redditch led by Bob Booth's deputy Detective Superintendent Stan Dixon (now deceased). This involved questioning more than 3,000 residents. We worked 12 to 14 hour shifts in pairs visiting households and carrying out thorough inquiries with householders as to occupancy of properties, sightings and noting anything suspicious. This type of work is painstaking and goes on day after day after day. It is boring and it is easy to get lulled into a false sense of security. To keep vigilant you have to continually remind yourself that each conversation and each person you speak to may have vital information that only your questioning and diligence will discover.

However, working in pairs is useful because you can take turns in questioning and completing the questionnaires. Towards the end of one very long day myself and a colleague were visiting houses in an area of the town I will describe as not very salubrious! The house stank and the carpet was covered with dog muck and looked like it had never been hoovered and certainly never cleaned. An electric fire was on full blast and the heat was excruciating. It was my colleague's turn to ask the questions and inevitably I sat back on a soiled settee and dozed off. I was awoken a few minutes later by my colleague at a point where the dog was being sick on the carpet and the stench had penetrated my nostrils. I started to heave and made it to the porch where I vomited, much to the surprise of my colleague and the householder!

None of these inquiries proved fruitful but were accompanied by a number of other sightings across the West Midlands of where the vehicle had been seen.

The case caused controversy between Staffordshire Police, Scotland Yard and West Mercia Police over the finding of Lesley's body in the mineshaft and whether or not it should have been found before during a previous search following an aborted ransom demand. These circumstances and the whole of the events surrounding the case were complex but eventually on 21st July 1976 led to Donald Neilson being sentenced to life imprisonments x 5 and sentences of 4 x 10 years and 1 x 21years for a range of post office murders/raids and the murder and kidnapping of Lesley Whittle.

Donald Neilson remained in custody until his death in 2011.

Motor Manslaughter at Bromsgrove

On another evening at around the same time I and a colleague Brian Smith who worked at Rubery were told to undertake late night observations for car thieves on the patch. This necessitated our travelling to Bromsgrove in a marked Police vehicle to pick up a plain car but travelling in plain clothes.

As we drove past a pub on the Birmingham road at Bromsgrove we could see that there was a crowd congregated outside and it looked like tension was brewing although no-one was fighting at that stage. Due to the fact we were in plain clothes we radioed to Bromsgrove to send uniformed officers to the scene and we carried on to Bromsgrove Police Station. Once we arrived we were immediately told that there was a report now of two road accidents which had occurred. One at the location we had just passed which was outside the pub and another one which had happened about a mile away in the town centre. We were asked by the control room to make our way to the town centre accident whilst uniformed patrols attended and assessed the pub accident which sounded more serious.

When Brian and I arrived in one of the side streets just off the main High Street we were confronted with a youth lying unconscious in the gutter but no sign of a car. He was alive but subsequently established to have broken his back. No one at the scene appeared to know what had happened but gradually reports came in that the young man had been seen hanging on for grim death to the bonnet of a car which had driven through the town centre at high speed. When the vehicle had turned off into the side street the driver had stopped the car, got out and thrown the young man into the gutter and then driven off.

This was serious enough but then reports came in that the incident outside the pub was in fact now a fatal because someone had been killed at the scene.

Gradually things became clearer and we realised the two incidents were connected and these were not accidents but deliberate actions and now we had a murder and possibly attempted murder to deal with.

The commotion we passed outside the pub had been the beginning of an argument between a group of youths one of whom had gone off in a huff, got in to his car and then the car had been driven into a group of people outside the pub. One person had been killed instantly and the second person, a young man had been injured and ended up on the bonnet of the car. The youth had then driven through the town centre of Bromsgrove with the man on the bonnet until he drove into the side street and threw him into the side of the road.

The rest of the night was spent taking statements, clearing the scene and tracing the driver of the car who was arrested very quickly.

He was charged and eventually went to prison for a long time convicted of manslaughter and other offences.

Fascism and Anti-Fascism

At around this time in the mid 1970's the National Front organisation were very prominent in demonstrating in major towns and were often confronted by those who had other views. This would usually result in violent confrontations in which the Police were expected to keep the peace. It was well before there was any formal riot training or protective equipment and you had to manage with the best you could get which was usually portrayed on television with officers using dustbin lids to protect themselves.

One morning we were ordered to cancel all rest days and parade at Bournville Lane Police, Birmingham on a Saturday morning at 6.30. The National Front were expected to march through the city and were to be opposed by a number of anti-fascist and left-wing groups who would be hell bent on preventing the march and would see the Police as proponents of the demonstration and everything the National Front stood for which was completely untrue.

Upon our arrival at Bournville Lane we were given a pork pie and a sandwich and told that it had to last for the rest of the day but we would be fed when we finished about 12 hours later. It is fair to say we were very grumpy and expecting a tough day.

Just when we thought it could not get any worse in walked a rather squat man in plain clothes smoking a huge cigar. He introduced himself as an Assistant Chief Constable and the man in charge of the Policing operation. He started off by thanking us all for volunteering to be there which was met by hissing and moans because no one was a volunteer and most of us had been directed at the last minute. He knew that and smiled knowingly. We expected a formal briefing but he said something like this.

'This is going to be a very tough day. All the intelligence we have received is suggesting that a number of those attending are hard core who are armed with razor blades, ball bearings and acid and intent on injuring you. However, we will prevail, because they are nothing but a disorganised rabble compared to you lot who are an organised rabble!

I want you to know that when you are getting the ball bearings, acid thrown at you I will be in charge, I will be there and I will be in complete control and not worried in the slightest. If you look up above you will see a helicopter and I will be in the helicopter looking down and thinking about you so that is why I am not worried!'

He smiled, hoped we would enjoy our lunch, wished us all the best of luck, thanked us, spun on his heel and left the room still smoking his cigar. We were speechless but then it dawned on us that he was being honest, no bullshit, not a lot more he could say but genuinely he knew what our fears were. In fact this was an inspirational speech that set the tone for the day. This Assistant Chief Constable understood what motivates Police Officers – honesty and a pork pie!

We were despatched to one of the side streets in Digbeth in the City centre. Someone found a pub open down the street and we took it in turns after opening to go and have a brew. Eventually we received notice that the demonstration was heading our way so we mobilised, linked arms strapped our helmets on and stood and waited. I noted we were under a railway bridge and feared that if the demonstrators or their opponents got there it would make a marvellous place from which to lob bricks at us. We could hear them approaching and chanting like a football crowd. We braced ourselves, gritted our teeth and not for the first time or last in my career I was trembling with fear.

Suddenly, the chants got quieter and we were told that the demonstration had changed direction and we were simply to remain there on standby. It was a freezing cold day and we were left standing around for hours. The fear gave way to boredom until I was almost praying the demonstration would return to give us something to do and break the monotony.

Eventually it all passed by without incident, for us anyway and we returned to Bournville Lane for a hot meal which never tasted so good.

I was fortunate in never having to undertake many other public order demonstrations and certainly never volunteered for any. The nearest I got to real action was in training in later years when they issued us with riot shields and got Police Cadets to lob bricks at us, which they did with zeal and some met their target!

The Murder of Carl Bridgewater

On the 19th September 1978 a young paper boy, Carl Bridgewater was murdered whilst delivering papers to 'Yew Tree Farm,' near Wordsley, Stourbridge. Carl was shot at close range with a shotgun. This location is actually covered by Staffordshire Police who immediately launched a murder investigation and were assisted by officers from the West Midlands Crime Squad. However, the location of the farm is situated right on the boundaries of Staffordshire, Worcestershire and West Midlands adjacent to the main A449 Kidderminster to Wolverhampton Road.

The events of that terrible day and the circumstances of the investigation that followed resulted in four men being convicted and incarcerated (one of whom has since died) for 18 years until their eventual release by the Court of Appeal in 1997. Alongside the convictions of the Birmingham Six bombers (referred to earlier) this again was described as Britain's worst miscarriage of justice and no-one has ever been brought to justice for the murder of Carl Bridgewater.

The tragic death of Carl touched the hearts of everyone and particularly impacted upon those of us in West Mercia both because of the proximity to the murder scene and because of events that were to unfold approximately two months later in the shadow of the Clent Hills, Worcestershire.

No-one was immediately charged with the murder of Carl Bridgwater and the investigation was still continuing at full pelt when on the 30th November 1978 two masked raiders, one of them armed with a sawn off shotgun burst into an isolated farmhouse known as Chapel Farm, Romsley and attacked the elderly occupants. They made off with approximately £300 cash.

Chapel Farm sits next to the very quaint St Kenelms Church from where it derives its name. At the time the Farm was resided in by Jack Smith aged 83 and his three elderly sisters Mildred, Kathleen and Henrietta. The old people were pushed around and one of them fell to the ground where they were all threatened.

The house was typical of many old farmhouses with little in the way of modern amenities and reminded me of what life was like back home. Although they were not seriously injured they suffered bruising and their treatment at that age caused them immense shock and all had to be taken to hospital.

Due to the nature of the robbery and the relative proximity, immediate links were made with the Carl Bridgwater case with the two forces West Mercia and Staffordshire making contact. Very quickly, because of a previous deception committed against the old people over payment for coal, links were made to a man named Vincent Hickey who had spent most of his life living in the south Birmingham area and Redditch and was known to the police. Vince Hickey was arrested and taken to Bromsgrove Police Station where he was interviewed in connection with the Chapel Farm robbery. Whilst in custody at Bromsgrove it was alleged Vince Hickey stated he had information on the Carl Bridgwater murder. A very long and convoluted inquiry then evolved which eventually led to the arrest of Pat Molloy, Jimmy Robinson and Michael Hickey (Vince's cousin) all being arrested in connection with the murder of Carl Bridgwater. This in turn led to Vince Hickey himself also being implicated with the murder. Eventually, Vince Hickey, Michael Hickey and James Robinson were all convicted of the murder of Carl Bridgwater and Pat Molloy with manslaughter. Michael Hickey and James Robinson were also convicted of the Chapel Farm robbery and the indictment against Vince Hickey was allowed to remain on file (not proceeded with).

Whilst James Robinson, Michael Hickey and Vince Hickey were in custody in North Worcestershire for the Chapel Farm robbery the potential case against them in respect of the Carl Bridgwater murder was still taking place. I was one of a number of officers drafted in to Bromsgrove Court where an application for remand in custody was being made in respect of the Chapel Farm robbery. If they had been granted bail for any reason then I assume we would have had to immediately arrest them on suspicion of the murder. Already there was a lot of media speculation around the case and publicly links were being made as to a connection between the two cases. Security at the court was of paramount importance. All three were remanded in custody and together with other officers I had the job of transporting them to prison. As we left the families of the men ran after the Police buses to wave and get a final glimpse. No-one at that stage could have envisaged the almost two decades of controversy that was to follow.

What I and many did not know was that day was the start of one of the longest running campaigns over a miscarriage of justice that has ever taken place in this country. Whilst the culpability of James Robinson and Michael Hickey for the Chapel Farm robbery has never been in doubt, the murder of Carl Bridgwater was a completely different scenario.

What followed were years of campaigning, years of allegations of falsehood and perjury against some of the officers in the case and a series of re-investigations and appeals to the Court of Appeal. Eventually, as stated above the surviving Bridgewater three were released from custody in 1997 on the basis that their convictions were unsafe due to scientific evidence which intimated that an alleged confession from Vince Hickey had been forged and subsequently shown to Patrick Molloy which induced him to make a false confession.

Instrumental in providing continued impetus to the campaign to release the men and quash their convictions was a lady who had been present in Bromsgrove Court at the time of the initial remands into custody, Ann Whelan, the mother of Michael Hickey. Standing in court that day as a young attractive mother of a teenage son she could not have believed that this case would lead her to have to sustain an 18 year battle to free her son from a murder charge and achieve national notoriety.

It has to be said that the case itself tainted the Police and the criminal justice system and provided further controversy against the West Midlands Serious Crime Squad which had been disbanded some years prior to the release of the Bridgwater three.

The introduction of the Police and Criminal Evidence Act in the mid 1980's placed much greater accountability and constraints upon the Police when detaining and interviewing suspects and also allowed for additional powers at the same time. Personally, I saw this as a positive step forward and now trials are much less about 'confession' evidence because everything has to be taped and formalities are much tighter.

This case was not good for anyone especially Carl's parents who will have lived through all of the above traumatic events and the twists and turns this entailed.

However, one thing that was missing from the majority media reports that surrounded the release of the men was any reference to the lesser known Chapel Farm robbery which is where this story began. Whatever the rights and wrongs of the Carl Bridgwater case, the fact that elderly people were subject to an armed robbery and treated violently is still very fresh in the minds of those Police Officers and others who were involved in that case.

Overall, this was an intriguing case providing you are not closely or personally involved with it. It was a piece of history that scarred the landscape of the West Midlands, and, will continue do so for many years. This is a piece of history that is well chronicled and debated but still poses more questions than answers.

Situated alongside the A449 Kidderminster to Wolverhampton road the old farmhouse where Carl was killed has now been converted into modern accommodation which still imposes starkly against the skyline behind high hedges that continue to hide the secret of, 'Who did kill Carl Bridgwater?'

CHAPTER 10

HIGH JINKS ON AND OFF DUTY

During the time we were at Barnt Green my section station was at Rubery which I described earlier. I usually popped in at least once a day to collect or drop off reports and to see Roger Cleveland the Sergeant.

There was a good team of officers at Rubery and I never minded on the odd occasion being drafted into assist when they were short of officers because they had to cover my patch when I was off duty.

We had some great laughs. On Armistice night it was a local ritual for the section sergeant to provide a barrel of beer and some food for the old soldiers of the village who would congregate in the back of the Police station. We would all start off by going to the Church service and then convene at the nick. We would lock the door, ensure there was cover from Bromsgrove and put the phones through. We then spent the evening drinking and eating with the old soldiers from the nearby British Legion and this went on usually until the early hours. We had fantastic conversation and it was a pleasure to share the company of such honourable and entertaining men.

However, I do not think such conduct would be tolerated now – we would probably all be sacked whatever the merits. Although we put ourselves off duty the use of the Police station for such occasions would certainly not be condoned nowadays!

We developed quite a rapport with the local licensees and one sunny day in summer set off on a trip to Torquay on an executive coach. It was about 6am when we set off. I have to say that by the time we stopped at the first services on the motorway most of us had been hitting the 'optics' on the coach and consumed quite a few shorts. Being pissed at 8am in the morning whilst having breakfast was a first for me but I am not sure it was for some of those on board the bus.

We arrived at Torquay and had lunch and of course a few more drinks. I was with a mate of mine who was a constable at Rubery called Dave 'Badger' Bartlett. We decided to get on a boat and go over to Brixham. Whilst wandering round Brixham both well oiled by now, Dave said in a slurred voice: 'We've betta gec somehowt fur the wivs,' so we embarked upon finding a present we could take back for the long suffering wives.

Actually, I am not sure Dave had a wife but that's immaterial? Anyway, we found a gift shop with a very attractive and attentive female assistant who was more than pleased to help us in our hour of need. I can't remember much except Dave said afterwards I asked the lady to marry me but she remarked if I was looking for a present for my wife that presented a few obstacles. Dave and I both left the shop with two furry gonks. To the uninitiated they were small furry toy animal puppets that were ugly but quaint and people used them to cover over small dustbins. I am not sure what possessed us to buy these and in retrospect it was probably not the best choice but when you are under the influence and looking for something that will deflect a good bollocking from the wife it is a case of anything for survival. It was our lifeline!

By the time we got back home it was the early hours of the morning. By now I was even more inebriated. Several things failed to register. The most important being that I had told Jud with usual male over-optimism that we would be back by about 10pm. I was wrong. Secondly, that even though I had clutched my little gonk in a brown paper bag for hundreds of miles it was now looking even more ruffled than it should and I did not realise I had dribbled beer all down it! The third thing that failed to register was that no matter how quiet you might be in at coming in women have a sixth sense and a nose that would detect the smell of beer at 10 miles!

Despite trying to be discreet, I was just at the point of taking my trousers off in the bedroom when I fell arse over tit into the wardrobe. Immediately, Jud woke up, on went the light and I was like a rabbit caught in the headlights. What followed was a diatribe which went something like,

'Where the hell have you been to this time of night, you are drunk and you stink etc etc.' My only saving grace now was my gonk which I produced like a magician pulling a rabbit out of a bloody hat. 'I've get yer a pressie darlin,' I said trying to put on my best sober BBC accent. I gave it her in the bag but failed to notice the state of it. Jud took one look at it and threw it back at me with words that indicated I should stick it somewhere where the sun doesn't shine. Lesson learned, I am not daft. I have never bothered with a peace offering since!

One of my favourite colleagues I like working with was Bob Middleton. I described Bob earlier as coming to my aid when trying to arrest a car thief at the top of the Lickeys. A big jovial man with a shock of red hair, a tremendous sense of humour and a big heart which belied an occasional temper to match his hair when roused. Bob was full of 'one liners' and little quips that used to crease me up. On one occasion during a bitterly cold and snowy day we were on patrol together at the top of Frankley Beeches near the M5 motorway when we came across a car parked up on the side of the road with the engine running and a hosepipe leading from the exhaust. We stopped and rushed out to investigate. The car was full of fumes and inside was a man who had obviously been in the car for some time because not only was there no sign of a pulse but he was stiff and quite obviously dead. It is routine in these cases to call for a doctor to attend the scene to pronounce 'life extinct.' We turned off the engine and called for a doctor via the radio control. Bob waited impatiently, puffing on his pipe and debating with me who should deal with the case. Suddenly, a Police Range Rover with a crew of two traffic officers arrived with blue lights on and claxton's blaring. They rushed up to the car, pushed us out of the way and dragged the man out the car. They laid him down by the side of the car and took turns to carry out mouth to mouth resuscitation and heart massage.

Bob looked on with amusement. 'He's bloody dead lads, even rigor has set in.' They carried on regardless and oblivious to our presence. Perhaps they were looking for a commendation as to the first cop who had ever revived a stiff? Being mindful that this poor dead bugger was lying in several inches of snow now on a freezing cold day Bob's next comment summed it up, 'Tell you what lads, if he wasn't dead before he will be now, of bloody exposure – we're off.' We drove off and left our two super heroes to it. They called us back to deal with the sudden death report and Bob had to deal with it because it was his patch. I cannot repeat his response.

The next incident reveals the other side of Bob. Proudly sitting on the side of New Road, Rubery and the last outpost before the boundary with Birmingham is the 'New Rose and Crown' pub. The licensee at that time was a man called Tom O'Reilly who was a legend in his own right. An Irishman with the usual fantastic Irish sense of humour. Tom had taken over the pub at a time when it had been run down and he was determined to get it back on its feet. Some of the locals from Northfield had virtually taken over the pub and Tom spent most evenings during the early part of his tenure chucking out any undesirables. Our job was to support him. Whilst visiting the pub one evening scaffolding poles were thrown through the windows by a bunch of aggrieved yobbos outside. On another occasion things kicked off inside the pub so fearing serious harm he set his Alsatian dog on them. Unfortunately, the only person it bit was some poor innocent woman who was not impressed. Eventually, Tom regained control of the pub and became a good ally to the Police in keeping it as a good pub.

It was during this time when one weekend night Bob and I were patrolling outside the pub when we could see a large bunch of youths congregated outside the pub just after closing time. They looked like a hard bunch from the estates of Northfield and Longbridge and we did not recognise any of them. They all appeared drunk and immediately started to abuse us shouting obscenities. We were well out-numbered; nearest assistance from our Force would be Bromsgrove or Longbridge if we were to call for West Midlands Police. I was more than happy to adopt a low profile, go deaf and walk away. Not Bob. He strode towards them and I felt obliged to follow. He told them all to shut up or they would be arrested.

The logistics of how the hell we would achieve this seemed to have bypassed Bob. I was also very mindful that the last time I had uttered these words to a group it was at Redditch and it ended up with me in hospital.

One of the crowd stepped out and made his way menacingly towards Bob uttering threats and baring his fists to fight. He started to throw a punch but Bob got in first and hit him so hard he bounced back into the crowd and did not reappear. Bob was now upset. He stood there like a raging bull, red faced, bursting out of his tunic and with fists raised ready for the next one. 'Come on, who is going to be the next one then?' said Bob.

I knew this was going to go one of two ways. Either we were going to be annihilated or they would back down. I have to say Bob looked a frightening figure and although I felt like disowning him and the Police at that moment I also braced myself for the onslaught and radioed for assistance. What they must have known was that everything was on their side. We did not know any of them and they could beat us to a pulp in a few seconds and be off before ever any assistance arrived. Bob repeated his invitation and then stepped towards the crowd inviting them to start. Amazingly they started to back off. Although they continued throwing insults not one of them was willing to step out of the crowd and be the first to meet Bob's wrath. Eventually they walked away and we lived to fight another day. Thanks Bob!

Tragically, whilst writing this book Bob died whilst still in his early sixties but long after he retired from the force.

Stray dogs were a regular feature at Rubery as well. A regular visitor who became very popular with colleagues was a big black Labrador called 'Bess.' Bess seemed to escape from her custody of home to the custody of the Police station at least two or three times a month. She was obedient, house trained and very affectionate. In fact, she would have made the ideal partner in life!

Situated in the corner of the front office was what I can only describe as an 'antique' telephone exchange switchboard with plugs that you pulled in and out to connect calls and little Perspex caps that opened and shut like eyelids each time a call came in.

Bess used to sit on the seat by the switchboard and put her paws on the table where she would sit obediently watching the switchboard for hours till collected by her owners.

Someone then trained Bess to wear a small Police helmet and sit by the switchboard.

A favourite trick was to put the lights on dim, leave the station door open and hide in the side office until a visitor came into the station. They would immediately start talking to what they thought was a police officer and then realise they had just declared their classified secrets and complaints to a dog!

Situated just on the West Midlands Police area but a stone's throw from the nick was Rubery Hill mental hospital. Some of the patients were in long term care and used to walk into the village. One of them had been a chef and another was a butcher. They would both walk down the street together but both dressed up in their respective uniforms.

On one occasion one of the patients came into the station and complained that during the night someone had stolen a button off his trousers and his false teeth. Despite every kind of reassurance he was not going to leave until an officer took a report of these crimes seriously and recovered the property. In sheer exasperation one of the officers went into the Sergeant's office and found a Sergeant's uniforms hanging up in a locker. He cut off a button and took it to the patient at the front desk explaining that during the night they had arrested a thief and recovered the button. The patient appeared pleased at this result but still insisted that we find his teeth. In further desperation the officer drew a picture of a set of teeth on a piece of paper and explained that we would circulate them as wanted on a poster. The patient appeared delighted, thanked us for our help and left the station where he remained outside talking to his friend who had been waiting patiently outside.

We were in the process of congratulating ourselves on ensuring we had another satisfied customer when in walked one of our colleagues who had just passed the two patients talking outside. 'Who are those two blokes outside?' he asked innocently. We explained what had just happened. ' Oh right,' said our colleague, 'It's just that they are having a right laugh about you lot and how one of them took the piss by coming in and pretending he had lost his button and teeth and how you lot swallowed the story, hook line and sinker!' Moral of the story is, 'He who laughs last, laughs longest and they certainly did!

One the highlights of working at Rubery were Sheila. Sheila was the station cleaner who came in most weekday mornings to keep the nick in good order. I used to wonder what the expression, 'salt of the earth' meant. Well, to me it means, loyal, honest, dependable, hardworking, unpretentious and generally an all round 'good egg.' Sheila was certainly all these things and also a very attractive lady with a great sense of humour and affectionate smile. Both Sheila and her husband Keith were good friends and had the respect of us all at the nick.

Sheila would do her best to keep the station tidy and us lot in order. She would cook us breakfast and act as cook, cleaner and counsellor. However, Police being great practical jokers it was a favourite trick to hide her mops, buckets and brooms and generally act the fool. Sheila took it all in good part and gave equal back but there were some occasions when she left having not completed her chores because of laughing so much with tears rolling down her cheeks. They were great days and sometimes we need to reflect that it is the 'Sheila's of this world, the unsung heroes who largely just get on with life, upon which we all depend that keep this country going. Bless you Sheila.

Overall, working at Rubery was a pleasure and working so close to the Birmingham boundary meant that we spent as much time working in Birmingham as we did in Worcestershire. I was forever in Longbridge and Bournville Lane police stations because all the villains we dealt with came from over the boundary. I learned a lot from colleagues in the West Midlands and it always felt more like working in a city than being a rural cop – sometimes the world of country life and Worcestershire seemed surreal against the backdrop of the estates in south Birmingham around Northfield, Longbridge and Selly Oak where I spent so much time. Most of the time it was quicker to nip over the boundary to execute warrants or serve summonses and carry out inquiries than to pass onto Birmingham officers to deal with.

I was forever in the Victoria Law Courts in Birmingham giving evidence and sometimes it did not feel like I was a West Mercia Police officer at all.

After working Barnt Green and Rubery for four years I was ready for a change and decided I needed to broaden my career and spend a short time on CID and at the same time pass the Sergeants promotion exam. What followed was a stranger path than I ever imagined.

CHAPTER 11

SEX IN SUBURBIA LEADS
TO PROMOTION

As I walked into the Force Training School at Droitwich I felt distinctly different. I was dressed in civvies and so were my colleagues. We were all there in order to undertake tests that would ascertain whether or not we were suitable to go on an accelerated promotion course to the 'college of knowledge' for the Police at Bramshill, Hampshire. Bramshill is to the Police what Sandhurst is to the Army. I felt different for two reasons. Firstly, I had not realised that this was a course in 'one-upmanship.' I noticed that everyone else attending was dressed in suits; some with waistcoats and little pocket watch chains. Also, they were all carrying broadsheet newspapers such as the 'Times' or the 'Telegraph.' Me, I was dressed in a sports jacket and a pair of flared trousers carrying the 'Sun' newspaper!

The other difference was that all the rest had applied and been 'paper sifted' to attend. I was eligible to attend because having passed the Police Sergeants Exam I was in the top 200 in the country for highest marks and therefore had an automatic right both to attend this course and subsequently to go forward for the formal interviews and assessments at Bramshill (referred to as Brands Hatch by many colleagues). Success at interviews at Bramshill would mean a scholarship at Bramshill, automatic promotion to Sergeant with promotion to Inspector guaranteed within two years. All those who obtained a scholarship were expected to graduate to the highest ranks in the service and certainly Chief Superintendent and beyond.

I was however totally unprepared and under the naive misapprehension that this course was to assist us in preparing for the more formal and later assessment process at Bramshill. Wrong! It was in fact a vetting process as well as a taster of what to expect.

We spent two days undertaking all sorts of tests on IQ and spatial awareness as well as debating sessions on for example 'The advantages of Real Ale?' The personal presentations were the best fun (I am being facetious) and I can remember having to talk to the rest of the class completely without warning for 5 minutes on the subject of 'How to strangle a jelly.' I am not sure if there was a deeply psychological bent to all of this, but, if there was then it completely passed me by.

The final sessions were two interviews, the first with two Chief Superintendents and a psychologist and the second with the Chief Constable and his deputies.

During the first interview I was asked the question, 'What do you think of the sun?' Now, because I had spent two days answering silly bloody questions I naturally assumed that this was some deep psychological trick question that required an extreme lateral thinking answer that would enable them to provide a psychological profile of me. My reply started like this:' 'The sun sir, rises in the morning in the east and sets in the evening in the west. It is extremely bright and our entire civilisation depends upon.........' I was interrupted, 'Not that bloody sun King, the Sun newspaper!'

Not to be put on the back foot I made an immediate recovery and answered the question as best I could. On reflection afterwards, I realised that the entire process depended upon evidencing that you read widely and read broadsheets not tabloids. My answer probably should have been something like, 'Well, I don't personally read it myself sir because I consider that it is right wing press and propaganda which I feel is neither impartial nor independent and reflects the converse socialist ideology and propaganda published by the Daily Mirror.' Unfortunately, I said something like, 'Well, the Sun is not a bad read really, I have it daily and it offers a quick glance at the main news when you haven't got time to read all the rubbish in those big papers that makes your arms ache!' In order to lighten the moment I was tempted to say something about the 'titillation' that appeared on page three but stopped myself because I realised their sense of humour may not match mine!'

Somehow, I don't think that was the answer they were looking for and the interview finished very shortly afterwards with me left with the distinct impression I had not done very well.

The second interview was with the Chief Constable – the renowned Alex Rennie where anything was likely to happen. Rumour had it that he did not particularly agree with the special course philosophy or accelerated promotion but was always obliged to put some officers forward from his force.

I won't dwell on the interview except to say that Rennie made mincemeat out of me. He was well known for being forthright and robust on promotion boards and gave me a number of scenario questions to answer before telling me that I would not be likely to succeed in the interviews at Bramshill (although he could not prevent me attending because of my exam marks) and that the force would not be recommending me because I was not the sort of person they would be looking for.

However, he was quite encouraging in other respects in telling me that he was convinced I was a bright young man with a good future in the force and that I should come back before him on the ordinary promotion boards once I had the 'bastard' put in me because I was too much of a nice young man. I asked him what he meant and was about to tell him that my wife could probably provide a very good reference to me being a 'bastard' because it was a form of endearment she regularly called me! He told me that I needed to go on CID for a while and undergo some acting-sergeant experience so as to develop a cutting edge. He then sent me off with my tail between my legs – not unlike the first occasion I met him when I joined from Cadet to Constable.

Initially I was despondent. It was the first time I had ever failed anything in the Police and nobody likes to be turned down. However, whilst I still retained the right to go on the Bramshill interviews I knew I would not have the backing of the Force and even if I succeeded then it would mean going to Bramshill College in Hampshire for 12 months and Jud had stated if I went she would leave me! So, I decided to broaden my career and go via the usual route of Force promotion boards instead of the accelerated route.

A few weeks later I was staying for the weekend at my parents' house and picked up the broadsheet newspaper my Dad always read, the 'News of the World!'

I was heavily engaged in reading the titillation when I spotted one of the sub headings which read: 'Sex in suburban Village.' I thought I would have a bit of that so read it with interest. The story was about a stockbroker belt village on the outskirts of Birmingham which had a sauna and massage parlour in which News of the World reporters had visited the premises and been offered sex. I was most intrigued until half way through the article I realised it my patch at Barnt Green! It immediately dawned on me a few questions would be asked like, why the hell I didn't know about it and what was I going to do about it?

The funniest bit of the article was when one of the local dignitaries' was phoned by the News of the World and asked what her opinion was on having a brothel in the middle of the village? Her response was that she thought it was awful, particularly because it came in the same week someone had the audacity to seek planning permission for a fish and chip shop as well! Whatever next?

When I returned to work on the Monday the phone started ringing and it was my Chief Superintendent, John Barnett. I told him I never had an inkling that the place was being run as a brothel and he told me I needed to sort it and seek whatever assistance I needed to do so. Whilst this sort of activity might now be fairly common even in rural stockbroker areas like Barnt Green at the time no-one had ever dealt with a brothel inquiry in West Mercia although they were fairly common in the neighbouring area of Birmingham. I therefore sought advice from colleagues at Bournville Lane Police Station in West Midlands Vice Squad. They offered assistance and told me the first thing we needed to do was to ascertain whether or not the premises were still operating and to keep it under covert observations.

I was convinced that by now with all the media exposure (pun intended!) the owner and those running the premises would have been frightened off. However, my initial assessment and observations using my own car in plain clothes showed that the premises were still very active and rather than having been put off by the publicity in the News of the World the owners were using it to their advantage and treating it as an advertisement.

I therefore arranged for further more discreet and formal observations to monitor the situation. This involved using the force observations van. I had to laugh when it arrived because it was an old 'Box' Van that had been used when we were Cadets to transport our kit whilst on adventure training courses to Bishops Castle and the Long Myndd in Shropshire. We knew it affectionately as 'ALF' because of its registration plate. It had been now been converted (loosely) into a van to carry out observations with blacked out windows and seating put in the rear including a mobile toilet if you got caught short during long periods of obs.

Although it looked nothing like anything that would be associated with the Police it was quite distinctive because it was so old and therefore when not in use I had to park it behind my Police house and station so that it could not be seen from the road.

The sauna and massage parlour was situated in the main village of Barnt Green almost opposite the local pub and adjacent to residential housing. Fortunately there was a road situated opposite the parlour where it was possible to observe the premises from a discreet distance. My colleague at the time at Barnt Green (who lived next door) was PC Dick Nunnerley. We took it in turns to carry out obs with one of us driving the van to the obs post in the morning and the other one hiding in the back to keep obs after the 'driver' had disappeared and left the vehicle. We were also assisted by my old mate John Price who had been my best man and was on CID at the time.

The premises seemed to open early in the morning and go on till late evening. We needed to establish the opening and working patterns and identify who seemed to be responsible for the premises as well as who was visiting. We set to with plenty of pens, papers, binoculars, night lenses and cameras and got to work. The hours were long and tedious. It was winter so daylight hours were restricted and inside the van it was bleeding cold.

However, we quickly established a pattern and noted who the main girls were that were opening up and working the premises as well as a couple of males who seemed to accompany them and appeared to have involvement in the parlour.

It became necessary not only to observe the premises but also to follow the 'girls' and their accomplices so that we could establish who they were and where they lived. Car registration numbers are always very limited.

I got in the habit of making sure my own private car was parked on the car of the Victoria pub so that at the end of the day after the premises were locked up I could follow them.

I did this on a couple of occasions and was lucky in following them to a pub on the outskirts of Birmingham where I stood next to them at the bar, was able to earwig their conversations and to clock a name and address on a letter in one of the girl's handbags.

Compared to methods used today this was very crude and unsophisticated stuff with little in the way of rules or guidance which was just as well really.

Next, we needed to identify who was the owner and current tenant of the premises. Inquiries revealed this to be a well known Building Society who had repossessed the premises and were acting as mortgagees in possession and during the interim period had rented the premises out to a tenant who was man from Kingsheath in Birmingham. Initially, they were very reluctant to help me both identify the client or to provide a statement. However, I quickly established that they had been visited by the 'News of the World' who had made them aware of their findings that the premises were being used as a brothel but despite this knowledge they had decided to carry on renting the premises out without even questioning the tenant. When I pointed out to them the implications of this and that as a major High Street building society they were actually the owners of a brothel and could be liable as such they suddenly became very helpful and furnished a statement and full details of the tenant.

The next stage was to ascertain evidence of sex actually being offered in the premises for payment to back up the allegations contained in the 'News of the World.' Because West Mercia has no expertise in this area (well, plenty of sex but not of brothels!) we decided to enlist the assistance of the West Midlands Police Vice Squad based at Bournville Lane Police Station.

My point of liaison was Detective Sergeant Dave Dixon and his team who were allocated to assist us where possible. Dave explained that we needed to 'test the goods' by putting undercover officers into the brothel in order to see if they would be offered sexual extras to the sauna and massage. I was quite intrigued by this and set about wondering how the hell you managed to get a job like this in the Police and would they accept a short term secondment! The answer was 'no' I was too ugly to pass the test!

Anyway, Dave arranged for a number of his officers to visit the massage parlour during business hours whilst we waited outside in the 'obs' van and filmed them entering and leaving. In order that there could be no allegations that the officers actually partook in sex the procedures was as follows. Before entering the Sergeant would search each officer and ensure they only had sufficient money on them to pay for the sauna and massage and not enough to pay for any sexual extras. They would also leave behind any identification card and then enter the parlour. Officers were under instruction not to procure sex but to elect for a massage and see what happened. At the point of being offered sex they were to ascertain the name of the masseuse, the terms and cost of the sexual extra being offered and then politely decline and leave making an excuse as to why they did not take up the offer.

This activity took place over several days using different officers. Each officer reported that they had been offered sex extras varying from masturbation, oral sex to full sex for various amounts of money.

Having reached this stage and acquired all necessary evidence it was decided to mount an operation to raid the brothel and arrest the tenant, the prostitutes and those males we had identified as involved in running the premises. The officer put in charge of this was Inspector Bob Dibble (yes, really, Officer Dibble) from Bromsgrove and together we started planning the operation. (Officer Dibble featured in a famous cartoon series called 'Topcat' which ran in the 1960's – this makes me feel really old).

On a crisp winter's day together with assistance from the West Midlands Vice Squad and a number of our own officers we raided the brothel and found activities at full flow including one or two of the regular customers who were in the act. We also found a stash of condoms, used and unused and a number of soiled towels. We seized the visitor's book, all evidential material and arrested the prostitutes. The punters were allowed to go with assurances we would need to see them again for statements.

The prostitutes were all interviewed at Bromsgrove Police Station and were very amenable. They implicated the main tenant as a man I will call 'Cameron' in the running of the premises and how the financial arrangements worked including his knowledge of what took place on the premises. Cameron was also arrested together with other identified men and all were interviewed. We released the prostitutes without charge, preferring to use their evidence against Cameron as being the main benefactor and living on immoral earnings of prostitution with which he was subsequently charged.

Despite quite overwhelming evidence when I interviewed Cameron he stated he was an honest businessman running a reputable business and had been the victim of unscrupulous women who contrary to his instructions and knowledge had turned a massage parlour into a brothel offering sex.

Eventually one man who was the husband of one of the women in the parlour appeared before the court and pleaded guilty of living on immoral earnings.

Cameron eventually appeared before Worcester Crown Court and pleaded not guilty to all charges. What we knew was that the evidence of the women who had been offering sex in the parlour was most important in implicating Cameron as both having knowledge of events and in receiving income. However, it all depended on their attendance at Court and in them giving the same evidence they had indicated in their written statements. My role was to produce evidence of the observations on the premises, the raid itself and the interviews with those involved.

By the time this case came to Court Jud and I were posted to work and live at Market Drayton in Shropshire. Unfortunately, when the trial dates were announced I realised it clashed with my annual leave. However, in those days there was no negotiation to change the trial dates and therefore I had to attend. Jud was not best pleased and had also taken off the same week so we decided to travel down to Crown court at Worcester, stay with my parents and then resume our holiday once I had given evidence. On this basis to try and placate Jud I told her I would not be committed for long and suggested she attend the Crown Court as a member of the public, watch the trial and then we would be ready to travel on whenever I had been discharged from the case.

This became a flawed theory for several reasons. Firstly, Police evidence is usually given later rather than earlier in the proceedings because of the chronology of events in such cases. Secondly, there is no guarantee how long proceedings take and thirdly as the main officer in case you really need to be there throughout the case to ensure all wheels are oiled and last minute hitches are dealt with.

Whilst most of the women witnesses from the brothel turned up, they needed reassurance to remain otherwise I feared they would do a runner. Nowadays there is a Witness Service in the Crown Court who welcomes witnesses, tells them where to go, explains procedures and generally provides support. Also, in most courts there are refreshments available for purchase. In those days there was no witness service and no cafeteria.

I therefore enlisted Jud to keep a watchful eye on the women and ensure they were taken care of until they needed to give evidence.

I have this lasting memory of Jud bless her making drinks in the Police room of the Crown Court for the women and muttering under her breath whenever we were private that this was not what she had signed up for when we married and basically I was taking the piss! Also, when could we start our leave?

On around the second day of the trial we hit a major problem in that one of the women whose evidence was crucial did not turn up for court. After giving evidence on oath as to the service of the witness subpoena the Judge issued a warrant without bail to arrest the woman and bring her to Court. Early next morning my colleague Dick Nunnerley and I were raiding her flat in Birmingham by 7am where we found her in bed with her partner. She was not impressed at being arrested and had to be taken into court in handcuffs. As we entered the court she looked at me and said, 'I suppose this was your idea you bastard!'

I did not envisage the evidence going too well but in fact I was pleasantly surprised. To say she was annoyed was an understatement. However, once in the witness box she turned her venom on the defendant Cameron and very articulately confirmed her evidence in her original statement that Cameron could not wriggle out of his responsibility for what had taken place at the parlour and she said it with convincing passion.

When it came time for Cameron to give his evidence he maintained his defence. However, careful dissection of his testimony by the prosecuting counsel around his lack of business records and accounts convinced the Court he was lying. The jury spent little time in finding him guilty and the Judge sentenced him to 12 months imprisonment for living off the immoral earnings of the women.

Immediately after the trial the Judge asked me to escort him to his car because he feared repercussions or lobbying from certain supporters of Cameron. I did this and remember feeling very relieved that we had secured a conviction and I could now resume my leave. The case gained national interest and the results were published in the 'News of the World' as evidence of their role in the affair.

Barnt Green villagers could now rest in peace that their very exclusive little village no longer contained a brothel but the planning application for the local fish and chip shop was granted and to this day has remained in the village.

During the investigation into the brothel I was formally posted to CID to undertake an aide to CID as a temporary detective. In between the inquiries on the brothel and preparing papers for the trial I worked on other cases at both Rubery and Bromsgrove but I guess I will always be remembered during this time for being the 'brothel King!'

After a brief spell on CID I was posted to Bromsgrove as Acting Sergeant on one of the shifts. I have to say that this was not without some trepidation.

All the sergeants I had known were 'oracles' of information, very experienced and generally very old. Here I was at 26 years of age, not very knowledgeable and certainly not that experienced.

I was not sure if my young age would undermine my authority. However, I worked on the premise that you treat others as you would wish to be treated and as long as you were shown to be sincere and fair, bobbies would make allowances for you.

Most bobbies can sniff bullshit at 100 yards. They don't want waffle, just decisions and that those that make them stand by them and accept responsibility especially when the 'wheel falls off' as it inevitably does. I had good tutors in the Sergeants I had worked for and respect for the way they always undertook to carry the can and if they did not know something to find out and then make a decision.

I found out very quickly that dealing with staff was just like dealing with the public. Be human and treat people with respect and they will both forgive and protect you when you foul up.

In those days there was less emphasis on management and much more about leadership from the front end, being capable and passing on your skills to those who needed to learn.

However, in policing, spurs have to be earned and wise cops will sit back and see how their leaders deal with the first bottle tests and whether they are up to the job.

My own Chief Superintendent John Barnett summed it up when he said, 'All my acting Sergeants wear three stripes so the public and most staff will assume you are permanent in the rank. You have the same authority and the same responsibility. If you cock it up, they will not make allowances for you, and, neither will I.'

Enough said. The rank of Sergeant is probably the most important rank in the Police service. The buck truly stops there – and, so it should.

Time soon passed until the next round of promotion boards which were held in the spring/summer of 1979. I got through the divisional boards thanks to my Chief Superintendent John Barnett. Barnett was a pragmatic and inspirational leader who truly led from the front. If he rated you, you could do no wrong. If he didn't then watch out. Fortunately, he rated me and supported me through to the central promotion boards.

Before we went on the boards Barnett briefed all of us nominated to go forward from the division. His advice was quite simple. If, when you are

erviewed and torn apart by the Chief Constable just think what
look like with his trousers down and inevitably you will be able to
.... t least I look better than him, and give him a wry smile!' I hasten
to add that that all Chief Constables at that time were men.

On a bright summer day in June 1979 I travelled with a colleague Geoff
Harding to the promotion board which was held at the Police Training
School at Droitwich. Geoff had several more years of experience than me,
was a competent detective currently on CID at Bromsgrove and favourite
to get through the board having been told it was his year. I and a couple
of other colleagues were there as rank outsiders and I regarded it as going
along for the experience and part of the ritual of promotion in preparation
for a future year.

Alec Rennie the chief constable was chair of the board sitting with his
deputy Barry Florentine. Both were formidable adversaries and I knew to
expect anything. I had been interviewed or rather savaged by Rennie on two
previous occasions and was not looking forward to a repeat performance.

Rennie had a philosophy. He was a hard man who won his spurs of policing
in the mining villages of Durham where he had a fearsome reputation. He
demanded loyalty to the job above all else from his supervising officers
and made it clear there was no compromise. Every promotion board was
designed to test that loyalty to the full. He also wanted to test whether you
had backbone. Rennie had probably never backed down to anyone ever,
even the Home Secretary – he did it his way and expected you to follow
him whatever the personal, family or professional consequences might be.
He could be robust, belligerent and at times very forceful. However, tales
also abounded of him being compassionate when the need occurred and
whether you liked him or hated him he made it absolutely clear that he
made the bullets and fired them!

Alex Rennie died in 2012 aged 92. Shortly before he died he published his
autobiography, 'From Farmhand to Chief Constable' which chronicles the
life of a formidable man who had a remarkable career including war time
service on a special assignment for Winston Churchill.

Rennie had inherited the force of West Mercia which was still harking back
to the culture of when it had been the four separate forces of Shropshire,

Herefordshire, Worcestershire and Worcester City. Despite 12 years having elapsed since they were amalgamated in 1967 the force still operated in these distinct areas and Rennie knew he needed to knock down boundaries. The best way of doing that was to ensure the staff were moved around at every opportunity. However, those officers who had served under the original county boundaries were given assurances that they could not be moved to another area post amalgamation unless it were on grounds of either promotion or discipline.

Therefore, Rennie's opportunity to move people around was quite limited and he sought every opportunity at either promotion boards or discipline hearings to ensure staff were moved to opposite ends of the Force which stretches from Ross on Wye in south Herefordshire to Whitchurch in North Shropshire. In my own case, I had joined West Mercia so could be moved anywhere at any time.

Geoff went in first and came out after about 45 minutes and was ashen. He had time to tell me that they had refused to promote him but were going to post him from Bromsgrove to Shrewsbury as a uniformed constable and he would lose his CID status. Geoff was not amused. Before I had chance to commiserate I was called through.

I walked in quite purposefully and saluted. Rennie invited me to sit down. Before my arse hit the chair Florentine (Deputy Chief Constable) said to me, 'Where was this brothel you dealt with then King?' Before I could answer Rennie suddenly cut in and said, 'Don't tell him King, he only wants to visit there,' and laughed.

It dawned on me that Rennie appeared totally relaxed with me and handed over the questioning to Florentine who persisted to ask me a series of questions about the brothel which led to me to admit that that yes it had been situated in the centre of the main village. Yes, I had been the local beat bobby for 4 years. No I did not have any inkling that it was being used as a brothel and yes it eventually took the News of the World to initiate some action. I just capitulated under the rapid machine gun style of questioning.

Florentine then leant back, smiled at having made me squirm and then handed over to Rennie to finish me off.

However, the brothel inquiry had obviously brought me to their favourable attention and Rennie was jovial and told me that this was the second time he had interviewed me for promotion. He told me that he was convinced I had a brain and a long way to go in the job and that he had no questions. He immediately told me that he would like to promote me to Sergeant and send me to a place called Market Drayton. I was now in a state of shock. Firstly, that after only a short mauling I had been promoted but secondly I didn't have a clue as to where the hell Market Drayton was.

I then said something which I have regretted saying for the rest of my life. 'Could you tell me Sir, where is Market Drayton? I have never heard of it?'

Wrong question. Rennie exploded and said, 'What, don't you know your Force area laddie, where the hell have you been till now.' I decided to back track and said, 'Oh, yes sir, I know of course it's where the horses run.' Wrong! Rennie's face contorted as he said words to the effect of, 'That is Market Rasen you idiot which is in Lincolnshire, I am talking about Market Drayton in North Shropshire, Shrewsbury division.'

To me it might as well have been in the centre of bloody Scotland, it was miles away, I had never heard of it and already was beginning to feel this was a big mistake.

Rennie then said, 'I want to post you to Market Drayton, I want you to live in a Police house and I will refuse permission for you to buy your own house because after 12 months I will probably post you again. Do you understand?'

I took this as an opportunity to throw myself on the sword and made several excuses why I would prefer to remain living in Worcestershire but was prepared to travel anywhere. I pointed out that Jud had a job in Redditch, that we were on the verge of buying a house in Redditch and that I could make best use of my experience in working the Birmingham boundaries as I had done for several years.

Surprisingly, Rennie appeared quite empathetic. He told me that he would consider the position and let me know his decision as soon as possible. I was then told to leave and that the Assistant Chief Constable Vickers would want to see me in due course.

I walked outside and was met by Geoff who still had a face as long as a violin string but was keen to know how I had got on. I didn't have the heart to tell him I think I had been promoted but was not sure when or where and in any case I was bewildered. So, I said nothing. We had a silent journey back to base and I made my way back to Rubery Police station where I was doing acting sergeant at the time. I was just at the point of picking the phone up to ring Jud when it rang. On the other end of the line was Rennie's secretary. She told me to return to Police Headquarters immediately and see Vickers the Assistant Chief Constable. She would not tell me why and I feared they must have found out about some misdemeanour I had committed and the game was up. It was an order not a request and I drove all the way to Police HQ feeling doomed. I did not ring Jud because I was not sure whether this was promotion or the sack!

When I walked into Vickers' office he stood up, smiled and shook my hand. I felt relieved. He continued, 'Mr. Rennie has had second thoughts about your promotion King.' I could have kissed him, I blurted out, 'Oh thank you, sir, I really wasn't looking forward to going to Market Drayton...........'

Before I could say anymore, Vickers interrupted and said curtly, 'No King his second thoughts are you are definitely going to Market Drayton and will posted there from two weeks on Monday. Lambs Removals of Worcester will be moving you, you are moving to a police house at number 3 Police Drive, Market Drayton. After 12 months we may well move you again so will remain in Police accommodation and can take it from me that any application to buy your own house during that period is refused. Do you understand?'

I meekly said something like, 'Yes sir, and that this had taken all the fun out of the decision making!'

Vickers retorted by say, 'Not really because Mr. Rennie did say you do have one decision to make. You can go there as a Sergeant or you can go there as a constable but two weeks time you are posted to Market Drayton. Which is it?'

'Sergeant, please sir,' I replied. I was fast getting the impression the talking was done!

'Best of luck then lad, off you go,' said Vickers and I left the office in shock.

I drove home and broke the news to Jud. We had a conversation that very much followed my conversation with Rennie about where the hell was it, never heard of it and so on.

We got out a map and followed the M5 north onto the M6 – when my finger reached Stafford I was really wondering if this was a joke because I could not see Market Drayton anywhere. Suddenly I saw it, about 18 miles north of Shrewsbury on the Staffordshire, Cheshire boundaries – what fun we were to have! All because of sex and a brothel!

CHAPTER 12

LIVING IN HELL AT MARKET DRAYTON

On a bright weekday morning in the summer of 1979 Jud and I made our way with a picnic lunch on board the car in order to view our new home and take stock of the village of Market Drayton in North Shropshire, which was about 65 miles from Barnt Green.

I took some consolation from the fact that Maelor Owen a very good friend and fellow acting sergeant had also been promoted and moved to Market Drayton. He and his wife Ann were allocated a house to live next door to ours.

We all decided to meet at Drayton Police Station. When we arrived, the section Inspector Colin Kenvyn was waiting to greet us. He welcomed us and then warned us all that the houses we were to live in were in very poor condition and that there was no money in the budget to do them up. He then gave us the keys and left us to inspect them.

Jud and I walked into the house to find that it was pre-war and looked like it was still in that era.

The walls were black from the smoke of open fires. There was no central heating, no cupboards in the kitchen, only a marble slab, the state of decoration was very poor and some of the walls were damp with paint peeling. Others were painted in khaki coloured paint. Every room was in need of decoration.

There were electrical sockets hanging loose off the wall and the toilet would not flush.

Compared to the Police house we had at Barnt Green this was a hell hole. I tried to put a positive spin on it but Jud sat in the middle of the lounge floor and cried. She looked at me in despair and told me she could not live there and would refuse to move from Barnt Green. I knew we had no choice, in a little over a week I was due to start at Drayton and that was not negotiable. There was no option for us to buy a house and the best I could do would be to move and then try to organise some repairs even if we ended up paying for it ourselves.

I was now starting to wonder what the benefits of promotion were but reflected that this was probably part of the loyalty test!

We met Maelor and Ann outside who took one look at the house they had been allocated (which was in the same state) and then they went straight to the nearest estate agent to buy a property. Maelor had only been advised not to buy a house whereas I was ordered not to. In view of the fact the force provided either free accommodation or a rent allowance they called the shots and had the power to tell you where you lived and with whom. You always needed their permission.

I managed to placate Jud and then Colin Kenvyn took us for a tour of the area.

Eventually we managed to get some repairs carried out to the house and finance for decorating but only after I threatened the Police county architect with calling environmental health.

Market Drayton is a small market town with a population of approximately 10,000 situated between Stoke on Trent and Shrewsbury and borders with Cheshire and Staffordshire. It is home to the Tern Hill, Clive barracks which at various times had been host to both the RAF and army regiments and in February 1989 was blown up by the IRA in a terrorist explosion which resulted in substantial damage but fortunately only one person was injured.

It is a very rural area and most of its economy is derived from farming. However, at that time it was the base of the famous Palethorpe sausage factory and now is host to Muller Yoghurts.

Drayton is also promoted as the home of the gingerbread biscuit which dates back to the 1700's.

Both Lord Clive of India and Oswald Mosley were born near Drayton and when I was stationed there it was home to an infamous poacher.

This was a self confessed professional and eccentric poacher. A man of the country, tales abound of his notorious stunts during his dealings with the law. On one occasion just before Christmas it is alleged he dressed as Father Christmas and sat on the roof of Shrewsbury prison with a sack of cigarettes and tobacco for inmates and repeatedly bellowed 'Merry Christmas' until he was removed and carted off by the Police.

On another occasion he appeared before court covered in manure and wearing a dead pig as a hat. He made another appearance in court dressed as a frogman which occurred just after he was practising for the world frog swallowing record attempt at a Market Drayton pub by swallowing a live frog which he washed down with a pint of black and tan.

Perhaps his most infamous piece of notoriety came after he nailed himself by his ear to a tree!

I had few dealings with him and much of the above occurred before my time at Drayton but his reputation lived on and he was always striding around town as if butter would not melt. Long live the eccentrics of this world and I hope he is still going strong and not behaving himself.

Typical of most small market towns Drayton had lots of pubs and only small shops. Main shopping had to be done at either Newcastle-under-Lyme or Shrewsbury which were both about 20 miles away. There was a Woolworths store though and Jud managed to get a transfer from Redditch to work in the local branch on a part-time basis so that made her feel better.

There was a local court in the town centre and once a week it was the job of the Sergeant to assist the Inspector with prosecuting cases – this was prior to the days of the Crown Prosecution Service. Prosecuting solicitors or counsels were employed to do the serious not guilty pleas but everything else was prosecuted by the Police.

The station itself was quite small but functional with a couple of cells. The one saving grace was a recreation room with radiators and a snooker table which became a godsend. Market Drayton must be the coldest place on the planet. No, I am not joking. Look at the temperatures that are forecast from nearby RAF Shawbury and you will see they record some of the lowest temperatures in the country. The police house we were in was so cold Jud and I used to regularly spend our evenings in the police station playing snooker where it was centrally heated. To begin with I used to give Jud a 30 point start, after a few weeks she was giving me a 30 point start on each frame!

The only other venue we frequented whenever shifts allowed was the Joiners Arms pub situated a few hundred yards from the house. Bob and Norrie were the licensees and we spent a lot of wonderful evenings and lunchtimes socialising with the locals.

Maelor and I were two of four Sergeants each with a shift of about 4 or 5 officers who worked to Inspector Colin Kenvyn. We covered the shifts and patrols of the section 24/7 but shared night sergeant cover with Whitchurch section which was approximately 12 miles to the north. North Shropshire sub-divisional headquarters were located at Oswestry on the Welsh borders. The main divisional headquarters were at Shrewsbury where the main highlight was patrolling Shrewsbury Town Football on a Saturday.

Sometimes we were required to travel to Shrewsbury via Oswestry and then return to Market Drayton which was a round trip of 70 miles. So even a divisional telling off from the superintendent required a packed lunch or a claim for expenses.

Probably the most pleasant bit about working at Drayton was Lorna and Judy who worked in the admin office and Sheila who was one of the receptionists. Other than that there were not many perks. All three were very pleasant and working between 9am to 5pm became a pleasure.

Police work is very much the same in a rural area no matter where you are. Always lots of routine inquiries to do, supplemented by the reactive responses to accidents, reports of crime, poaching and yobbish behaviour both in the town centre and on the estates. Then there is the violence, fights after closing time and the inevitable domestic disputes, neighbour disputes and family feuds.

Drayton has two major 'A' roads which converge at a spot called Tern Hill where the A53 meets the A41. This was a notorious cross-roads where we were continually called to deal with serious or fatal road accidents.

Fatals, as they are known are common but one of the most traumatic incidents officers attend. The job of the sergeant is to supervise the scene and make sure all evidence is collected either to prosecute a driver or to present to the coroners court. One of the most difficult tasks is ensuring that there is continuity of the deceased from the point where they die at the scene or later, to the mortuary and then carry out identification with relatives and attend the post mortem to identify the body to the pathologist.

Once all inquiries are complete then the role of the officer dealing and the sergeant is to record all the evidence in a comprehensive and factual file of evidence which is always a painstaking and complex piece of work in order to ensure nothing is missed.

One of my first tasks at Drayton was supervising a fatal accident where four people were killed in a two vehicle head on crash which occurred just the Whitchurch side of Tern Hill crossroads. A car being driven by a young man with his father as front seat passenger tried to overtake a lorry and collided head on into a Morris Marina being driven the other way which contained an elderly man and wife. Both they and the young male driver were killed instantly. The father (passenger) died later in Shrewsbury hospital. This was the first fatal accident I had supervised and it came home to me how quickly life can be turned upside down or end in a split second of misjudgement.

On another occasion my shift was on early turn (6am to 2pm). I paraded and briefed them whilst having a cup of tea and read out the briefing log of messages to note and observations for vehicles or people wanted. One of the messages related to a non-stop road accident which had occurred on the Staffordshire police area in a village just over the Shropshire boundary. An elderly lady had been crossing the road late at night when she was struck and killed by the driver of a red Audi car who had stopped momentarily afterwards and then driven off at a fast rate of knots. The message was requesting observations for the red Audi car which was likely to have damage to the front. No registration number had been obtained and Staffordshire were struggling to identify the car or driver.

My friend and fellow sergeant Maelor was now in the process of buying a house and had put in a bid on a house that was on one of the estates in Drayton. One of the officers on my shift was an old sweat called Cliff Bryan who was friends with Maelor. Once we had paraded Cliff decided he was going to drive out on patrol and have a look at the house that Maelor was buying.

After a few minutes Cliff called me on the radio and said, 'Sarge, what was that message you read out about obs for a red Audi car?' I reiterated the message whereupon Cliff told me that whilst looking for Maelor's house he had come across a red Audi parked on a house driveway which had a damaged headlight. On closer inspection he found that there was what appeared to be the remains of someone's scalp (hair and skin) left in the headlamp.

I immediately joined Cliff and examined the Audi to confirm what Cliff had said. Sure enough, it looked like we had found the car wanted by Staffordshire Police. We knocked on the door which was eventually answered by a middle-aged man who was small and scrawny with a mop of untidy hair. He was either very tired having just got out of bed or feigning tiredness. When we inquired about the car on the drive he stated it was his and he had used it the night before. When it came to the crunch question about the damage he stated that he had been driving back from Birmingham the night before and thought he had hit a sheep. He alleged he stopped, could not see the sheep so assumed it was not injured and decided to drive home.

Once inside the man's house I could smell stale alcohol on his breath and could see the remnants of a bottle of wine on the dining table. He stated, as expected that he had not been driving under the influence of drink but had consumed most of a bottle of wine after arriving home.

So here we had what was a case of a man who had been involved in a fatal road collision. Whether or not he was to blame for the accident had yet to be determined but one thing was clear, he had left an elderly lady dying in the road and driven off. Drink may well have been a factor involved in the accident and the reason why he left the scene. However, he had come up with the usual defence which existed at that time which was that he had been drinking since the accident after arriving home so even if tested and over the limit it would be very difficult to prosecute. In those days there was no means available to do back-calculation of blood or urine tests to determine forensically what may have been consumed both pre and post driving incidents.

However, we decided this did not matter. The seriousness of the situation meant we must follow the procedures and worry about what could be proved later. We breathalysed the man and the crystals turned to show a positive test. On this basis he was arrested and taken to the station for a second test and to obtain blood or urine specimens. This was before the days of the intoximeter breath-sampling machines that now exist and give immediate results.

This meant that we were able to get his car forensically examined and recovered to the station and then allow opportunity to interview him formally about the accident and give his account to Staffordshire officers who came to Drayton.

What was the result of all this? Potential death by dangerous driving, leaving the scene of an accident where an elderly woman died and possibly drink driving? Well, life is about what can be proved in evidence and the law as it existed at the time.

I attended the inquest hearing on the old lady which was held at Stoke-on-Trent. Result - accidental death. She had stepped out in front of the Audi car without giving the driver chance to avoid the collision. The coroner was a stern elderly man with a monocle which fell out of his eye every time he raised his eyebrows which was quite often during the proceedings. He summed it up by saying that it was not for him to determine whether or not the driver was drunk or to deal with the fail to stop afterwards, it was merely to determine cause of death. Leaving the scene of the accident was not considered to have been instrumental in causing the death.

Later the blood specimen came back negative (below the limit) so there was no point in prosecuting for that. There was no evidence of dangerous driving so it just a matter of the fail to stop after the collision which was dealt with by a magistrates court in Staffordshire but could not at that time have resulted in much more than a fine or endorsement on his driving licence.

Only he will know the full story of what occurred that night and whether drink was a factor in the accident. However, had it not have been for the nosiness of Cliff Bryan looking for a house for sale then it is unlikely he would have been traced at all!

During the time I was at Drayton I had some real characters of officers on my shift. One of those was a young officer who had transferred to us during his probation from Shrewsbury I shall refer to as Kevin. Kevin could not drive Police vehicles or in fact any vehicle other than a motorbike (which was his pride and joy). He had very little experience of dealing with anything prior to arriving on my shift and was in desperate need of close supervision in a section where it was necessary very often to work alone.

The first time I sent Kevin out to get a statement it was from a lady who had witnessed an accident and was potentially a first rate independent witness. Kevin established from the lady, who was even more eccentric than he was, that at the time she was walking her cat along the road on a lead. Yes, I know a bloody lead! Kevin's statement consisted of a first rate description of the cat, the lead the walk but little or no detail of what the lady had witnessed! He was despatched to retake the statement.

Kevin became ill and was in single quarters so Jud and I were worried how he might cope on his own. Jud cooked him some beans on toast and we took it round to his quarters.

Kevin answered the door and was eating something cold from a tin with a fork. However, what amused us was the way he looked. Kevin appeared to be wearing very little except for a great long black Police gannex mac. He had a thick black droopy moustache with a daft grin on his face and underneath the long mac were these pair of thin spindly legs covered in matted black hair. It took Jud a long time to recover and I have to say it was sight to behold.

Whilst working nights Kevin and I were called out to the Bear Hotel in the village of Hodnet to a report of a domestic dispute between an estranged husband and wife. When we arrived the man was complaining because the woman had found him at the pub with another woman and ripped off the wing mirrors from his car. He was quite calm and just wanted things to calm down but she wanted to scratch his eyes out and we needed to get her away.

I got Kevin to put the woman in the front passenger seat of the Police car whilst I spoke to the husband alone. I was getting some details when suddenly I heard Kevin screaming, 'Sarge, Sarge, help me, help.' I turned round and could see that the woman was trying to get out of the Police vehicle and make her way back towards her husband. Kevin was valiantly trying to prevent her by holding on to her arm but in the process the woman was so strong she had dragged Kevin out of the driver's seat of the police car across the passenger seat and was now dragging him across the car park on his back where he was still holding on. I could not assist because I was bent double in laughter and the husband did a runner. Seeing a Police officer being dragged backwards across a car park in full uniform by a woman was one of the funniest things I have ever seen.

Eventually, the woman calmed down, we drove her home, gave words of advice and then made a fast exit.

I eventually managed to get Kevin trained to drive Police vehicles which at least meant he could work on his own. However, I found that was the start of another problem. Kevin had spent years riding a motorbike. The problem was he drove a police car like he rode a motorbike.

On nights we used to double up and patrol the section villages together where usually Kevin would drive and I would act as passenger and observer. Firstly, Kevin used to drive at a fast rate of miles per hour everywhere. I tried to explain that on nights the idea is you patrol slowly, looking for suspicious activity and checking for burglars and so forth but it was to no avail.

What made it really disconcerting was that when Kevin negotiated a bend he would lean right over (as motorcyclists tend to) anticipating this would change the direction of the vehicle rather than relying on the more

x method of the steering wheel. However, probably the biggest
is that he believed that the car was the same width as his motorbike
through the same gaps! By the time we got to the station I was
usually legless and a quivering jelly.

However, Kevin was a nice guy, entertaining to work with and I believe he
became a competent officer and had a long career. Bless him!

I had another officer on the shift for a short time I will call Ralph. He
was a little bit of an intense character but always willing and respectful.
Sometimes he did odd things.

My shift was working 2pm x 10pm but Ralph had some time off. We
were on quick change over to 6am x 2pm the next day and Ralph was
due to work. Because he had been late on a couple of occasions before I
had warned him that I expected him to be on time for his early shift and
parade at 5.45am.

I was alone in the station and just about to pack up and go home at 10pm
when I could hear what I thought was an animal or someone groaning.
Upon listening more intently I realised that it was snoring but I could not
find out where it was coming from. Eventually, having followed a process
of elimination I realised it was coming from a rather large broom cupboard
situated in the corridor. I opened the door with some trepidation mixed
with intrigue to find Ralph. There he was fast asleep having made a bed
in the cupboard. I rather rudely awakened him and asked him what the
hell was going on. He replied to the effect that he was concerned about
oversleeping so he decided to sleep in the cupboard on the basis that if he
did oversleep he could not be in trouble because he was already 'on the
job' at the station! I closed the door and left him to it trying very hard to
work out the logic?

The military influence of having the Tern Hill barracks nearby and RAF
Shawbury just a few miles down the road was never far away.

Just after we arrived at Drayton, Maelor Owen was taken out for a tour of
the section by one of the Inspectors and they went to RAF Shawbury and
watched the helicopters landing and taking off.

Maelor asked one of those questions that you should never ask, 'Has one of those ever, crashed?' The Inspector replied that to his knowledge, no. Maelor went on to comment that in the event it should ever happen he felt he ought to read the major incident manual so he was prepared.

By the time they got back to Drayton a call came in to say that a helicopter had crashed!

The Inspector and Maelor collected the Major Incident Book and then made their way to the scene. The incident was fairly well contained and I do not think it was too serious. However, the press attended and the Inspector went to brief them, allay their fears and explain that it was a minor incident and all under control. One of the press reporters then asked the Inspector if it was such a minor incident why was he was carrying around a Major Incident Book?

Quick as lightening the Inspector replied, 'This is not a Major Incident Book today, it's a just in case we have one book!'

The one thing I learned very quickly at Drayton was that everyone knew everyone else's business and that everything is incestuously linked. When you arrested someone and then took them to the Police station it was not long before the rest of their family, friends, solicitor and someone bringing flask and sandwiches turned up. Life was very parochial and local trouble makers got to know the Police very well.

I immediately realised that when confronting people who were drunk and ready to fight it was best to adopt a non-confrontational attitude and try to talk them round without the need for arrest. This was on the basis that the nearest assistance was about 12 miles away at Whitchurch which would consist of probably one officer and the next nearest help was at Shrewsbury probably half an hour away. A lot can happen in that period of time when you are on your own and severely outnumbered. The other reason was that once someone was arrested the Sergeant was confined to the station for the rest of the shift until the prisoners were sober enough to interview and release which meant no more patrolling.

About half way through my period at Drayton I dealt with a most interesting case of 'abstracting electricity.'

Early one evening in the winter I was called by the local electricity board company to attend one of their staff who was in need of assistance at an old mansion house out in the country.

When I arrived I was met outside by one of their inspectors who informed that he had just carried out an inspection of the property we were at and had found that the seals on the meter had been tampered with and that this combined with the fact that the owner seemed to incur very low electricity bills led him to believe that electricity was being falsely obtained without payment.

The property itself was indeed a splendid old residence in the style of an old mansion house with several bedrooms and living rooms and was in the process of gradually being renovated. There were all the numerous electrical devices any household should have and seeing that it was towards the back end of winter the previous electricity bills did seem very low for previous quarter's use of electricity.

The male occupant was a well educated middle aged man who I believe may have had a background in physics or something scientific. He was very aloof, astounded that we should be questioning his integrity and denied all knowledge of the allegations made that he was defrauding the electricity company.

Together we all inspected the meter which was found to be on a board that could be swung round meaning the meter could be placed upright or on its side. We noticed that when it was on its side the meter stopped rotating and registering units but did not affect the supply of electricity. Also, the seals on the unit had been crimped with an ordinary pair of pliers compared to the ones used by official engineers which contained a special stamp. Something was obviously amiss so, the meter was seized together with every pair of pliers we could find and the occupant arrested.

I sent the whole lot off to the Forensic Science laboratory where it was established that someone had tampered with the interior of the meter so that when it rested on its side and with the use of magnets then it stopped registering use of electricity. At the point where it came near to having the meter read then it would be put into its usual position to appear normal.

The man of the house was charged with illegally abstracting electricity and appeared before the court but I was never informed of what the result was.

I understand this type of ruse cannot be repeated now!

One of the bug-bears of being a Sergeant was dealing with accidents involving police vehicles which seemed to occur in my experience on a regular basis. It always meant a full investigation and a long report as well as having to suspend the police driver from driving police vehicles if they appeared at fault.

I was on duty one night when at 4am I was called to deal with an accident involving one of my officers who had driven his police panda car into a postman who was riding his cycle past a junction on the way to work. Nothing too serious occurred but I did have a conversation with the officer which was something like this. 'At Market Drayton at four o'clock in the morning there is only ever likely to be one police officer, one police vehicle and one lonely postman on his way to work and probably every other bugger in the world is asleep. Can you tell me how on this basis in a town of 10,000 population and God knows how many square miles you have to patrol you have managed to collide!'

He was unable to answer and I thought it was a reasonable question. However, it didn't end there.

About two weeks later we were working early turn shift (6am to 2pm) when there was a report of a post office robbery taking place in one of the local villages. One of our beat officers Jim Hudson from Hodnet leapt into his police van parked at the front of the police station and reversed out very quickly. At the same time the local postman (thank goodness a different postman, because the other one was still off sick) was driving a post van through the police yard to deliver letters to the houses at the rear of the station.

Jim reversed squarely into the side of the post van causing damage to both vehicles.

The irony of the Police driving into two postmen in less than two weeks had passed me by because I was more concerned about the paper work.

However, I did receive a call from the local postmaster who demanded to know if the police had a conspiracy against his staff and could we refrain from driving at them.

There were positives working at Drayton and some lighter moments. I struggle to remember what they were but here goes.

One weekend Jud's sister Ruth, her husband Dave and two children Sarah and Nigel visited us to inspect our new abode. Dave was always in the habit of picking up a newspaper and engrossing himself in the news to ignore the kids and Ruth. Nigel found my handcuffs and snapped one cuff onto Dave's wrist. We were not worried because I confirmed I had the key. Nigel then snapped the other cuff on the same wrist. Again we were not concerned because I had the key.

After a few minutes Dave asked if we could slacken off the cuffs because they were a bit tight on his wrist. I approached Dave with the key and was then confronted with a problem. The cuffs had been snapped on the one wrist with the key holes facing inwards and there was insufficient room to get the key in either of the locks due to the tightness of the link and because Dave's wrist was now beginning to swell up. Suddenly Dave became rather pre-occupied by this and threw the paper down. At least we had his full attention now; it was like having his privates in a vice! He was in pain and getting worried but we thought it was hilarious. We were at the point of calling the fire brigade when I managed to break one of the links of the handcuffs and that enabled us to spread the cuffs sufficient to place the key in the lock and release them. Dave was relieved, the kids couldn't stop laughing and Ruth reminded Dave to pay more attention in future to his family commitments or else he might find himself locked up!

I have always been interested in various forms of motorcycle sport and one of the best day's duty I enjoyed was supervising the national motorcycle circuit at Hawkestone park whenever there was a big meeting. It meant minimum hassle and maximum opportunity to watch the racing which in those days was usually televised, a free meal and drink and a great opportunity to meet normal people.

By now Jud and I were getting into snooker and were avid followers of the world championships. On the 5th May 1980 Jud and I were watching the final frames of the world championship between Alex 'Hurricane' Higgins (Northern Ireland) and Cliff Thorburn (Canada) which was a cliff hanger from the beginning. We were also waiting to go out to a Police social night at Whitchurch golf club but did not want to drag ourselves away from the telly. Suddenly, the snooker was interrupted by news that the SAS had stormed the Iranian Embassy in London where terrorists had been holding hostages for six days. Dramatic scenes were shown as the action was happening and the world was on tenterhooks wanting to know what the outcome was. Then, the coach arrived to take us to the function.

When we arrived at the club everyone just wanted to watch the telly and catch up on either the snooker or the embassy siege. It was one heck of a night in terms of national events. Cliff Thorburn won the snooker after a knife-edge finish and the SAS ended the siege successfully and received world wide acclaim. Eventually, we enjoyed a night out.

Towards the end of my time at Drayton we had a new Inspector arrive called Dave Borthwick who had transferred from the Regional Crime Squad and was a CID man through and through. Within a few days of his arrival one of my officers submitted to me a file which consisted of numerous obscure traffic offences which I did not really understand. In those days the Sergeant made recommendations and the Inspector would then countersign the report and mark it up with a decision as to prosecution. I decided to take a chance and put the file through with my best guess as to recommendations because to research everything would have taken ages. I was working on the presumption that Dave being a CID man would not know either and would countersign my recommendations and if it went to court it could be sorted out there.

I was surprised to receive the report back with a load of red ink on it from Dave correcting my recommendations and giving me constructive advice about lack of traffic knowledge. I went to see him and said, 'I thought you were CID and wouldn't know about all this traffic regulation stuff and construction and use.'

Dave then told me that for many years he had been on traffic and had always kept up to date his knowledge on road traffic despite the fact that he had since specialised in investigating serious offences on CID and the

Regional Crime Squad. He proceeded to tell me that the job of a supervisor was to know a bit about everything and he certainly did.

Dave was quite happy interviewing a robber or investigating serious crime but could give sound advice and had amazing knowledge about every aspect of Policing, including obscure subjects such as betting and gaming and protection of birds which was a mystery to most of us. He was a natural policeman with tremendous ability. A complete all rounder who prided himself in working hard and was an inspiration to all those that worked for him at that time at Drayton.

Although Dave had received a side-ways move from CID back to uniform if he had any regrets he did certainly did not show it and his philosophy was always that nothing and no-one would ever stop him working and doing the job he loved. During the short time I worked for Dave I learnt a lot and have always tried to follow his work ethic but not always successfully!

I was approaching the 12 month anniversary of being posted to Drayton and actually Jud and I were now quite enjoying ourselves. The social life was good, we had made numerous friends through the local pub and from attending mess functions with the army. We were even getting used to the house although I have to say we always treated it as camping rather than living there.

One morning I received a telephone call from the Assistant Chief Constable Vickers. He told me my 12 month penal servitude was now up and asked if I wanted a move. I did not want to sound too keen but indicated yes at the same time with some trepidation as to what might follow. He offered me the job of section sergeant at Hagley back in north Worcestershire and to live in a Police house that had recently been modernised in the village of Belbroughton. I was so happy I could have kissed him. I rushed home to tell Jud who was also over the moon until it came time to leave. The final night we had a leaving do at the Joiners Arms and Jud cried because she didn't want to leave all our friends!

CHAPTER 13

RIDICULOUS TO THE SUBLIME

As I looked at the young man sitting in the driver's seat and the young woman sitting next to him I could see they were both dead. Sometimes you just know, but there were obvious signs like a trickle of blood from the ears that indicate a fractured skull combined with absolutely no movement.

In the immediate aftermath of a fatal collision there is usually an eerie silence. The traffic has stopped and everyone present is shocked as if frozen on the spot or appears to be in slow motion. It seems to go on for eternity but in reality does not last long before panic, hysteria, sirens and intense activity of emergency workers change the false serenity into a hectic place where chaos has quickly to be changed back to normality.

However, it will never again be normality for some. The lives of the two single mothers of both the young man and the young woman would never be the same again.

The two young male drivers of the other two cars involved although not injured would never be the same again. The motorcyclist who had followed all three cars and been first on the scene would never forget what he saw that morning.

For myself and Taff Rogers the constable who attended the scene emotions will be controlled and checked whilst at the scene but afterwards thoughts will be reflected upon, self analysis of actions will be conducted and memories filed alongside hundreds of other experiences in the library of the mind for future reference.

This was the A456 near Hagley on a damp but clear spring Saturday morning. The A456 at this point was a notorious stretch of road and one of the busiest in Worcestershire that leads up to the M5 motorway and Birmingham.

The sports car had hit a tree in the central reservation with tragic and terrible consequences for the attractive young couple in it who were about to get married and had just put a deposit on house.

As a cop at the scene there are a hundred things to do and all at once. Firstly, protect the scene to ensure it is safe and traffic diverted. Ensure required assistance is on its way. Tend to the injured and save life until fire and ambulance can take over.

Ascertain what has happened from witnesses and get their details. Check what vehicles are involved and who was driving.

Make sure that all evidence of how the accident has occurred is preserved such as skid marks, debris and ensure vehicles are not moved. Consider if drivers have been drinking and if there are immediate and obvious causes of the collision. Try and get immediate explanations from drivers and witnesses as to their version of what has occurred. Note the road conditions, weather and visibility.

Carry out registration checks for identity of drivers and to check whether vehicles may be stolen, drivers disqualified or insurance offences.

Ensure valuables of those involved are taken care of and arrange recovery of vehicles. In the case of fatal collisions call specialist investigators to draw a scale plan of the scene and police scenes of crime officers to photograph the scene.

Ascertain where casualties or the deceased are being moved to and in the case of those that are dead ensure you have the names of the ambulance staff who convey the body so that continuity for identification from the accident scene to the mortuary can take place.

Once the immediate scene is clear then it is a case of informing relatives, interviewing witnesses and drivers, arranging for vehicles to be examined by specialists for signs of defects and investigating thoroughly to put the facts together until there is sufficient evidence to decide how the accident occurred for the purpose of an inquest and the coroner and to determine whether or not anyone should be prosecuted.

The work of ambulance and fire brigade is largely completed once back at base. The work of the Police will continue for weeks or months and may not be concluded for years. There is no greater responsibility for a uniformed officer than investigating a road death. The diligence of that inquiry will be analysed by Police supervisors, coroners, lawyers, courts, insurance companies and civil court procedures.

What appeared to have occurred in this instance is that two young men in separate sports cars were seen by a witness to be travelling very fast in the outside lane of the dual carriageway. However, this was approximately one mile before the accident occurred. There were no witnesses to the actual impact but what we established had happened was that the first sports car was in the outside lane overtaking the young couple in their car in the inside lane when the front passenger side of that car had struck the front driver's side of the young couple's car causing it to swerve off the road and hit a tree in the central reservation. The friend of the driver of the first sports car was following behind and managed to avoid the collision.

We left accident investigators to piece together the scene of the collision to work out exactly what happened.

The following morning was a Sunday and one that I will never forget. Taff and I travelled to the mortuary to meet with the mother of the young girl and carry out formal identification of the body. When she saw her lovely daughter she cried, looked at me and said, 'Mr. King, this is my only child, I lived my life for her. My life might as well be over.'

As a professional there is nothing that you can say that will help, only to show that you care and to sympathise. I could have cried with her but that would not have helped either.

Later that week we attended the post mortem (PM) of both the young man and young woman. It was Taff's first PM and he was nervous. We were also both upset in view of the overall circumstances. However, one of the mortuary workers was a character of a man who realised it was

Taff's maiden flight. He also had the ability to throw his voice like a ventriloquist. He was in the process of working on one of the other corpses from a post mortem completed earlier. He winked at me and when Taff's back was turned he shouted 'Ouccchhhh' in a voice that sounded as if it was coming from the body he was working on. Taff almost jumped out of his skin but when he realised what had happened he did see the funny side of it and eventually became quite intrigued by the whole process of watching a PM despite the sadness of the situation.

As we built up the case it looked like a very good case of death by dangerous driving on the part of both drivers of the sports cars. There was no evidence to show that the young couple had in any way been to blame. There was clear evidence that the other two cars had been travelling very fast for the conditions and that the collision had occurred because the driver of the first car veered across the path of the young couple's car causing them to lose control.

However, at a point during the investigation it all started to fall apart. Firstly, early legal advice made us realise that the evidence of the cars racing was well before the collision and did not prove conclusively that they had been speeding or racing at the exact point of the collision. Secondly, during interview the first driver stated that he had hit a patch of water in the outside lane which had caused him lose control and veer to the left.

My heart sunk because although I did not believe it I did not think we would be able to disprove it.

I immediately called the accident investigator who told me that he had noted the patch of water on the road and would run some further tests. Some days later he told me that he had run a mathematical formula and from the depth of the water (which he had measured immediately upon attending the scene), taking the weight of the driver and the weight of the car he could confidently predict that it would have been impossible for the car to have aquaplaned off the water. Phew!

However, because of the uncertainty over speed at the point of the accident, what started out as a good case of death by dangerous driving ended up as a dodgy case of driving without due care and attention. The driver of the first car pleaded not guilty but following trial was found guilty and fined for due care and attention and no insurance.

Not really justice and no comfort to the families of the young couple but at least we secured a conviction.

This then was Hagley Section: a stockbroker belt of North Worcestershire near to Stourbridge and a dormitory village for commuters to the local conurbations of Birmingham and the Black Country and sitting in the shadow of the beautiful Clent Hills.

It is traversed by two roads namely the A491 which leads from junction 4 of the M5 and the A456 which leads direct to Birmingham.

These roads are two of the busiest in Worcestershire and during the two and half years I was stationed at Hagley I would deal with fatal accidents on virtually every intersection and road leading off those two roads within the boundary of the Section.

The other busy area of work was burglaries at houses in both Hagley and the neighbouring parishes which provided rich pickings for burglars travelling over the border from Halesowen, Stourbridge, Cradley Heath and Quinton. Add to that numerous thefts of and from vehicles in the beauty spots of the Clent Hills and a few acts of spicy indecent exposures in the woods, straying animals and people lost and that was Hagley.

The estate of Lord Cobham known as Hagley Hall was resided in by the 11th Viscount John Cobham (now deceased) and his wife Penny. Penny Cobham was a dynamic business woman and turned the family mansion house into a successful conferencing and banqueting venue. The hall was also host to many major events such as an annual motor show and a fireworks display which attracted thousands of visitors. I seemed to be forever writing up contingency plans and operational orders for these events which necessitated extensive traffic diversions and road policing.

The hall itself had a complicated myriad of liquor licences in force which applied to different rooms within the mansion house and laid down specific requirements under the Licensing Laws. It was complicated but I made it my business to research it so I was on top of knowing what licences were in force and how they should be applied. Lady Penny Cobham was a very attractive, articulate and assertive lady who had carried out her own research. When I rang her one day to advise her about an aspect of licensing at the hall she strongly disagreed and we parted company on quite frosty but polite and formal terms. Not long afterwards the licensing was passed formally to a private company who took on responsibility for the liquor licensing so my debates were with a new licensee.

Hagley police station itself was and still is situated next to the A456 Birmingham Road where it meets the A491. In those days it consisted of one big room which was partitioned with glass to make a small sergeant's office. Recreation facilities consisted of a kettle and an outside toilet without a bolt where ablutions were regularly interrupted by members of the public thinking it was a side entrance to the nick.

I had four shifts of two officers on each shift who covered the section 24/7 whenever possible.

One of the most popular officers at Hagley was also the most eccentric. PC 492 Terry Reed was a legend in his own lifetime. A short, thick-set man with steel grey hair and a very posh voice, Terry was well educated and a totally loyal and dedicated officer but worked in unorthodox but enterprising ways.

One morning I made my way into the garage where we kept one of the police panda cars. I saw a couple of the officers smiling to themselves but dismissed it as one of those things.

As I walked into the garage I was confronted by this awful smell and suddenly stepped into a load of horse muck! Now call me old fashioned but I did not expect to find horse muck in a panda garage. As I was concentrating on scraping the contents off the bottom of my shoes and trousers I noticed something else. The inside of the aluminium garage door was buckled out from the inside and looked like it had been kicked in from the inside.

When I went back into the nick the lads were rolling about belly laughing at my caustic language and surprise. When they had stopped laughing and I had calmed down they told me what had happened.

The day before Terry had been sent to a report of a horse straying along the A491 dual carriageway. Now, most officers would have said, 'Area searched, no trace.' Or, if they had found it they would have put it in the nearest gated field. Not Terry, no, he chose to either lead it or ride it back to the Police station and then put it into the panda garage whilst he made diligent inquiries to trace the owner.

Unfortunately, during the interim period not only had it crapped all over the place and kicked the same out of the garage door. It had also injured its hooves in the process which necessitated Terry calling out a vet and incurring a very large bill which I was left to explain to the Finance Officer at Kidderminster who was not impressed!

Terry's exploits did not end there. Situated at Clent was a children's home called The Field House which housed young girls held in care on behalf of social services. Some of these young girls had led terrible lives and were quite vulnerable. Despite this on occasions they would be desperate to resume their lifestyle despite the consequences and would frequently abscond, sometimes for weeks or months at a time.

Terry was the local Police liaison officer for these missing persons and dealt with most of them so that we could maintain continuity. One afternoon a report was received of a young girl having just absconded and sighted on Hagley Hill. Terry went with PC Shane Lewis to apprehend the girl knowing that if he did not catch her it may involve months of work to track her down. They drove along the dual track in the direction of Birmingham and then saw the girl on the opposite side of the carriageway.

Shane dropped Terry off and whilst he darted to the opposite side of the road Shane drove to the next intersection until he could safely turn round and go back in the opposite direction. This only took literally a few moments but in that time Terry and the girl were no-where to be seen.

What happened was this. Terry grabbed hold of the girl and then proceeded to stop the first car that came down the hill. It happened to be very well-to-do gentlemen in a Rolls Royce. Terry stepped into the road, stopped the Roller and told the driver he was commandeering the car in the name of the law. He then bundled the girl into the back of the Roller and directed the driver to take them straight to the Field House.

Eventually, Shane got to find out what had happened and drove to the Field House to pick Terry up. When he arrived he was bemused to observe Terry and the driver of the Roller fighting with the girl on the front steps of the home in an attempt to drag her into the house. Fortunately, no bills were received from the driver of the Roller who was more than pleased to have been of assistance to the local constabulary!

On another occasion I turned up to work to be told by Shane that Terry was at the scene of a house fire in which someone was burning to death in the centre of Hagley village.

I had this image of Terry literally fighting the flames single handed without any thought for himself so I rushed to the location.

When I arrived I found Terry had the situation under control and the fire had been put out. However, it was not a nice scene. An elderly lady had burned to death having fallen onto an electric fire and smouldered overnight. The only thing that was left was her legs from the knees down and the rest was ashes. The local postman had found her and to put the fire out had thrown a bowl of water over the lady which added to the macabre scene and mess. The postman was traumatised by his discovery and eventually we sent him home. Besides verifying what had occurred we were left with three major problems.

The first was that the inside of the house was black and covered in fat just as if there had been a chip fan fire. A quick search of the house to verify her identity and details of next of kin revealed a treasure trove of money hidden in every nook and cranny including the drawers. This meant sifting through the body fat in order to collect and secure all valuables which was not a pleasant task.

The second problem was carrying out a formal identification of the corpse in view of the fact there was little left except the bottom half of her legs. A couple of days later we did this by using the local district nurse to identify the ulcers on the remaining parts of the legs which the nurse had tended and bandaged for a number of years.

The third most pressing problem was to convey news of the death to the lady's only remaining relative which was her sister who lived in

Birmingham. Several journalists and radio broadcasters were at the scene and it would not be long before word spread. The worst case scenario for the family is that they learn of the news from the media before being informed personally.

PC Shane Lewis and I sped off to Birmingham to break the news to the sister. When we arrived she was on her own and we called a neighbour to be present.

I broke the news that we believed her sister had died in a fire at her home address, that there was nothing suspicious but that it would be a case that needed to be investigated by the coroner. I was not prepared for the next question, but on reflection I should have been.

The elderly lady said to me, 'Oh dear, bless her, where is she, when can I see her at rest?' I was dumbstruck. In the rush to get the news delivered before the press announcements I had not thought through the consequences of explaining that the only bits left of her sister were the bottoms of her legs and that everything else was destroyed. Such moments draw upon many years of experience, tact, diplomacy, sensitivity and poetic use of words so, I turned to Shane and asked him to explain, which he did brilliantly!

I would ask Terry to type as much of his work as possible on the grounds that I could never decipher his hand writing which resembled a spider that had crept out of an ink pot and crawled over a sheet of paper. Not only that but he wrote copiously in very small letters. If Terry had a sheet of paper the size of a wall he would have filled it and needed more. He was aware that 'succinctness' was an art he had yet to learn.

The office typewriter developed a problem in that it would not print either of the letters 'I' or 'T'. This was a real problem for us all but especially Terry who needed it more than the rest of us and meant all his reports had to be signed off 'erry' Reed. We applied for a new typewriter or for it to be repaired. The response from the Admin department was 'no'. Terry then proceeded to type a very eloquent report full of missing 'I's and 'T's and submitted it to the superintendent to make the point. Sure enough, it was repaired.

I have two final memories of working with Terry. The penultimate memory was on a Boxing Day when the local Hunt used to meet at Hagley Hall and then everyone would convene afterwards at the Lyttelton Arms Pub where the licensee would put on lunch and few bevies for the Police. It was a popular occasion for hunt saboteurs who would very often get into fisticuffs and aggravation with the local hunt supporters.

On one occasion two of them were fighting in the grounds of the hall when who should attend but Terry. He grabbed hold of both of them by the scruff of the neck and shouted out in his very best posh accent, 'Stop thar fighting young men or I shall box thy ears for you.' So surprised at his authority and demeanour and probably confused by the old fashioned grammar they scuttled off with their tails between their legs.

The final memory is of Terry both arriving and leaving work. When he arrived he was prepared for anything. Haversack, flask, sandwiches, emergency rations, change of clothing, in fact Terry could have existed on the Clent Hills lying in the snow for days at a time and would still have survived. He rode a motorcycle on his journey to and from work. His favourite trick was dressing up in his full motorcycle gear and helmet before he left work and then remembering that he had forgotten to phone his beloved wife Val to let her know he was on his way. Knowing that it would take eternity to take off his helmet, telephone and then put it back on he would ring his wife, leave a reasonable time for her to answer it and then say, 'Val, it's me. I am just leaving and I am assuming you can hear me. However, do not bother to answer because I can't hear you, I have my helmet on. See you soon, bye,' and then he would put the phone down.

Terry was a wonderful, kind, loyal, conscientious cop and when they made him they broke the mould. It was a pleasure to work with and to have known such a character of a man. Sadly in 2011 Terry died and I went to his funeral to pay tribute to a man who made a mark on West Mercia that will be long remembered by many of us.

We were now living in a detached modernised Police house in the village of Belbroughton, not far from Hagley and on the outskirts of Stourbridge. It had all the mod cons such as central heating and had recently been refurbished. Compared to living in the pre-war monstrosity we had been forced to live in at Market Drayton this was pure luxury and definitely a move from ridiculous to the sublime!

Two things conspired to ensure that it was not long after (within a month) of taking up residence we conceived our first daughter Amanda (known as Mandy). The first was probably having a warm bedroom that did not necessitate sleeping in pyjamas and a roll neck sweater. The second thing was that the house was situated immediately next to the side of the road and motorbikes used to roar past until the early hours of the morning!

However, although the house had been modernised we soon found out that the water tank had not! Every two weeks it was my job as section sergeant to prosecute cases from Hagley section at Bromsgrove Magistrates Court. This was in the days well before the advent of the Crown Prosecution Service who now prosecute all cases.

I was in the middle of formally outlining a case to the magistrates when the usher rushed up to me and stuck a note in front of me which read, 'Phone your wife immediately, water pouring in through the ceiling at home!'

I requested a short adjournment and rang Jud who told me that it looked like the water tank had burst in the loft and that water was running through the ceiling and down the stairs. I tried to tell her how to turn off the water supply, rang to arrange an emergency plumber and then went back into court to hastily finish off my cases.

Fortunately, no serious damage was caused and by the time I got home things were reasonably under control.

Prosecuting was always fraught with unexpected problems. We had two Clerks to the courts. One was a friendly amicable man who always did his best to assist me. The other one was less helpful. I would turn up at court with a big thick bundle of papers which were marked with case numbers in sequential order. I relied upon the court clerk to announce the case number of each case as the defendant was called in order that I could access the relevant file quickly. On one occasion the unhelpful clerk was presiding and he insisted on reading the name of the defendant and then quietly announcing the case reference number to the bench of magistrates quietly which I could not hear.

I quickly looked through the court list for the name of the defendant he had just announced which was a very common name like Smith and cross referenced it to the numbered list. I searched out the relevant file and eloquently outlined the case of indecent exposure which had occurred on the Clent Hills and involved an erect penis which had frightened an elderly lady and her little dog called 'Peebles' who were out walking across the hills. (I wasn't sure about Peebles being frightened but thought I would add it in any way!).

I was in full pelt and explaining how traumatised both the lady and 'Peebles' had been as a result of this act of wantonly, lewdly and obscenely exposing his erect penis when I was rudely interrupted by the defendant who shouted, 'Excuse me, I am only here for speeding, not indecency.' He was right – wrong case. I wanted the floor to open up!

CHAPTER 14

FAMILY CONNECTIONS WITH THE ORIGINAL PC PLOD AND ENID BLYTON

For the second time in our short marriage and career Jud and I were living in a beat station and I was the 'Sherriff' of the local patch of villages that made up Hagley Section.

It was perhaps fate that Jud should both marry a copper and become a beat officer's wife.

Why? Well, Jud had an Uncle called Christopher Raymond Rone, known as 'Ray.'

Ray was an ex guardsman and upon leaving the army joined the Police where he served in Dorset. At one point he was the local beat bobby for the village of Studland.

Enid Blyton used to stay regularly with her husband at the old golf club in Studland and got to know PC Rone very well who would visit her when passing by on his bicycle. In later years she revealed to a journalist that her inspiration for the character of 'PC Plod' in her Noddy books was Jud's Uncle Ray Rone. He was the archetypal village bobby and there is no doubt that the image of PC Plod epitomised the avuncular nature of the English beat bobby worldwide alongside the familiar figure of Jack Warner who played the TV character, 'Dixon of Dock Green.'

This is a true story and was later outlined in an article in the Daily Mail newspaper on May 27th 2000 at a point when Dorset Constabulary were about to close Studland Police Station following the retirement of PC Rone's successor. The irony was not lost on the press! PC Rone the original PC Plod retired in 1970 and died in 1990 aged 75. His inspiration in the shape of PC Plod of course continues to live on, long after the death of both his creator and inspirer!

It is fair to say that both Jud and I were very happy and contented living at Belbroughton and I was thoroughly enjoying life being the beat sergeant at Hagley where I had almost complete autonomy over how we operated the patch.

However, with the smooth goes the rough and it was not long before the fragile nature of life was to come over to me in dealing with an incident that was least expected.

I have never bothered too much about working over New Year because they come and they go. What starts off as hail fellow, well met, Happy New Year is very often followed by drunken fights and violent domestics or stabs in the back both metaphorically and in reality so I have always felt it all a rather hypocritical and pointless exercise. Yes I know, 'Bah Humbug.'

When I went to work on New Year's Day 1981 I was feeling very much like this and it was not long before my philosophy was borne out.

One of my long term colleagues whom I had joined the force with 11 years earlier as a cadet was PC Gerry Newton who was one of my constables at Hagley.

Early that morning I got a call via the control room that Gerry was at the scene of the death of a baby and required the attendance of a supervisor.

When I arrived I quickly established that a young baby boy just a few weeks old had been found dead that morning by his parents on trying to rouse him for an early feed.

The parents were married but both very young. They were absolutely distraught to the point where it was impossible to glean any form of information from them.

Deaths involving young children are one of the saddest incidents anyone will have to deal with. Not only that they are the most traumatic, it means that as a Police Officer you are representing the coroner and the baby's interest in establishing what has happened. It means asking questions that are unthinkable and no matter how sensitively or tactfully they are asked, in order to establish the facts the parents will sense an inference that they are being blamed for the death. Questions like: 'When did you last see the baby or feed the baby?' 'Were you sleeping with the baby?' 'Did you hear him/her?' 'Did you check on him/her?' 'In what position does the baby sleep?' 'Is he/she on medication?' 'Had he/she been ill?' 'Are you breast or bottle feeding?' 'Had you been drinking?' 'Are the parent's drug users?'

Also, in those days we would have to seize all bed clothing, mattress and clothing worn by the baby in order to establish whether suffocation was a possibility.

These are tough questions to ask, and tough actions to undertake, they are insensitive and intrusive at a time when parents and family are in emotional turmoil, grief and trauma. However, the bottom line is this. The vast majority of deaths in infant children result in explanation or are diagnosed as infant death syndrome (cot death). However, at the point of attending the incident the Police officer does not know this. It may be that the death was caused intentionally or because of neglect and no-one else is going to establish those facts other than the officer attending the scene who is acting both in the interest of the child and on behalf of the coroner.

In addition, as this book has reflected most deaths involving adults have an element of humour that can be used privately by emergency workers to displace the grief and sadness they feel as a result of dealing with the darker side of life. However, this is not the case when dealing with the death of children. There is no place for humour. Grief and the stress of dealing with the death have to be absorbed alongside an outwardly professional detachment and demeanour. This incident was particularly traumatic. They were very young parents who were absolutely traumatised and grandparents who were equally distraught. A house that was decorated full of the signs of love and affection to a young baby boy on his first Christmas and New Year with all the hope and aspirations that the future would bring. I looked at one card that read, 'To our wonderful grandson on his first

Christmas, lots of love.......' I felt like weeping, I felt sick and angry that such a horrible thing could be allowed to happen to someone so innocent.

Gerry and I dealt with the scene and the baby was conveyed to the mortuary to await a post mortem. We established what we could and there was nothing that indicated anything other than this was a totally unforeseen and tragic death.

That evening I went home to the comfort of my house and Jud. As I entered the kitchen I saw Jud who was by now 5 months pregnant sitting on a stool. I looked at the little bump in her tummy and was overcome by feelings of guilt, anger, suppressed sadness and hopelessness of wondering what the hell life was all about and how unfair that a young child should die when so many evil bastards were literally getting away with it.

I started crying, shouting and throwing things around the kitchen. It took some time before I was calm enough to explain to Jud what had occurred. It is times like this when the home becomes sacrosanct and sharing emotions with someone you love and trust with a licence to say anything, anytime is the only way to release and cope with pent up feelings. Then, you can move on. Sometimes, this can only be done with colleagues because of the confidentiality and sensitivity of the occasion, sometimes it can only be done with the people you love most who do not worry about seeing chinks of weakness or that you are human.

The result of the post mortem was 'natural causes' in that the baby had been suffering a slight cold and infection and during the night had suffered breathing problems, became stifled and died in his sleep. So sad. However, a couple of years later I saw the couple standing by a bus stop with a young child in a push chair and I assume by then they had another child and they looked very happy. I hope they had a great life together.

Years later as an Inspector I had to give a talk to a 'Cot Death' support group in Redditch. They all had examples of losing babies and where they believed the officers attending had acted insensitively. They were emotional and desperate for their messages to be heard and for an explanation as to why the Police should act as they did. In some of the examples they gave there was no explanation. However, when I relayed my experience above it is fair to say you could have heard a pin drop, we shed a few tears together and I think they appreciated that the feelings exist on both sides and that overall Police have a very difficult job to do. I left the meeting with my shirt stuck to my back in sweat and reflected that this was one of the toughest meetings I had ever attended.

Our own daughter Amanda was born in the May of 1981 at Bromsgrove General Hospital and thankfully everything went well. Our second daughter Caroline was born six years later in 1987 at Worcester and again there were no serious problems. However, the above incident will always be at the forefront of my mind, not least in making me realise how precious and lucky we were to have two healthy babies.

I have always enjoyed investigating. To me it was one of the most fascinating aspects of policing. However, most inquiries you carry out are routine and can be fairly boring. Occasionally though something comes along that tests your powers of persistence, observation, attention to detail, evidence gathering and interviewing skills to the full. Then it is like a game of cat and mouse where your wits are pitted against someone who will do everything to escape detection.

What follows is an example of what started as a fairly routine non-stop accident and ended up as a full blown Crown Court case resulting in a conviction for reckless driving and attempting to pervert the course of justice.

During the early hours of Saturday night into a Sunday morning a young man who had just left his girlfriend's house in Belbroughton was driving his treasured possession of a second-hand Ford Escort around a traffic island on the outskirts of Clent village when he was confronted by an Audi car being driven the wrong way around the island which crashed into him. The driver of the Audi failed to stop and drove off at a fast rate. The driver of the Escort was unhurt but stunned and the vehicle sustained extensive damage.

Fortunately, the driver of the Escort obtained the registration number of the Audi but because his car was not driveable he had to run back to his girlfriend's house before he could report the accident.

Meanwhile, two police officers (one of which was my close colleague Gerry Newton from Hagley) were driving an unmarked Police car along the A491 feeder road in the direction of Bromsgrove when they were overtaken by the same Audi and noticed that the front nearside headlamp was badly damaged and rubbing on the tyre causing it to smell of burning rubber.

The officers followed the vehicle for several miles and the driver tried to lose them. The Audi contained four occupants including the driver. Eventually, the Audi came to a sudden halt and one of the rear seat male passengers got out of the car whereupon the Audi was driven off. The officers spoke to the passenger and noticed that his mouth was bleeding. The passenger just told the officers that the driver of the Audi thought they were just being chased and did not realise it was the Police. He took the officers to the address of the driver which was on the outskirts of Birmingham. When the officers and passenger arrived at the address neither the driver nor car was anywhere to be found and the driver's girlfriend stated that he had left and gone to a club and she did not know when he would be back.

At this point, due to radio problems the officers were still unaware of the accident that had occurred at Clent and assumed that they were dealing with a drunk driver who had made off and got away with it so they returned back to Hagley. Eventually, two and two was put together and the incident was left for myself and PC Andy McGill to follow up on the Sunday morning.

Andy was a very down to earth 'brummy' who prior to joining the force had been a motor mechanic which both myself and several colleagues found very useful on more than one occasion. Andy was full of one-liners and used to crease me up when he spoke.

He was on my section at Hagley and usually teamed up with Terry Reid. Like Terry, Andy had terrible hand-writing which meant that for 8 hours of every 24 when they were working I could not read a bleeding thing they ever wrote.

However, like Terry, Andy had a heart of gold, a great sense of humour, was hard working and I enjoyed working with him.

Andy and I read all the papers relating to the overnight accident then decided to visit the Audi driver's address again in Northfield, anticipating we might now get a more forthright explanation when seeing him in the cold light of day.

We were completely taken aback when he denied driving the Audi car the previous evening, admitted that his company owned the car (with the registration number taken by the driver of the Escort and Police) but refused to say where the car was located and inferred that it would probably have been driven by a friend whom he refused to name. He was most obstructive, most arrogant and made it plain he would not assist us. We had no power of arrest at that stage. He was completely sober and we had to leave the house knowing that it would be a matter of serving formal notices on him to disclose the driver of the vehicle, or prove it was him, which was going to be difficult. The best evidence we had was the passenger who had been in the car whose identity we did know. We needed to speak to him and start afresh.

The man we guessed was the driver of the Audi car was called Arnold. Arnold was a self-employed businessman who ran a company in the Black Country. Imagine our surprise on the Monday morning when Arnold went into his local Police station and reported that his car had been stolen from his business premises over the weekend giving him what he thought was every reason to allege the car was stolen at the time of the accident and that he was not involved.

However, what about the man who had been seen getting out of the passenger seat of the car on the night they were chased by Police? His name was Flint and we were now desperate to see what his story would be. When Flint was interviewed he was surprisingly forthright and confirmed that Arnold was driving the car at the time of the accident and named the other occupants of the car and gave us the full story as he knew it. However, we were still not out of the water yet. We knew that Arnold, who was a very intelligent man would probably still deny what took place, convince the other friends in the car not to give evidence and do his best to discredit what Flint was saying.

Eventually all this was proved correct, Arnold claimed that Flint was completely drunk on the night in question and must be mistaken and the other passengers all declined to say much at all. Events became much more serious when we discovered Arnold had also made a claim on his insurance policy for the theft of the car which was virtually new and was never recovered. We suspected it had been taken to a breaker's yard and destroyed or otherwise disposed of because it disappeared completely and was never found. What had started as a simple fail to stop accident and driving without due care and attention had now become a case of potentially perverting the course of justice and attempting to defraud the insurance company. However, we needed to prove beyond reasonable doubt that Arnold was driving the car and to corroborate Flint's evidence.

Every time we went anywhere near Arnold's home or business to make inquiries or attempt to speak to him he made complaints of harassment and on one occasion even alleged that the officers following him in the Police car that night had a crate of beer on the back seat and were drunk (presumably alleging Flint had told him this).

The gauntlet was thrown down, but this was going to be difficult and it is where persistence, good old fashioned detective work and attention to detail combined with lady luck comes to bear.

Firstly, we had been told by Flint that on the Sunday morning he had driven Arnold to Frankely Services on the M5 where he dropped him off to collect the Audi car which had been left overnight on the services and he could see it was damaged. Andy and I carried out a Police National Computer check on the registered number of the Audi to see if it had been checked at all overnight. We travelled to Police headquarters at Hindlip near Worcester and searched through hundreds of vehicle checks recorded on computer spread sheets that had been made by Police Officers over the period when the Audi was left at the services to see if it had been checked. Bingo! We found that it had been checked overnight whilst at the services by a motorway patrol crew who because of the damage had checked to see if it was stolen. When the result came back negative (because at that stage it had not been reported stolen) they decided to leave it.

Flint also told us that on the evening in question all the party concerned had visited a restaurant at a pub near Belbroughton. We recovered the receipts and order for the meal which was in Arnold's name and this together with the details of the vehicle being checked at Frankley completely corroborated Flint's story.

However, we still needed cast-iron proof that Arnold had been driving the car at the time of the accident and using it over the weekend. Over a cup of tea and a cigarette Andy and I contemplated what more we could do and employed some lateral thinking.

Suddenly, Andy said, 'Got it Sarge, credit cards!' In those days credit cards had not been around long and were generally only used by the rich or those in business with only a limited number of companies being on the market. Cheques and cash were generally the norm but Andy was right, Arnold was likely to use credit cards. We then phoned every credit agency in the country to ascertain if either Arnold or his company name were customers. Two companies came back and confirmed he held cards with them. We then asked them to check their records for the period between the Friday evening and the Monday morning before the car was reported stolen to see if there was any record of transactions relating to fuel. This was important because in those days whenever you purchased fuel the service station required you to provide a security code which was the registration number of your car. So, if Arnold had made purchases of fuel and had given the registration number of the Audi then we had proof he had been using the car over the weekend when according to him it had been stolen.

One of the companies came back and informed us, yes, they had records of fuel purchases on Arnold's credit card over the relevant weekend, signed by him and in which he had given the registration number of the Audi. Double Bingo! At last we had something positive in addition to the evidence of the passenger Flint.

Eventually came the day to formally interview Arnold and because of his constant allegations of harassment I got an Inspector to sit in the interview as an independent observer. Andy said afterwards the interview was like a game of chess.

I went through the circumstances of the accident and Arnold predictably denied all knowledge or responsibility and maintained his story that he had not been driving the car in question which had been stolen. Eventually, we came to the business of the credit cards. I was looking forward to this because there was no way he could know we had acquired such evidence. I cautiously approached the subject and he confirmed, yes he owned credit cards, no he had never had any stolen or lost. I asked him to check the receipts and he confirmed his signature. I then pointed out the fact that they contained evidence of purchases of petrol in which the registration number of the Audi car he had reported stolen during the same period had been noted by the cashier or given by him to the cashier. Gotcha! Arnold was stunned but only temporarily.

He recovered composure and then immediately retorted that his company owned two identical model Audi cars with similar registration numbers. Also, that over the weekend in question he must have been using the other Audi temporarily and that because he was normally accustomed to driving the Audi that had been stolen he was in the habit of just ensuring he gave the registered number of that car to service station attendants as a security code for the credit card. He then gave us the number of the other Audi car and confirmed it was usually used by one of his employees at another factory near Manchester and intimated he may have borrowed it that weekend as he did occasionally.

Blast! Andy and I were blown away. What we had assumed was cast-iron evidence had suddenly thrown considerable doubt on the entire events. We immediately confirmed that what Arnold told us was at least partly true. The new registration he gave us was another identical Audi car with a very similar number (in fact, only two digits different) and was indeed registered to one of Arnold's companies at Manchester.

We waited until we knew Arnold was out of the country on business and early one morning Andy and I drove straight to Manchester and visited the company. Sitting outside was the second Audi car, nearly new in pristine condition.

Andy and I went inside, announced who we were but left them to assume we were local Police making routine inquiries about Audi cars used in crime and that we needed to eliminate the whereabouts of all identical cars over the period of a certain weekend. One of the bosses at the company came forward and said he normally used the car. We interviewed him, being coy as to what we said and avoiding any conversation about Arnold. He gave us irrefutable evidence backed up by records that he had been using that Audi car over the weekend when the accident had occurred and no way had it ever been loaned to or driven by anyone else.

Armed with this evidence we left Manchester as happy as a dog with two bones! Now we had sufficient evidence to move forward.

With this evidence combined with Flint's explanation, the evidence of the Police officers and other extensive corroboration we now had enough evidence to pursue a prosecution.

Arnold eventually appeared before Worcester Crown Court charged with Reckless Driving and Attempting to Pervert the course of Justice. Faced with irrefutable evidence collected over the period of a 12 month investigation he pleaded guilty. He escaped imprisonment but was fined a total of £1,500, disqualified from driving for two years and ordered to pay prosecution costs. In addition of course the insurance company refused to pay out for the value of the Audi which was £6,500 and at long last the young man who had his car written off would be able to recoup costs from the insurance company.

If Arnold had admitted liability for the accident he would have probably had a small fine and licence endorsed.

During the inquiry it was fed to us from sources close to Arnold that he thought we were 'country bumpkin coppers' who would never prove the case against him.

Immediately after the case Arnold approached me, he apologised and said, 'I have been a fool, I am sorry.' I replied, 'Absolutely, and as a businessman you broke the fundamental rule of underestimating the opposition.' He nodded and walked away.

Now you might think as an intelligent man he would have learnt a lesson by this. I certainly thought so until I read in a local newspaper in 1987 that following a late night Police chase around a midlands town he was alleged to have driven at speeds of up to 100mph in a 15 mile chase. This included driving the wrong way around a traffic island. Arnold appeared before Wolverhampton Crown Court charged with reckless driving and driving whilst disqualified but was given leniency before the court because reports suggested he was suffering from an epileptic condition. Such is life!

However, Andy McGill and I did not have as much luck when we set out one fine summer's afternoon to catch car thieves working on the Clent Hills. We parked my Talbot Alpine car in one of the lay-bys by the side of the road and I carefully placed one of Jud's handbags on the back parcel shelf in full view of the road. Andy and I then secreted ourselves in a tree nearby hoping to catch the regular thieves. After a couple of hours on this hot sunny afternoon and bored out of my tree, I fell out of the bloody thing and at that point we decided to give up and go home. The bait did not work and Jud got her handbag back!

A few weeks later whilst on patrol with another officer, we had better luck though. I have always believed that you make your own luck through positive policing. What do I mean? Well, every commendation for good police work could probably just have easily ended in discipline if it went wrong and sometimes it does. Coppers who get results are usually observant, industrious and risk takers who push the boundaries and have a good nose to sniff out those involved in crime. When it goes right you get plaudits, when it goes wrong you are on your own and can drop in the proverbial. In days gone by such activities were condoned and officers were usually protected where they were shown to be doing the job for the right reasons. Now, things are different and the Police are risk averse as an organisation and officers must comply strictly to the law and procedures.

Rightly or wrongly that is what society expects, or does it?

Anyway, I was out on patrol with PC Martin Jordan and again we were looking around for car thieves. We came across a an old black car parked up on the top of the Clent hills with four male occupants in the car, all of which looked suspicious. Why, well let's just say it's a feeling you get in your bladder when you feel things aren't right. We stopped and spoke to them. Four local lads from the Black Country area of the West Midlands who said they were just out looking to eye up any girls and passing the time of day.

The vehicle details checked out with the driver so I asked if we could search the car and they agreed. There was nothing much of significance in the car or boot except a black leather jacket pushed down in the rear passenger footwell. I asked whose jacket it was and one the lads said it was his. I asked what was in the pockets and he said 'Nothing'. I searched the pockets and found a very nice wristwatch. I asked the supposed jacket owner who owned the watch and he said he did. I asked him to describe it but he couldn't and neither did he know what sort it was. I then proceeded to arrest all four on suspicion of theft of the jacket and cautioned them.

We called for assistance to convey them to Kidderminster and it was during this interval that Martin indicated to me that he thought I might be pushing this in arresting four men on suspicion of theft because one of them couldn't describe his watch! I told him to hold his nerve. However, as we were driving to Kidderminster I was beginning to question what the hell I was going to say to the custody sergeant at Kidderminster to convince him I had acted in accordance with reasonable suspicion.

As we were en route we received a request to attend Adams Hill, Clent where a driver had just returned to his car and found that it had been broken into. Lo and behold his black leather jacket had been stolen together with a very expensive wristwatch.

What a result! These four young men eventually cleared up about 50 thefts from motor vehicles on the Clent Hills and a substantial amount of property was recovered from where they had dumped it over a period of time in a nearby pool.

Martin and I received a commendation for these actions but I did reflect that in other circumstances it could have ended up as complaints and discipline for unlawful arrest and false imprisonment. I forget to say that alongside positive policing you always need a little bit of good fortune!

Another example arose from a simple complaint of a motorcycle being ridden dangerously off road by two young men again on the top of the Clent Hills near Wassel Green lane which is on the outskirts of Stourbridge. When I got there I checked out the motorcycle and got the details of the two riders but all seemed OK. The motorcycle had no plates but a Police National Computer check on the serial number of the frame did not reveal it was stolen. The one lad alleged he had purchased it recently for a few quid from some lads he only knew as casual acquaintances purely to ride off-road.

Although the bike was in good condition his explanation appeared reasonable. However, I decided to follow him home with the bike to check it out with his family and confirm where he lived which was on the Pedmore estate at Stourbridge. On arrival his Dad was there and confirmed the lad's story. I could do no more so I left it at that.

The next day, still being somewhat unconvinced I traced the frame serial number of the motorbike via the manufacturer to a registration number. When I carried out a stolen vehicle check on the number it came back as a stolen bike which was reported stolen from Dudley a few days earlier. Unfortunately, there was always a few days delay in getting the serial numbers recorded on the Police National Computer hence why it came up no trace when we had checked it the day before. I was annoyed. Even though the theft of the motor-bike was on the West Midlands area and the lad I had stopped also lived there I decided to have the pleasure of locking him up myself. I called for Martin Jordan and together we visited the lad's Dad at the Pedmore address. On reflection this was to be a big mistake!

When we arrived at the house, the Dad, who was an oldish man, answered the door and the lad was nowhere to be found. Not only that but the old man was in a different frame of mood, refusing to elaborate on any questions and denying any knowledge of the motorbike or the whereabouts of the lad.

I asked to search his garage. Reluctantly he led us to a lock up garage on the estate where I expected to find the motor-bike. What I found was another bike stripped down, again without any registration plates. I asked the Dad who this bike belonged to and he said it was his. When I asked if he could produce any documentation for it he told me to sod off.

On that basis Martin and I arrested him on suspicion of theft of the bike and took him to Stourbridge police station where I relayed the facts to the female custody sergeant who I knew quite well. She suggested we do an immediate check on the serial numbers of the bike in the garage to establish whether or not it was stolen and ascertain the owner. The old man seemed to be protesting too much and I was convinced it would come back stolen. Imagine my surprise when the checks revealed the bike was not stolen and was in fact registered to the old man.

The custody sergeant who was a very attractive policewoman looked at me quizzically and reminded me that what we now had was a situation where we had the Dad locked up for stealing his own motorbike. We had a stolen motorbike from Dudley but we didn't know where it was or where the potential thief was? I had to admit that was about the strength of it and at that point the sergeant invited me to release the old man and get the hell out of her police station and stop wasting her time. Suddenly, she did not seem so attractive but I persisted and asked if before we finally released him could I go back and search his flat and the garage thoroughly. She reluctantly agreed and gave me the keys to his house.

I then noticed there were two garage keys and formed the opinion he must have another lock up somewhere nearby. We got the old man out of the cells and took him back. We searched the first garage which was seemed OK. I then asked him outright where the second garage was. At first he denied having one but at the point we started to try the second key in the locks of all the garages he told us which one. As we opened the door the old man collapsed on the floor, feigning illness. No wonder, when we opened the door we were confronted with a garage which was stacked floor to ceiling with car parts and would have done Halfords proud.

The old man told us more or less straightaway that the parts were stolen and he was holding them for someone else. We then went to his house and searched that. In the loft we found another Aladdin's cave of house-ware and both ladies' and gents' clothes including some very sexy knickers!

Basically, it took the rest of the night to empty the flat and garage and convey it all to Stourbridge police station where the local cops were not too impressed at having to finish off our work. Eventually the lad was arrested for stealing the motorbike but I was never informed of the eventual result and was warned by my staff to keep my nose out in future. However, justice was done!

In the final case I will outline before I leave Hagley you could argue that justice was not done and to me sums up the irony of how things sometimes turn out.

On a fateful day at the bottom of Hagley Hill at the point they refer to as the cattle market lights on the main A456 Birmingham road a lorry and trailer appeared to run out of control and collided into a tanker and several other vehicles including a van and cars. Five people were killed and several injured. The first officer who arrived at the scene called for assistance and described it as a 'bloody disaster.' He was confronted with some awful sights and I will spare the details for the sake of everyone concerned.

I was off duty that day but went to the scene where it was dealt with by the traffic department. It took many months to investigate and during the course of the investigation the brakes on the lorry and/or trailer unit were found to be defective which may have been a contributory factor to the accident. The driver had been killed at the scene so of course no explanation was available.

The companies who owned the trailer and lorry were summoned for failing to maintain the brakes on the units and I had the job of prosecuting the case at Bromsgrove Magistrate's Court. In cases such as this it is very routine. The company secretary gets summoned on behalf of the company where they can plead guilty by letter and the maximum penalty is a fine. In this instance I was not allowed to mention that the vehicle concerned had been involved in a fatal collision because the case had to be judged in isolation. The magistrates must have wondered why I was standing in court with a file about one foot thick for a relatively simple case. No-one from the company was present because during the interim period it had gone into liquidation. A relatively small fine was granted and the magistrate's clerk went onto the list of creditors.

What may seem complete irony has to be seen and judged on the merits of what can be proved. Pursuing cases of corporate manslaughter where substantial penalties can be incurred requires extensive evidence of neglect and recklessness. Relatively recent legislation in 2007 has brought about new offences and liabilities for companies that were not available to the same degree in the early 1980's.

CHAPTER 15

SUGAR BEET AND SHIFTS
AT KIDDERMINSTER

I was happy at Hagley and they could have thrown my personnel file away and left me there for the rest of my career. I was surprised one day to receive a call from the superintendent at Kidderminster who told me it was time for me to transfer to Kidderminster in order to experience working a busier area and to have the opportunity to carry out duties of Acting Inspector. It was non-negotiable so I went.

We had already bought our own house in Kidderminster where we had lived for a few months, so it was no great problem.

I took over as one of the sergeants on Shift 2 at Kidderminster. My colleague on that shift was John Hunt. John and I already knew each other and got on well. He had a very dry wit and sense of humour which used to crease me up.

The work at Kidderminster as a sergeant was different. It was back on full 24 x 7 shifts, busier workload, lot more officers but less autonomy and responsibility than I had been accustomed to whilst working smaller sections such as Hagley.

It was a case of either being on patrol, supervising officers, or, taking turns at being the station sergeant. This meant covering the cells, checking officers' paperwork and keeping an eye on the control room which was the centre which housed switchboard, front inquiry office and the radio and where all incidents were received and monitored by police officers and civilian operators.

Kidderminster was well-known for its carpet industry and the smell of sugar beet which emanated across the town every autumn from the sugar beet plant at Foley Park.

The carpet industry has since dwindled and the sugar beet factory closed several years ago. Kidderminster is a medium-sized market town and the capital of the area known as Wyre Forest. As a Police Officer I found it a violent place where drunken behaviour and nasty domestic disputes were common. One of the first incidents I attended was on a notorious estate where as we approached the house a washing machine came flying through the front window. Now that was one strong man who was feeling very angry!

On a New Year's Eve you expect trouble, but my first at Kidderminster was a belter. Everything was deathly hush and surreal until just before midnight. We received a 999 call to say a fight was taking place at the Land Oak pub on the Birmingham Road.

Several of us were driven there in the back of a Police riot van. As we approached the Land Oak lights we could see two men were fighting, but both lying in the centre of the road with the traffic driving round them. 'Bloody fools, they deserve to be driven down,' somebody shouted.

Suddenly one of my team shouted, 'Sarge, shit, one of them is Mickey Benting.' Mick was a detective based at Kidderminster and was working nights with us but in plain clothes. I looked more closely and could see it was Mick and he was struggling with a young lad in the centre of the road who was struggling like mad with Mick trying to restrain him. We stopped the traffic and then tried to get the young fighter in the back of the Police van after Mick informed us he was under arrest for failing the 'attitude test.'

Mick had turned up at the pub when a fight was in progress and the young man in question appeared to be the main protagonist. Mick arrested him whereupon he broke free, Mick ran after him and then the two of them ended up in the centre of the road.

I have to say; in 33 years in Policing I never saw anyone as violent or struggle as hard as this man did when we tried to place him in the police van. He was not particularly big but he was very wiry and strong. He kicked, punched and spat all the way into the van even when he was lay on the floor of the van being restrained by several of us.

The irony was that in the middle of all of this whilst calling us all the 'wankers' under the sun and a few other choice words in addition to still trying to spit, gouge and kick, it was bang on the stroke of midnight. Now, it was no place to stop, link arms and sing 'Auld Lang Syne' but PC Derek Hughes who was driving the bus did put the radio on so it screeched out the famous rendition whilst we all sang along. The young fighter did not seem to appreciate the sentiment!

We got to the Police station, booked in the prisoner and then we had a call to attend an Indian restaurant on Comberton Hill. The report that came in was that our Acting Inspector Bernie McDermott had been trying to calm down a load of drunken revellers outside the restaurant when someone had hit him over the head with a flagon of cider and thrown him through the front glass window of the restaurant. Now, from memory, I cannot exactly remember if that was correct but either way Bernie was not well and had to be taken to hospital. When we arrived in the riot van all hell was breaking loose.

There were a number of separate fights involving several men who were outside the restaurant and spewing out into the street. We all exited the van and grabbed the first person we could find fighting whereupon they were arrested. I arrested one man who came quietly and I then led him back to the van, handcuffed him and remained with him for security (secure cages in vans had not yet been invented). All was well for a short while until my colleagues started pouring more prisoners into the van and leaving them with me to supervise. Some were handcuffed and some not. When it reached the point that there were 4 or 5 in the van it suddenly dawned on both them and me that they completely outnumbered me.

In my haste I had made the false assumption that the rear door was locked. When the first one jumped out of the back door I realised it was not! Then the rest decided to follow suit. I clung on to the one man I had arrested, determined that he didn't escape at all costs. We both ended up on the floor of the van between the seats with me trying to pin him to the floor.

Now some situations are surreal and this was one of them. I have this image of me lying on the floor of the van, with my officers still trying to arrest offenders and sticking them in the back of the van. They were using my head as a stepping stone and then nipping straight out of the back of the van. Fortunately, a policewoman on the shift, Wendy Dawson had realised what was going on. As they were alighting from the back of the van Wendy was hitting them full pelt with her handbag. She floored a couple but others ran away where another officer pursued them and using a mixture of brute force and a karate chop floored another one. It was probably like something out of keystone cops but that is the nature of policing when chaos ensues.

Eventually we nicked five and took them back to the Police station. When I arrived it was still chaos in getting the officers to identify who they had arrested. Eventually we got it sorted. The rest of the night was also hectic. With my Inspector in hospital and the other sergeant on duty finishing at 2am I was the only supervisor left and it was one of those nights where you survive by the seat of your pants and great teamwork.

When you finish a night like that it is so satisfying to go home, have a drink and slip into bed knowing that the world will wake up with a hangover whilst you can sleep in a deep slumber. That is coppering and I guess it always will be. The relief of knowing you have survived whilst others celebrated.

The result of the fight outside the restaurant was that five offenders were initially charged with causing an affray, which is a serious public order offence. To me this made sense. All we needed to prove was that each individual was fighting and the public including ourselves were frightened. Bernie would vouch for that one! Unfortunately, the prosecuting barrister in his wisdom changed the charge of affray to one of unlawful assembly which basically is harder to prove because it requires a common purpose to be shown amongst those present. In addition they were charged with various individual assaults on officers. The unlawful assembly charges got chucked out. Fortunately, the jury at Worcester Crown court did find them guilty of the individual assaults and some were sent to prison. Job was done as far as we were concerned but it almost went down the pan!

One of the greatest pleasures was carrying out the job of station sergeant and supervising prisoners in the cells. Well perhaps pleasure is too strong a word, but it was always entertaining.

Bill was one of the bobby's on the shift who was driving through the Horsefair at Kidderminster one afternoon in a marked liveried Police car. He was driving slowly in a line of traffic when an elderly man came out of a betting shop, picked up a brick, threw it straight through the windscreen of the police car and hit Bill on the head. Bill was not impressed so he stopped arrested the man and brought him into custody. The prisoner was actually a man called 'Bob' who had walked out of Lea Castle Hospital, just outside Kidderminster and had severe learning difficulties. He had walked down to the bookies, put on a bet, lost all his money, walked out in anger, picked up a brick and the first person he saw was Bill so he wanged the brick straight through the windscreen of the police car.

There was no point in trying to prosecute Bob but I needed to detain him in a cell until I could get him picked up by the hospital staff. After making numerous telephone calls it became apparent that the hospital could not pick him up and we needed to escort him to the hospital. On going to the cells to get Bob out I found that he had managed somehow to jam the dividing door between the cell and the toilet off its runner and he was now trapped in the toilet where we couldn't get him out. On looking through the spy-hole into the toilet I realised he knew exactly what he had done because he was sat on the seat telling us to 'Fuck Off' and flashing the V sign with his fingers whilst laughing at the top of his voice. It took a winch and several hours of labour to eventually extricate him out of the toilet.

I then decided to personally take Bob back to the hospital with a couple of other officers. I sat in the back of the police van with him. Bob told me was from Ross-on-Wye in Herefordshire and he spoke with a deep country Herefordshire accent. When I told him I was from Herefordshire and was a Bromyard boy we became best mates. He told me in a rich rural dialect, 'Yoom aright officer, but that other bugger (Bill), he's a bassard!'

I just had to agree.

When we arrived at the hospital I was intent on just off-loading Bob, getting a signature from the staff on the detained person's sheet and making a quick exit. We did all that whereupon Bob suddenly decided to run off again, straight up the corridor and out into the grounds. We gave chase but suddenly realised no-one from the hospital was following. They explained there was little they could do because they had no legal authority to detain him and that because it was dark they were convinced he would not go far and return for tea.

I decided we would leave. I had by now had enough. I have a lasting memory of Bob as we drove out of the grounds appearing from behind a tree where he shouted words of a couple of syllables and again flashed the 'V's whilst laughing. I think he had achieved his ambition of having a very entertaining day at our expense.

That was the last I ever saw of Bob but he was one of many mental health patients that I dealt with.

A lady called Sylvia was a resident of 'D' Block at Kidderminster General Hospital. The hospital is about a mile from the police station. Sylvia would regularly go missing but when she got hungry, usually about lunchtime she would turn up at the police station and ask for a lift back to the hospital for her lunch. We usually obliged because it was one way of at least ensuring she was returned safely.

I took her back personally on one occasion and rang through first to the staff in D Block to let them know I was on the way. On arrival the door to the block was answered by a lady who was in a smart suit and immediately tore a strip off Sylvia and profusely apologised to me for wasting police time. She ushered Sylvia through to the ward and then I obtained a signature in my pocket note book for handing her over. The lady signed my book and then on handing it back she said to me, 'You know officer, I love the Police, and I always have since I had my bike stolen. Her name was Henrietta, do you know Henrietta, she, was lovely you know, did you ever find her?'

I suddenly realised I had handed over one patient to another patient and mistaken her for a member of staff. Such is life! At least Sylvia made it for lunch.

One Sunday I was the 2pm till 10pm station sergeant with responsibility for the prisoners. The cells were empty and it was fairly quiet. I was told that one of my officers, Derek Hughes had been called on early and gone with a colleague to London to pick up a prisoner who was wanted on warrant at Kidderminster and had been arrested by the Met Police overnight.

When they arrived Derek took me aside and asked to speak urgently. 'Sarge, this guy is an Irishman, a really nice man but he is adamant that it is not him we are after and we have a case of mistaken identity.' Now, it wouldn't be the first time a prisoner in custody has lied so I didn't get too carried away by his protestations but I did decide to speak with him personally whilst booking him into the cells and make some further inquiries.

Now, we will imagine his name was something like Mick McConnell. When I met him I was confronted by a man who was one of the nicest and most polite prisoners I had ever met but he appeared totally confused and was adamant he was not the man in question.

He said to me: 'Sarn't I've never heard of this place bloody Kiddleyminster before in my life, let alone ever been here.' It had more than a ring of truth.

I sent Derek scuttling off to the collator's office where I guessed we would have a photograph of the wanted man on record.

After a few minutes Derek came back with a photograph and looked rather bashful. I looked at the photograph and I looked at Mick. Suffice to say that the only resemblance was one of approximate age and the fact they were both male. I was totally convinced with one look that our Mick was not the man wanted on warrant!

I said to Mick, 'Listen mate I am sorry about this, I believe you, but how did you get arrested in the first place?'

In a broad Irish accent he told me, 'Last night I went out on the piss, cos I go on the piss every Saturday night. When I got home it were the early hours and I was hungry so I put the pan on. But I fell asleep; when I woke up there had been a fire. The Police were there and 'Trumpton' (the fire brigade) had pissed water everywhere. The Police asked me for my name which I gave them. Then they checked me out cos they must have thought I might be a bloody terrorist, for Gawd sake. The next thing I know, they told me to get my coat and nicked me. They said I was wanted by the Police at Kiddleyminster. I knew it was bollocks but they wouldn't listen.'

I gathered from Mick's explanation that his real name was an alias used by the real man wanted on warrant and nothing to do with him. This was a cast-iron case of mistaken identity.

I apologised profusely and could see this was a big issue. False imprisonment, civil claims – I could just see the newspaper headlines now!

'Look Mick, what can I do for you, I appreciate this has been a cock up,' I said in an attempt to placate him.

Mick replied, 'Well, Sarn't the first thing I need is something to eat and drink. The second thing I need is a lift back to London, cos I am working on a building site in the morning and I can't afford to miss a day.'

The first two requests were easy, the third one, getting him back to London was more of a problem I needed to ponder.

I sent out for a meal for Mick and decided that he was obviously a man who liked a drink so I asked him if I could get him a pint of lager from the Police club bar which was still open from lunchtime.

He smiled broadly, nodded and then as I made my way to the bar he shouted to me, 'Sarn't can I have something else.' I said, 'Mick, whatever you need you can have and deserve.'

He smiled again and said, 'Do you think I could have two pints of lager!'

Two pints of lager and a meal of fish and chips later Mick was quite chirpy but I still needed to get him a lift back to London.

The problem was because he was no longer a prisoner I could not authorise using a Police vehicle and an officer for a round trip of 240 miles whatever the merits, particularly if they were ever involved in an accident. Also, because it was a Sunday I had no access to cash to pay for a train or bus and this was long before the days of corporate business cards.

I went to see the duty Inspector and explained the predicament. 'Give him a rail warrant,' he said pragmatically. I pointed out respectfully, (as you do to senior officers) that rail warrants could only be issued to members of HM Forces or serving Police Officers. Neither of these categories fitted an elderly man who was only about 5'5" and had long shoulder length, unkempt straggly hair and was unshaven.

The Inspector replied, 'Well you find a way round it and I will sign the warrant. At the end of the day, we will have to pay one way or another, the rail authorities don't care as long as they get their money and we will explain to admin what we have had to do.'

That afternoon I sent a Police officer with Mick to the railway station to convince them that the warrant was a genuine Police rail warrant.

When he left the station he was very gracious and said to me, 'Sarn't you lot at Kiddleyminster are real gentlemen, different to those bastards in the Met.'

Mick never complained and took it on the chin. A very genuine man who could have taken us to the cleaners but instead took it in good part due to having a fantastic sense of humour.

As he left his parting words were, 'Wait till I tell the buggers on the building site tomorrow how I spent my Sunday. If they don't believe me Sarn't can I ring you to tell them?'

I took my hat off to him. Admin were ok as well, no comebacks on the warrant. In those days ends justified means, not any longer!

The Wyre Forest has the river Severn running through it. A lovely, picturesque sight during most seasons, except, sooner or later some bugger jumps in it and drowns.

I was early turn shift on a Sunday. The evening before a middle-aged couple decided to venture from the Black Country out to a pub which is situated near the banks of the river Severn. In fact, they were not strictly a couple. The man had been in a common law relationship with the same woman for a number of years where they had lived together as husband and wife. The lady who was with him that evening was not the same woman he lived with.

They sat and enjoyed a romantic few drinks together beside the river whereupon, the man, possibly having achieved some 'dutch courage' decided to show his new lady how he could wade across the river. In the cold light of day you may consider this was not a wise move. However, the combination of testosterone and alcohol I have found from experience is a great inhibitor of 'wise moves' and this was to prove no exception.

The problem was that the 'beau' in question whilst showing off to his lady friend was not a proficient swimmer. He was OK until about mid-way point across the river because he managed to find a line of rocks to walk on. Unfortunately, he did not appear to realise that the depth of water at this point of the river was quite deep. Inevitably, he slipped off the rocks and was suddenly taken away by the current. Before the unfortunate lady in question could raise the alarm the man had disappeared into the river.

By the time the emergency services arrived it was too late. The man was no-where in sight and the search had to be abandoned because of darkness.

The following morning I was despatched with an underwater search team to find the body. The search commenced at the point where he was last seen but due to the fast current quickly expanded down-stream. We were there for hours with no sign of the man.

It was approaching lunch-time and I was due off at 2pm. I knew that for some reason I was on a three line whip from Jud to get home on time for a late Sunday lunch and was looking forward to a meat and three veg. It had been a long time since breakfast and I have to say that a part of me was now hoping that the search team would break for lunch so I could be relieved by the afternoon sergeant and get home reasonably on time.

Suddenly as I looked at my watch about 1.15pm I saw the thumbs up sign from one of the divers which was a sign they had found something. Sure enough it was the body of the man. They quickly recovered the body to the embankment and it was then I saw something quite unusual, well to me anyway. Rigor mortis appeared to have set in and the man was rigid in a position where he was as if in a sitting position with his hands stretched out in front of him. The head diver explained to me that this was perfectly natural in drowning situations where the body appears in what they call the '*driver's*' position. It is so called because when someone drowns the last thing they do is raise their hands above their heads in the water to gain attention and then as they sink to the bottom the hands gradually lower and very often the body ends up in a sitting position with the hands in front as if they were driving a car.

Now, I have often wondered if the diver was having one over me but no-one has ever refuted this explanation and I could see it made sense. However, it caused a bit of a problem. We put the body into a body bag but because of the rigor position of the body we had difficultly zipping it up. Bearing in mind that the body was also full of water it made it difficult to carry. We were situated on a river bank, several hundred yards away from the near vehicle access so it meant carrying the body for some distance. Muggins caught for the upper body end which was the heaviest. By the time we reached our destination I could feel my back go and when we reached the nearest gateway I was bent double and in agony.

I called for a funeral director who took ages to find the location. Eventually, we got the body loaded into the hearse and headed towards the mortuary at Kidderminster General Hospital. I followed behind in a police vehicle. I was still in pain and somewhat distracted. However, I suddenly realised I had made a big error. I had not had the body certified dead by a doctor. Now, it may seem a bit irrelevant to the likes of you and me that if someone has been lying in a river for almost 24 hours, completely submerged in water that you need a doctorate to tell if they are dead. However, I did know that morticians and pathologists get very annoyed if bodies are brought into the mortuary before they are officially declared as dead and it is one of the rules that is sacrosanct.

I immediately put on the blue lights, overtook the hearse and flagged it down. I told the driver to ensure that when we reached the hospital he must stop outside casualty so that I could find a doctor and get the body certified before we took the body round to the mortuary.

The undertaker did exactly that. I rushed in to the doors of the hospital and immediately dragged the first person I came across wearing a white coat out to the hearse and asked him to ensure the man was dead. The 'doctor' looked at me pathetically and then explained that he would love to help me but he did not feel qualified to do so because he was only a 'technician' passing through casualty on his way to somewhere else.

My embarrassment was compounded by the smirks on the faces of the crew in the hearse.

I ran back inside and eventually verified the qualifications of the next man I found in a white coat who told me he was definitely a doctor. He took great care in examining the man in the body bag and eventually pronounced he was dead. I did feel like announcing that I could have told him that and it did not take six years at medical school to state the obvious, but I resisted the temptation.

We got the body into the mortuary and did the necessary tagging, seizing valuables off the body and arranging for the identification.

I then drove back to the Police station to carry out the paperwork and as I reached the Police station the control called me on the radio to ascertain my location. I assumed it was Jud who had taken out a bounty on my head because I was now several hours late and no doubt lunch was spoiled. However, the control room proceeded to tell me that they required my assistance in the front inquiry office where the very angry common law wife of the man who had drowned was there demanding to know the identity of the wanton woman who had supposedly killed her 'husband' the night before and wanted to know all the facts!

I knew this would require a great deal of time, tact and diplomacy, all of which I felt distinctly lacking at that moment in time.

Fortunately, someone else took on the task and I eventually got home to face a different sort of trauma!

Death is never far away in policing. However, some deaths, indeed murders are harder to understand than others, particularly when they involve killing in the family.

As a shift sergeant it was routine to attend and supervise all sudden or unexpected deaths where a doctor is not able to confirm and certify a cause of death as natural causes.

One morning I attended a sudden death on an estate at Kidderminster involving an elderly man who lived alone. One of my officers, Derek Hughes was at the scene and he was suspicious as to what the cause of death may have been. The man was lying on his side and appeared to have an injury to one side of his head which could not be explained.

He had no particularly relevant medical history and because he lived alone we could not verify if money or anything else was missing from his flat which had been found insecure. I agreed with Derek that we needed to treat it as suspicious. The term used nowadays would be 'unexplained death' which is a much better explanation because that is exactly what it means. Precautions need to be taken to preserve all evidence and not make assumptions until a cause of death has been established and the possibility of foul play has been eliminated.

We called CID, scenes of crime, made house to house inquiries and did all preliminary work before leaving the scene under the supervision of other officers so that we could go back and brief both the Divisional Chief Superintendent and senior CID officers. They needed to decide if a Home Office pathologist and forensic scientists need to attend the scene before the body was removed.

Derek and I briefed the senior officers, which resulted in them asking Derek to lie on the floor, play dead and imitate the position which the body was in when he found it. The scenes of crime officer at the scene had found a cup which had rolled under the furniture and appeared to resemble the mark left on the man's head which may have been the cause of the injury.

It was looking more likely that the man had collapsed due a heart attack or similar and had fallen onto the cup he was holding at the time which had struck him on the head.

Derek was playing out the various scenarios of how this could have happened and in the process of getting an Oscar for his work.

I left the room and went through to the control room to see what else was happening because CID were now involved in this and I needed to supervise the rest of the incidents that were taking place.

Suddenly one of the operators said to me, 'Sarge, I've got Eamon Croft on the line and he needs to speak to the Detective Superintendent immediately, he's got something urgent.'

Eamon was a mate of mine and was the Detective Inspector at Ludlow which was a very quiet little market town where very little happened. I decided to speak to him and explain that the Detective Superintendent was engaged in dealing with a suspicious death and could he phone back.

Eamons response was blunt and to the point. 'Les, whatever he is dealing with there, I have something bigger and more serious. I have four people dead with gunshot wounds and the house has been set on fire, now put me through to the boss!' I put him through immediately.

Derek, who was still playing dead on the carpet of the gaffer's office described the situation beautifully. Apparently, after I put the phone through the Detective Superintendent took the call and after speaking to Eamon he explained to the Chief Superintendent that there was slight change of plan and emphasis and he was needed elsewhere!

The death at Kidderminster turned out as natural causes. The other deaths were a different matter. It transpired that a man had shot his entire family dead and also the pet dogs and cats. He had then attempted to set fire to the house and then killed himself.

This was a terrible tragedy and although I was involved in making the initial arrangements for specialist officers to attend the scene I am glad that my involvement was on the periphery. Sometime later I was privy to the photographs and I have to say that the scene that confronted those attending must have been horrendous.

Unfortunately, this type of incident is not in isolation and the subject of why parents kill their families and sometimes themselves has been subject to considerable criminological research, particularly in the United States.

I have no idea what sparked off the incident and draw no association between that incident and subsequent international research which has been carried out.

However, that research does indicate that the reasons why women and men carry out such atrocities is different. Women (who are in the minority of offenders) have been found to be mentally ill and frequently suffer from post-partum (natal) depression. However, in men the situation is different. Known as 'Family Annihilators' men who commit these atrocities are not usually mentally ill and factors may include impending divorce, male sexual jealousy, extensive debt combined with an obsession of control and possessiveness where the family is at the centre of their life. The crime may also be pre-planned and calculated. The reasons and factors involved are complex and almost impossible to diagnose at a point that would lead to preventing an incident taking place. Many perpetrators will be regarded as respectable family members who have never before come to the attention of authorities.

When it goes wrong it has devastating consequences. However, because the perpetrators very often kill themselves, there is no murder trial or media frenzy at the conclusion, just a sombre inquest verdict in which the headlines are very often quickly forgotten by those not directly involved.

CHAPTER 16

AFFAIRS IN THE COMMUNITY

It was my first time ever, giving a talk to a bunch of kids on what the role of the police did and the danger of strangers. However, here I was as a Police Sergeant, in a First School at Kidderminster on a bright sunny weekday afternoon talking to about 25 miscreant pupils aged between 5 and 6 years old.

They seemed a lively lot so I thought to calm them down I would show them my truncheon, helmet and handcuffs as I tried to explain to them the perils of talking to strangers. What I hadn't realised was, they were the bloody danger and I was the stranger in controlling a classroom full of kids.

I passed round my equipment and forgot about the golden rule which is do not show any visual aids until you have given your talk otherwise they will lose concentration.

I should have remembered the other golden first rule which is, never work with animals or bleeding kids.

After about two minutes I noticed one of the pupils who was wearing my helmet was screaming because the little bugger sitting next to him had banged it down right over his eyes and nose to the point where he could hardly breathe. As I was trying to retrieve the helmet back, being careful not to rip his nose off I heard another scream behind me. I turned round to see one snotty-nosed little kid who was holding my truncheon and appeared to a potential domestic violence merchant for the future. Why, because he took one look at it and then banged it down over the head of the little girl sitting next to him who burst into tears. He took great delight in the immediate gratification of his actions and before I could stop him he banged it down on the head of the lad sat in front of him who immediately retaliated and a fight started.

After managing to separate them, calming the little girl down and retrieving the truncheon and helmet I thought I was out of the woods until I saw two lads in the back row who had handcuffed themselves to the radiator in such a way that it took me ten minutes to release them.

Eventually, with the help of a couple of the teachers who had come running in upon hearing the noise and screaming and took pity on me, we managed to get everything calm.

I gave my lecture in the quickest possible time because all I wanted to do was get out of the place. As I spoke the little sod who had banged the girl over the head with the truncheon kept interrupting and asking me stupid questions with a sick grin on his face whilst picking his nose and flicking it at the kids sitting in front of him.

When it became time to leave the teacher asked me to stand by the door whilst the pupils filed out of the classroom and thanked me personally. When it came to the turn of the kid with the snotty nose whom I had already stereotyped as a potential future criminal he beckoned me with his finger to stoop down so he could whisper in my ear. I was wary because it did occur me this might be his opportunity to put the nut on me. However, he surprised me completely by saying, 'Mr. Policeman, thank you for coming, I love you,' and kissed me on the cheek. I was not sure whether to laugh or cry but was definitely both moved and confused!

After, checking the helmet for head lice, wiping the truncheon and handcuffs and massaging my pride I reflected on my experience, learned my lessons and was ready for the next onslaught.

This was the role of Community Police Sergeant, working in a department known as 'Community Affairs.' It was a specialist role because after 11 years of operational roles it was time I did something that was different to enhance my career route to Inspector.

About 12 to 18 months earlier I had turned down the offer of a post as a Detective Sergeant on CID. Whilst I welcomed the opportunity and knew I would enjoy the role, at the time I had good family and domestic reasons for turning the position down. What I did not realise was that this would in effect be held against me and delay any future promotion opportunities. However, in a long career, things happen. I knew I was right at the time to turn it down and have never regretted the decision despite the fact that it had long term implications for me which were to manifest several years later.

Working on Community Affairs was fantastic. After a number of years of working 24/7 shifts and operational pressures this was something different. I was working weekdays and evenings, every Saturday and Sunday off and worked to a diary in which I could be as busy as I chose.

There were several facets to the job. One, as described above was liaising with schools and giving talks to pupils of all ages on a range of Police subjects such as stranger danger, keeping safe, crime prevention, drugs, alcohol and substance misuse. We also supervised activity for the Duke of Edinburgh's award scheme and arranged visits to police stations and talks to adult groups plus some after dinner speaking engagements.

A major part of the role also involved weekly meetings with social services deciding whether to caution or prosecute young offenders and attending child protection conferences where young children were considered to be at risk of harm.

We covered not only the area of Wyre Forest (Kidderminster, Stourport and Bewdley), but also, the south Shropshire areas of Ludlow, Bishops Castle, Church Stretton, Craven Arms, Cleobury Mortimer, Clee Hill and Bridgnorth in addition to all the rural villages, some of which I had never even heard of.

There were five of us in the department all with different roles. The boss was Inspector Roy 'Basher' Burrett who had been one of my sergeants at Redditch when I joined. Roy was still the big, burly character of a man he had always been, having earned the title of 'Basher' the hard way and was truly a hard man. However, he was now in the twilight of his service doing a more gentle job and like most of us had mellowed with age into the kind, caring and supportive man that he really was who cared passionately about his family and the job. Roy had a wicked sense of humour and exuded many talents. However, he still had his moments when a short fuse would ignite very quickly because he did not accept fools lightly.

On one occasion I was on the phone talking to a vicar's wife and arranging when I could give a talk to the local Women's Institute when Roy exploded into the office. He had been out to a child protection conference with social services. I heard him open the downstairs door (our offices were in the bedrooms of an old Police house) and start to stomp up the stairs muttering under his breath. I remember thinking, Roy's not happy!

One of Roy's party tricks that he had practised to perfection was to throw his briefcase at an angle up the stairs and across the landing where it would hit the office door with such force it opened the door and then landed in the office next to his desk.

On this occasion Roy threw the briefcase with such vengeance it not only hit the door open in the room where I was talking on the phone but also hit a four drawer filing cabinet causing an almighty bang and all the ledgers to fall off that were perched on the top if it.

This was followed by Roy saying something like, 'Bloody, social workers, they will be the death of me.' A few other choice words were issued and then Basher burst into the room. The fact that I was on the phone did not appear to faze him one little bit and his tantrum continued until I put my hand over the phone and said something like, 'Boss, this is a vicar's wife, I am trying to arrange a talk.' Roy continued muttering and stormed off into the other office to make a drink.

I then resumed my composure and the vicar's wife, who seemed very concerned about my safety asked if everything was OK. I told her that a prisoner had tried escaping from the cells but we had now captured him and everything was in order! She seemed grateful and I terminated the call as soon as possible.

Mick France-Serjeant was the crime prevention sergeant whose role was giving advice to the public and business owners on how to secure their premises and prevent crime. Mick was a 'Geordie,' again with a fantastic sense of humour and a smile to match who could charm the birds out of the trees. Mick was happily married but like most of us had the occasional domestic tiff. During one particular week he was going through a difficult period when he had the misfortune to reverse his car off the drive and straight over his wife's beloved cat. To Mick it was an unfortunate and tragic accident that was completely unintentional. Despite all his best offers, apologies and explanations I understand that Mick had some difficulty convincing his wife otherwise but eventually peace resumed and Mick hoped that the subject would never ever be resurrected.

Roy was quite an artist. Never being one to miss an opportunity in taking advantage of Mick's bad fortune he drew a beautiful picture of a black cat on a piece of flat cardboard, lying on its back with paws outstretched in a prone position. He then left it behind Mick's office door so that it would be the first thing he would see as he opened the door. When it happened, I was unsure of what the response might be. Fortunately, Mick saw the funny side of it but I don't think he took the picture home for posterity!

Dennis 'Jumper' Collins was the recruiting and training sergeant whose job was just that.

He also toured schools and colleges in an attempt to recruit either Police officers or volunteers for the special constabulary and would go anywhere for a good cup of tea and a cake. The antics of Jumper would probably fill a book alone. He was a man who had been in the merchant navy, toured the world and as they say been round the block a bit. Once again a man with a very dry wit who took very little seriously and spent a lot of his time buying and selling second hand cars, even on one occasion to the Chief Constable. Jumper was renowned for his practical jokes which bedevilled the senior ranks to the point where they had given up trying to get one over on him.

Jumper thought the world of his wife 'Mary' who was seriously disabled with rheumatoid arthritis. On one occasion we were talking in his office when he suddenly looked outside and said, 'Its bloody raining got to go.' He then went off at a fast rate of knots to go home and get the washing in off the line, knowing Mary would struggle to do so.

The final member of the team was our secretary Cheryl who did her best to keep us all in order. Cheryl was ultra efficient and a very speedy typist who could knock out a report as quick as you could blink. However, she always emphasised that she had difficulty in checking her own work and insisted we always proof-read her typing.

Mick did a crime prevention survey on a high-class gent's outfitters and drafted a report for Cheryl to type who left it in his tray for checking and posting.

When he checked it he found an error. A sentence that referred to 'Please keep all your expensive shirts out of the front window on display,' had been typed up, 'Please keep all your expensive *'shits'* out of the front window on display.'

Mick then proceeded to destroy the top copy and then sign off the copy as if it had been posted. He then wrote a separate note dated a couple of days later pretending that the recipient had rang up to complain about the indecent nature of the letter and demanding to know who the insolent typist was!

When Cheryl read the note she was devastated and was about to ring the man concerned and apologise when Mick had to admit it was a wind up.

My last memory of that incident was Cheryl chasing Mick around the office threatening to staple his vital bits to the inside of his trousers. Lessons learned by both.

This then was my life for just over two years. A life of continual laughter, where work was such a pleasure it was almost a hobby and I felt guilty for being paid.

It was also busy and I learnt many new skills and gained extensive experience and confidence in public speaking and teaching, both to adults and children. We also attended many voluntary groups and special schools where I developed induction processes and resources for the Police in communicating with the mentally handicapped.

I have always been interested in communicating with people and communities. In 1985 I was sent on a two week 'Community Involvement' course in Lancashire. One of the lecturers was a lady who counselled children subject to sexual abuse but was a teacher by profession who specialised in teaching how to communicate with people who are deaf, blind, suffering strokes, victims of abuse, or in the act of threatening suicide. Her lecture was about 'empathy' and how to stand in someone's shoes and look through their eye sockets. This was probably the most prophetic, instructive and insightful lecture I have ever attended.

I could not write down the notes fast enough. Every sentence contained practical hints and steps on how to communicate with a range of people in every potential situation of crisis. One of the lessons I learned about was how to communicate with someone about to commit suicide. This was to come in very handy not long afterwards and I will describe this later.

On the same course a renowned lecturer from Manchester spoke to us about how the responsibility for preventing crime did not rest with the Police but was influenced by schools, education, family protection, jobs, housing, health and income. His message was that the Police alone cannot prevent crime unless they work closely with those organisations like local authorities who have ownership of the resources and environment to put it right.

The following year I attended a project at Bushbury in Wolverhampton where residents were being assisted in regenerating and refurbishing their own estate by building up their own capacity to manage the estate facilities and set up leisure centres and support for children and young families. This meant that they took a pride in their estate and would effectively ensure no-one committed crime because for the first time they felt a responsibility for the communal areas having been involved in building and maintaining facilities working alongside the Police, local authority and voluntary groups.

The three experiences above changed my perception of how to prevent crime in communities and why the vulnerable and those most at risk are sometimes the victims, one day and the perpetrators the next day. As a 'die-hard' lock them up and throw the key away copper, I now realised both the problems and solutions of crime were extremely complex and were beyond the remit of the Police alone. This may sound obvious now but it was not at that time. For too long the Police had shouldered the responsibility for tackling something they certainly could not do alone.

Yes, their job is to enforce the law when required but it is also to mobilise the efforts of other agencies to work in partnership and ensure they face up to their responsibilities.

The experiences I had during this time changed my perception of the role I was undertaking and was to have a profound effect upon my future career.

Alongside this I started to specialise in the world of drug and solvent misuse which in the middle 1980's was just starting to receive national concern around the proliferation of heroin and cocaine.

At the time there was a thirst from both the general public, schools and local groups to have greater awareness of the signs and symptoms of drug misuse including being able to identify street drugs. I did a lot of background reading, spoke to officers on the drug squad and then produced a number of pseudo drugs to resemble real substances. For example I used cow cake as cannabis resin, gravy browning as cannabis oil, talcum powder as heroin and manufactured a concoction of crystalline materials to resemble cocaine.

During lectures to adults we were able to use the real stuff. This consisted of a box with examples of every type of illegal drug that had been seized over a period of time. There must have been literally thousands of pounds worth of drugs in that box which required extensive close scrutiny as it was passed round amongst audiences. All the drugs were sealed and we counted them before anyone was allowed to leave the room.

It's fair to say that people were largely unaware and naive during the 1980's about drugs. Most had never come across illegal drugs, even cannabis and most did not believe they existed in the villages and towns of Worcestershire.

The majority were fascinated by the experience and wanted to know what cannabis smelt like. I used to burn a piece of cannabis resin on a block and pass it round amongst the audiences so that they could familiarise themselves with the odour which once smelt will never be forgotten as an acrid smell like burning rope. On one occasion a man in the audience who had spent some time in North Africa suddenly enlightened us by saying,

'Ah, I will always remember that, it reminds me of camel shit!'

Someone else in the audience said, 'That doesn't help me a lot, I have never smelt camel shit and hope I am never close enough to the arse of a camel to do so!'

I developed a reputation for giving these lectures to the point where I was inundated for requests to do presentations to all sorts of audiences. At the same time I researched the current thinking around preventing children from taking drugs and the contemporary thoughts on drugs education in schools. I also produced a set of drug awareness guidelines for operational police officers and became a member of the first wave of Government Drug Rehabilitation Groups that were set up around the country.

During this time I had gone on two sets of Inspector promotion boards and failed both.

The legacy of turning down a position on CID was pointed out to me as the reason why my commitment was being questioned.

However, I felt I was now starting to regain the earning of my 'spurs' and went on the third board where I was successful. I was overjoyed. The date was the 28th August 1986, my Dad's birthday. I did not appreciate it at the time but in fact my promotion would not actually take place for a further three and a half years until April 1990.

I was summoned to Police headquarters to see the Assistant Chief Constable Bernard Drew who congratulated me on being promoted but stated it would not take effect for at least 12 months because he had a specialised job for me to do. He explained that because of the reputation I had gained in the world of 'drugs' he was going to second me to work with the education departments throughout Shropshire, Hereford and Worcester to work with teachers and youth workers in order to improve their awareness of drugs and to develop drug education packages which could be used in schools with pupils of all ages as part of personal, social and health education.

Whilst I was disappointed about not being immediately promoted I realised this was a golden opportunity and if I turned it down I probably would not get promoted for 12 months anyway. I was learning.

I immediately accepted and in September 1986 I was posted as Police Drug Liaison Officer to work in the Local Authority Education Building situated in Blackwell Street, Kidderminster.

CHAPTER 17

INCOMPATIBLE BEDFELLOWS
- DEALING WITH DRUGS

On commencing the 'Drugs project' I was told to develop my own terms of reference which meant making it up as I went along.

The first part of the project was working with a Deputy Head teacher from Waseley Hills High School Rubery called Tony Bradley who was also seconded to the project. The aim was to develop or buy in the latest drug education packages and cascade them out to all schools and train teachers how to use them. This meant improving their awareness of the basics of drugs to deal with practical situations in schools where they came across incidents and also ensuring they were able to implement the drugs packages as part of the curriculum. I had to replicate this in Shropshire and Telford by working with health and education specialists based at the old Cross Houses Hospital, near Shrewsbury.

The second half of the project was to work with Youth workers both permanent and voluntary staff and do more or less the same thing. The idea was to familiarise them with drugs and education packages that could be used in an outreach or informal capacity.

Hereford and Worcester Youth service seconded a lady called Mary Parnell to the project who joined us a few months later.

We needed administration support and this was provided by Carol Gordon who did a sterling job for us in making some order out of chaos. We all developed a very close relationship and remained friends by keeping in contact for many years after the project ended.

Tony was extremely knowledgeable on the subject, had loads of contacts and was well organised to get things underway. Although Mary came into the project later she was very experienced at dealing with young people and understood the politics and culture of the youth service which was very necessary to get staff on board.

It is important to understand the context in which we were working. Drugs in the middle 80's were a mystery to most people. The conservative government at the time recognised that there was likely to be a proliferation of heroin coming into the country from Pakistan. Although some people were aware of Cannabis and knew it existed, the vast majority were unable to believe that heroin, cocaine, LSD and other so-called party drugs were common on our high streets or that illegal drugs were being used by pupils in a social environment and occasionally being brought into schools.

There was a lot of complacency about the subject, a disbelief that it could ever affect other than a small number of people and that the rise in importation and registered addicts was increasing year on year.

Although prevention was regarded as key to making young people aware there was conflict as to what approach should be made. Some believed that the short sharp horror story approach was best and that this would put young people off ever experimenting.

Unfortunately, that approach had been tried in vain particularly around the subject of smoking. It had failed abysmally on the basis that no-one believes it will happen to them and in the case of young people it can seek to glamorise the issue and make it more attractive. The other thing is youngsters are not daft. They mix with drug users and know that if you use cannabis like millions do you are very unlikely to suffer death or serious illness.

At the other extreme some teachers and parents believed that the best thing to do was to ignore the problem and not say anything so hopefully the problem would go away. The same approach of course used to be made over sex education but most of us know that eventually you do find out and sometimes with tragic results.

I had always worked in Police stations and now I was based with local government staff in a local government building in the centre of Kidderminster. It was a culture shock to me after dealing with the rough and tumble world of cops and I appreciated very quickly that their sense of humour was totally different and robust bad language was not the done thing.

However, Tony Carol, and Mary were great and we shared some fantastic laughs in the privacy of our own office.

Tony and I travelled miles together across the country and got to know each other extremely well despite the cultural differences. Basically, as a police officer I did not believe in the subtle approach and my usual approach to any challenge was to be bold and kick the door down. From Tony I learnt that there are other more diplomatic ways to approach a problem and that sometimes if you knock the door first or go round the back you may find the door opens easily.

When Tony left the project he gave me a framed copy of the poem 'Desiderata' by Max Ehrmann dated around 1920. The poem starts:

"Go placidly amid the noise and haste, and remember what peace there may be in silence.'

Wise words which I took on board from a man who was older and wiser, well, definitely older!

Tony and I shared many platforms and experiences together as we lectured to hundreds of school teachers and staff across the counties of Herefordshire and Worcestershire and visited dozens of schools.

We developed very interactive methods of teaching teachers in a way that we would want them to teach the subject to their pupils and using the same materials. We used role play, quizzes and games to get the message across and developed good reputations with the educationists.

A lot of the lectures we did were to staff after hours or to parent teacher associations to create basic awareness of the signs and symptoms of drug misuse.

Just before Christmas we visited a school at Peterchurch which is in deepest south Herefordshire. It was after school hours had finished and was dark when we arrived.

We entered via the front entrance and I can recall a scene that was surreal as we lectured on drugs with me, burning some cannabis with one hand and balancing a cup of tea and a mince pie in the other hand.

When it came time to leave we were ushered out of the rear exit and walked across the car park which was in pitch blackness back to Tony's car.

Suddenly in a flash Tony disappeared from in front of me followed by a scream, a grunt and the sort of bad language he was not normally associated with. Before I could utter a word suddenly the world opened up in front of me as well and I fell sharply into a big hole straight on the top of Tony who felt the full weight of my 14 and a half stone in addition to the large box of drugs I was carrying.

I was OK but Tony was in a sorry state. Basically, we had fallen into a large hole that was being excavated in the centre of the playground and was completely unprotected.

By now both of us were making a fair bit of noise and Tony was telling me in no uncertain terms to get the hell off his back. As we were both climbing out of the hole a member of the health education service who had been in the audience drove his car up to us with the headlights on full and shouted, 'It's OK, I have called the Police, have the muggers got away?'

At this point I realised he thought we had been mugged for drugs and started to see the funny side of it. However, Tony had distinctly lost his sense of humour and when he emerged into the headlights of the car I realised he had cut his eyebrow open which was streaming blood and had broken his spectacles as well as being covered in mud.

There was no way Tony could drive so I drove his car to the local GP surgery in the village. At this point my impetuous nature was not lost on

Tony and he looked distinctly nervous that I was driving his car but he had little choice.

We walked into the surgery and I have to say God bless the good old NHS and the doctor's receptionist. Tony, who was covered in shit and holding his eye with a handkerchief soaked in blood woefully explained his injury and asked if he could receive medical attention. Without even a hint of irony the receptionist asked if he had made an appointment. Tony tried to explain that up until five minutes before he had not known he would need one and had not planned on visiting the local doctor due to an unfortunate accident.

However, there was no way in getting past the receptionist and she despatched us to Hereford General Hospital accident and emergency department.

When we arrived they were more receptive but insisted on going through a long questionnaire. Tony, with the patience and quiet disposition he was known for answered all questions whilst still holding his eye and feeling very, very sorry for himself.

However, at the point where they asked if he had taken any drugs and I was still holding the drugs box full of illicit drugs I literally broke down in laughter to the point where tears were rolling down my cheeks. Tony just did not see the funny side of it at all.

We worked very closely with a national training organisation called TACADE (Teachers Advisory Council on Alcohol and Drugs Education) who were specialists in providing resources and training on personal, health and social education. They published an international magazine and I wrote an article for them entitled, 'Incompatible Bedfellows' referring to the unique project that Tony and I were involved in with Police and education working so closely together. I received correspondence back from as far as Australia and there was considerable interest in the work we were undertaking which was regarded as pioneering at that time.

In May of 1987 Tony and I were running a course for a number of teachers at Pitmaston House in Worcester when my second daughter Caroline was born on exactly the same day as when her sister was born six years earlier.

This left me in a dilemma. Jud was in hospital having Caroline, Mandy was only six and needed getting to school and I was supposed to be helping Tony run the course.

Fortunately, we had contingency plans. I took Mandy to school, visited Jud and Caroline in hospital and then went to Pitmaston House to help Tony and enjoy the buffet lunch. From there I went home, picked up Mandy from school and then we both went into the hospital to meet her new sister. This was much to Mandy's disgust who just wanted to enjoy her birthday and play with her new toys. Having a sister on the same birthday was a bit of an inconvenience!

When it came to the time for Tony to leave the project I commenced the second half of the project with Mary concentrating on awareness and teaching to voluntary, part-time and full-time youth workers across Herefordshire and Worcestershire.

This was both different and difficult for a number of reasons. They were of a different culture, not a captive audience and much of the training had to be done at evenings and during residential weekends.

Mary had a lovely personality and a unique way of communicating with both colleagues and especially young people. She was one of the few people in life I have met who actually enjoyed working with teenagers and could have them eating out of her hand.

Whilst I had been working with Tony I met a lady who I would describe as the most formidable teacher and public speaker I have ever met called Eileen Bruce.

Eileen was a teacher by profession but at the time I met her she was a health education officer in charge of the Health Promotion Unit situated just north of Bromsgrove.

Eileen was blessed with many attributes, not least a charming and magnetic personality combined with a twinkle in the eye and a dose of wisdom and judgement that only comes from years of experience in teaching, life and communicating with people.

Over the period of a couple of years Eileen and I shared many public speaking platforms together on the subject of substance misuse. I would usually start, like a warm up act until Eileen came on and wowed them with her down-to-earth and magical delivery that was both a pleasure and privilege to watch.

With her white hair, twinkly eyes, infectious smile and occasional wicked humour Eileen would regale the audience with teaching tales and the foibles of youngsters until she had the audience eating out of her hand. Then when she had gained her credibility and they were truly warmed up and receptive she would put across the serious message of how to communicate with young people on the subject of personal, health and social education issues such as drugs and sex education. Whether teachers, health professionals or parents the audience would heed every word and sit on the edge of their seats waiting for the next anecdote or vital piece of information.

Few people ever have this skill, which is, the natural ability to read and communicate with an audience at their level and to both entertain and educate at the same time.

I learnt a lot from listening and watching Eileen and I am sure I am not alone.

Whilst training the youth workers we spent a couple of nights away on a residential course with them at the national sports centre at Lilleshall in Shropshire. This involved Mary, myself and Eileen taking it in turns over the three days to train the youth workers who were all from Hereford and Worcester Youth service.

It was an intense course and unfortunately fraught with difficulty. Eileen had done something to her leg which was bandaged up and had to be kept elevated. Determined not to let us down Eileen turned up to do her bit but not only had to keep her leg up when lecturing but also had to keep disappearing at regular intervals to put ice packs on it to reduce the swelling.

On the second evening I went to go in for tea and was preparing for my session which was to due to take up several hours of the following morning on drugs, signs, symptoms and identification of illegal drug use.

As I sat down to tea I had a message to ring Jud urgently at home. When I did she told me Caroline who by now was a few months old was suffering from severe stomach pains and the doctor had advised she must be admitted to hospital immediately. Jud needed a hand to cope both with the hospital admission and to care for our eldest daughter Mandy who was only about 6 yrs old. I immediately told Jud I was on my way back home and would meet her at Kidderminster hospital.

After putting the phone down I realised I had two problems. The first was I had travelled with Mary to get to Lilleshall and had no transport to get home. The second problem which was not so imminent but equally important was how the hell was I going to get to Kidderminster, sort out the family and then make it back again for 9am the next morning when I was due to lecture to the youth workers. It did not escape my notice that literally thousands of pounds had been invested in the course, I was the only person who had the information to present from the Police at such short notice and the organisers were going to be less than happy if I cancelled, let alone my bosses.

Well, first things first, I borrowed the Hereford and Worcester Youth service mini-bus that had been used to bring some of the delegates to the conference and drove that to Kidderminster. I wasn't sure quite how to explain if stopped by the Police that an off-duty police officer was driving a Hereford and Worcester youth mini bus in Shropshire whilst on a personal errand of mercy but fortunately the opportunity did not avail itself.

On the way it did occur to me that I now had a double reason to be back in the morning otherwise about 16 delegates couldn't get home from Lilleshall the next day.

When I arrived at the hospital Jud and Mandy were worried and Caroline was quickly admitted for tests. I told Jud to take Mandy home and I would wait at the hospital.

In the middle of the night the nurses told me Caroline had suffered an obstruction of the intestine but they had cleared it using a barium meal test.

In the morning they told me that Caroline seemed to be OK and would be released later.

I then telephoned Jud who sent Mandy to school and then came to relieve me at the hospital.

I then drove the mini-bus home, had a quick shower, changed and drove back to Lilleshall where I was able to carry out my lectures. Fortunately, even without sleep adrenalin is a marvellous motivator and it wasn't until I got home that evening that I started to feel tired and catch up on 36 hours without sleep. Another example of where business and home life get mixed together!

Just before I left the drugs project I was sitting in the Education Authority office at Blackwell Street Kidderminster when a member of staff rushed in and in a panic blurted out that a woman was trying to throw herself off the top of the multi-storey car park opposite in an obvious attempt of committing suicide. Our offices overlooked the car park so I went to look and could definitely see a woman who had one leg straddled over the wall of the top level and was looking down to the ground below. I said the first thing that came into my mind which was, 'Call the Police!' With more than a hint of irony the woman who had spotted the incident said, 'For Gods' sake, I thought you were the Police!'

'Yes, OK but get some bloody uniformed Police here whilst I go and have a look,' I retorted.

At this point I wasn't sure what the hell I was going to do but I knew I had to be seen to be doing something. I ran out of our office building, across the street and into the bottom level of the car park. I was in civilian clothes so I realised the woman would not know I was in authority. I tried to take the lift in an attempt to get to speak to the woman. The lift was not working so I decided to run up the steps to the top level of a number of floors.

I have never been noted for my physical attributes, particularly running and it is fair to say that by the time I got to the top of the stairs on the top level I was completely knackered and gasping for breath. At that point I realised I need to stop and regain composure otherwise I was in danger of a heart attack. Fortunately, these brief few moments gave me time to think. I referred earlier to attending a course where a woman counsellor lectured to us on how to communicate to someone who was in the process of committing suicide. The words etched in my brain were to do and say something to the prospective suicidal person completely out of context that they will least expect. This will have the effect of taking the heat out of the situation and give you time to think and assess the situation – it also takes the onus away from the crisis. The example the counsellor gave was of entering a flat where someone is about to electrocute themselves and asking if they have any teabags to make a cup of tea.

I didn't really think that example would work very well in this situation so I racked my brains trying to think of something whilst I walked over towards where the woman was.

I could see her still perched on the wall and as she saw me approaching she cocked both legs over the wall and sat facing the ground.

I just sauntered over and said, 'Excuse me love, sorry to bother you but have you got change for 50p for the parking machine?' For a moment she looked at me like I was gone out but then paused and got off the wall where she bent down to pick up her handbag which lying on the floor of the car park. She was now safe so I rushed forward and grabbed her just as a Police car and two colleagues also arrived. They placed her in the car and took her away for a mental health assessment. As she drove away she looked at me completely confused and seemed to be wondering why I was no longer interested in money for the car park machine. However, that was one lecture I was able to put into practice.

My time had now come to resume operational policing duties and hand the project over. It was January 1988. I was still pending my promotion to Inspector which had been announced in August 1986. I was told that I was going to be posted back to Kidderminster where there was the opportunity to carry out acting inspector duties pending my promotion which was expected imminently. Unfortunately, nothing could have been further from the truth. Promotion for me was still to be over 2 years hence and during the interim period I was to face one of the most difficult periods of my career due to a combination of unfortunate events.

CHAPTER 18

TOUGH YEARS

On Monday 18th January 1988 I was the early turn Acting Inspector at Kidderminster.

At 6 o' clock in the morning the place was relatively calm but was soon to be buzzing as it had been since the day before. On Sunday 17th January a 14 year old newspaper boy called Stuart Gough was reported missing whilst carrying out his paper round in the leafy commuter village of Hagley situated in the foothills of Clent on the outskirts of Stourbridge but well within the boundary of Worcestershire.

Stuart was a responsible young boy from a loving and caring family and from word go it was suspected that Stuart had been abducted. It would have been completely out of character for him to have disappeared without trace. Unfortunately and tragically this was to prove true and what followed was one of the biggest inquiries into abduction and murder that West Mercia saw in the years surrounding 1988.

On the Sunday there was still hope that Stuart would be found alive and that some explanation would be found for his disappearance however odd. Extensive searches nearby had already been conducted but to no avail. Unfortunately, as next day dawned it looked less likely that Stuart would be found alive and well following a winter's night of cold exposure even if he had been lying injured somewhere.

I knew the press and radio stations would be ringing in early for immediate news and as the duty inspector I would be the first point of contact. I scoured the press releases left behind from the previous day but they were all dated.

I had a fair idea of what Monday would consist of so I decided to put together a 'holding' press release until someone more senior came along and then they could take over.

It is hardly ever appropriate just to tell the press that you have no news or to offer no comment so I decided I would wing it and give a statement as required.

I decided to give a couple of key messages. That there had been no news or developments overnight, that whilst we still had hope, increasingly we were getting concerned as time went on and on that day we would be concentrating on extending our previous day's search and we would welcome members of the public to assist in that task under control of the Police. Also, that it was proposed to set up an incident room and that we wanted any members of the public with information to come forward. I knew that would not be in conflict with anything senior officers might say and that at least it made the news contemporary for that morning and sounded like we were on the ball.

I was not experienced at giving media interviews but like most cops you have to be prepared to do anything as the need arises. My first interview was with the news channel that at that time piped out national news to all of the commercial radio stations throughout the country. The first broadcast was live but I decided to go for it and followed my script, I got through it without stumbling words and felt quite relieved until the presenter asked me for the telephone number of the incident room for the public to phone into! At that point there was no incident room and no number designated, worse than that I could not remember the number of Kidderminster Police station either so I blabbed something out about just contact your local police to contact West Mercia.

When I later listened to the broadcast on tape I was most embarrassed with my pregnant pause and waffle and had to ring in again (once I got the telephone number) to amend the statement which was re-run for remaining bulletins and sounded more professional. Another lesson learned!

Almost two weeks of hectic inquiries and activities took place across the West Midlands area before the fate of Stuart was known. During that time the press activity was immense and during nights our uniformed shifts had to staff the mobile incident room and caravan that were set up at Hagley community centre.

The person who led the abduction inquiry was Detective Chief Superintendent David Cole, a very experienced and able detective who had an excellent reputation and paid meticulous attention to detail in every investigation and was proud of his knowledge in relation to the forensic science and pathology of cases working very closely at that time with a renowned Home Office pathologist, Dr. Peter Acland.

However, the man who bore the brunt of the media and maintained the public profile for the Police was the Divisional Chief Superintendent at Kidderminster, Tony Warren. Tony also took on responsibility for maintaining contact with the Gough family. Tony did an excellent job in dealing with the media, day after day in keeping the news fresh, inspiring hope and keeping the public up-to-date with developments. At the same time he retained the confidence of the family and came across to all as the genuinely caring professional face of the police which must have encouraged hundreds of people to come forward with information. In those days we had no formal training in dealing with families in these situations and largely Tony performed this duty but also involved a policewoman on my shift called Sally Nicholls who provided the daily support and communication.

It quickly became apparent that Stuart's disappearance might be linked to another attempted abduction of another paperboy at Hagley and a serious sexual assault on another young male in a village near Hereford. Both these incidents occurred around the same time and the sighting of a car and description of a driver and offender eventually led to the arrest of a 32 year-old suspect called Victor Miller and his flatmate 46 year-old Trevor Peacher. Miller owned a car similar to that seen in the vicinity of the other incidents at Hagley and Herefordshire.

Peacher had initially provided an alibi for Miller which later proved untrue but he could not be connected with the incidents. However, Miller eventually confessed to the abduction and murder of Stuart Gough and almost two weeks from the date when Stuart had been abducted led detectives during the middle of the night to a location at Bromsberrow near Ledbury where he had buried Stuart's body in a wooded gully.

It was in the early hours of Sunday 31st January 1988 that I was on duty at Kidderminster Police station when we received news in the control room from detectives that Stuart's body had been found. Officers and staff had lived with the inquiry for two weeks and we all held out a glimmer of hope that Stuart would be found alive. There was a sombre air and a few tears shed but now the truth was apparent and someone had to tell the family that Stuart was dead and this was definitely a murder inquiry.

We arranged for uniformed officers to attend the house and to support detectives in breaking the news and contacted Sally to befriend and assist the family.

Miller was initially brought before Hereford magistrates court on his first appearance where he instructed his solicitor to make a statement to the effect that he publicly accepted responsibility for Stuart Gough's death and wished to receive the maximum possible sentence and wished to avoid causing more distress to Stuart's family.

On the 3rd November 1988 Miller appeared at Birmingham Crown Court having been charged with the abduction and murder of Stuart Gough. He pleaded guilty and was sentenced to life imprisonment. The Judge referred to him as a sadistic sexual psychopath and the murder as deliberate, premeditated and cold blooded.

Trevor Peacher was later sentenced to three years imprisonment for providing Miller with a false alibi.

The epitaph on Stuart's headstone sums up in one simple sentence the aftermath of a crime of such enormity to the family: *'The silence hurts.'*

In later years I got to know, Stuart's father, Geoff Gough quite well when he became a volunteer at Bromsgrove Victim Support where I was the local police liaison officer. By then Tony Warren had retired from the Police and taken over as chair of the local committee. Geoff expressed the wish that he wanted to do something to repay the police and community for what they had done to assist him, his wife Jean and their family during and after the murder.

This was a crime that rocked the nation and particularly the little village of Hagley which is no stranger to tragedy and a place that I will always hold with particular affection.

Earlier in this book I told the story of the multiple fatal accident that occurred at the bottom of Hagley Hill. Almost six years after Stuart was abducted, on the 18th November 1993 a mini-bus full of pupils from Hagley RC High School were travelling along the M40 motorway near Warwick whilst travelling back from a concert at the Royal Albert Hall when a terrible incident occurred. The mini-bus which was being driven by a female teacher collided with a maintenance truck which was on the hard shoulder. It resulted in 12 of the children and the teacher being killed and two other pupils being injured.

Again, this was something that tore the heart out of the community and especially the school. I had no direct involvement in this incident having since left the Kidderminster division but it is a memory that will live on forever for so many and serves to illustrate that Hagley has seen more than its fair share of tragedy.

Early in 1988 after resuming back to Kidderminster on shifts and whilst still acting up as Inspector I was invited to address the national annual drugs conference run by the Association of Chief Police Officers which was being held at Lancashire Police Headquarters. This was to be a prestigious occasion because it meant that the West Mercia Project would receive national acclaim which was good for both the force and the education authorities. I was to share the stage with David Stanley. David was the Chief Education Officer for Hereford and Worcester and whose idea the project had been in the first place. I knew that my own Chief Constable Tony Mullet and Assistant Chief Bernard Drew would also be present and for me personally this should have been a good career move.

At the conclusion of the Drugs project I had been formally presented with a county shield by Hereford and Worcester County Council as a token of thanks for the work we had done with teachers. My career was now at a very high profile point and I knew things could only get worse! Unfortunately I was right.

As I stepped off the stage at Lancashire and took a seat my Chief Constable turned to me and congratulated me on my performance. He told me I must aim for the highest ranks in the Police service and pointed to the ACPO chair which at that time was held by Sir Hugh Annesley who later went on to become the Chief Constable of the Royal Ulster Constabulary.

Although I was flattered I did not take this seriously and unfortunately made some flippant remark like, 'Well, I have been on the promotion list to Inspector for about 18 months now so if I got that promotion it would do for now.' Mullet looked surprised at the delay, muttered something but said no more.

I drove back home after the conference and arrived late evening. When I got in Jud said we had to make an instant decision by next morning following a telephone call she had received from the Chief Superintendent at Kidderminster.

The telephone call was an offer of promotion to Inspector at Hereford to take place immediately but it would mean moving house, they would not accept me commuting the round trip of 70 miles daily.

Jud and I sat and discussed the pros and cons for several hours. It was not an easy decision. Over the period of the past 12 months all of the family had been in hospital for one thing or another. We had been involved in a car accident in which Jud and I had both got whiplash injuries and the final straw was when Jud was diagnosed with having rheumatoid arthritis. We were at the point families reach sometimes when they are worn out and cannot face anymore hassle. Moving house and Mandy's school at a time when we were feeling so debilitated was not something either of us felt we could face.

The following morning I telephoned the Chief Superintendent, briefly explained the position and then declined the offer of promotion if it meant moving house. However, I made it clear I was prepared to travel to Hereford if that was the only option. The Chief Superintendent sounded surprised but appeared to accept what I said and then explained that by turning the offer down I may well go to the bottom of the list again. I accepted that but did say I had already waited for 18 months at their request so if any vacancies did occur then I would appreciate the offer.

After a relatively short period of time a vacancy for the position of Inspector in the Force Operations Room was advertised. This was based at Hindlip Hall, near Worcester and being a distance of only 15 miles was very commutable. It was open to both those in the rank and those awaiting promotion such as me. I made inquiries with Police HQ personnel department and was told that I was not eligible to apply because I had a complaint pending against me from a member of the public and it was policy not to promote someone whilst pending a complaint in case it was founded and discipline was necessary. I pointed out that I was already pending the same complaint investigation when I was offered the first promotion to Hereford so if that was the policy why was I offered the promotion then?

No real answer was forthcoming and I started to smell a rat and suspected that I had obviously upset headquarters and that some games were now being played. The bottom line they told me was that I must be free of any complaint record before being promoted.

This was confirmed when I was advised by my local Chief Inspector to submit a report and explain the reasons why I had turned down the promotion to Hereford on the basis of compassionate grounds and that it may be in my best interest to have this on record.

Worse was to happen. I was then posted into the custody block where I became a permanent custody sergeant processing and supervising prisoners whilst in detention.

Whilst I did not mind the job, in fact, it was very good experience, it was the best possible way of attracting complaints from prisoners and sometimes their solicitors!

At this point in the late eighties there was no CCTV to protect you against unfounded allegations. There was very little assistance given to the custody sergeant and sometimes you were dealing with up to 15 – 20 prisoners on your own. Prisoners vary from those that are drunk and violent, or under the influence of drugs to those that are mentally ill or suicidal. All prisoners are an accident waiting to happen. A number may be young, vulnerable or just downright devious. All of the results of society's ills pass through the custody block of a police station. Not only do you have to protect them and ensure they get their rights and procedures are adhered to but you have to continually review their detention and ensure there is sufficient evidence to both detain and charge them.

The prisoners are very often extremely abusive, their legal representatives and relatives can sometimes be obnoxious and so can Police Officers if you are making decisions regarding bail or release from detention without charge that they do not like. It can be the most unpopular place in the world and this is why most sergeants do not relish the prospect of being the dungeon master! Since the introduction of the Police and Criminal Evidence Act 1984 (known as PACE) the codes of practice under PACE have ruled how prisoners must be treated whilst in the detention of the police and relate to every aspect of investigating, evidence gathering, welfare and rights of detained persons. The responsibility for ensuring that these rules are maintained rests very clearly with the custody sergeant and woe betide you if you are found to have broken the rules. Not only will cases be lost but discipline can follow.

So, it is very easy to see that in this environment, as hard as you try to be good then you will get complaints made against you. The motto in the Police is if you are not getting complaints then you are not doing your job. Not always true but many commendations for good police work could just as easily have been a complaint or discipline because positive policing and getting results in those days meant very often leaving yourself vulnerable to false or malicious allegations that you have done something wrong.

Over the next 2 years I was to receive about nine complaints from members of the public. At least all of them were for doing the job, rather than not doing the job. Some were minor and trivial, some were serious and worrying. They ranged from allegations of minor infringements of PACE through to allegations of forgery, assault and inferences of perverting the course of justice. As fast as I got one complaint cleared and written off by the complaints department then another one would arrive. Several of them involved giving evidence in trials where I, along with colleagues were accused of lying and various other misdemeanours. The problem was that all this time my promotion was being delayed and I became very despondent and frustrated.

I reached the point where I wondered if I would ever get promoted and started to seriously wonder whether this was a conspiracy because I had turned down the first vacancy. I requested to be moved out of the front line of policing for a while until the complaints had been reduced to an acceptable level to promote me. That was refused.

In desperation I made an appointment to see the Assistant Chief Constable who I had worked with on the Drugs project to see if he could find a solution for me. We had worked closely together on the project, he knew I had agreed to initially postpone my promotion for 12 months in order to do the job at his request and we had got on well.

I went to see him at force headquarters and immediately realised this was now different territory. As opposed to being usually quite friendly and calling me by first name he was polite but very formal and just kept referring to me as Sergeant. He listened to what I had to say, made some brief notes as to where I was prepared to travel to but made it clear there was little he could do because the decision rested with the Deputy Chief Constable and he was not prepared to challenge it. When I made some further points he terminated the interview and told me he had a lunch appointment whereupon he ushered me out of the office.

I realised now that no longer was I an opportunity but a liability for the organisation and how quickly you can go from being the bee's knees to being completely out of favour.

I was now feeling angry and I have to say I developed an attitude of abrasiveness towards senior officers where I would challenge decisions vociferously. Whilst I was OK towards my staff it didn't take me long to upset the senior management at every opportunity.

I knew I was stressed and I felt that I needed to be straight with my own Chief Superintendent and get it off my chest. I tried several times to see him but he was always busy. I suppose I was like the proverbial bear with a sore bum and had a face that was as sad as a Labrador which has lost its bone.

Eventually the Chief Superintendent called me into his office one day quite unannounced. For a few seconds I was relieved because I thought at long last perhaps they had decided to promote me. However, I quickly realised quite the opposite. The Chief Superintendent read out a report that he said he was going to send to headquarters about me. It read that I was the most difficult and truculent officer he had on the division and requested that I be promoted or moved to the further possible point at the earliest opportunity. I was astounded, angry and upset. What followed was a slanging match that lasted for almost two hours where I made my points and he made his.

The following morning after a poor night's sleep I went back to see him again. He told me he had watered down the report as a result of my representations but it still requested I be moved out of the division as soon as possible.

Within a week or so a memorandum was received back from the head of personnel which said that the Deputy Chief Constable had considered the report but that there was no way that I could be promoted or moved whilst I was pending so many complaints. However, the final paragraph in the memorandum which I have kept to this day stated, 'In the interim period please continue your counselling efforts in respect of Sergeant King.'

I reflected that the three hour bollocking I had received over two days was obviously 'counselling' and I should be grateful. I had to smile and suddenly the whole thing started to lift. I had by now after almost 3 years given up the notion of promotion and decided that the best thing I could do was probably keep my head down, keep soaking up the complaints, be polite and respectful and just get on with the job. I had to admit to myself that there is never any place for bad attitude, particularly in a disciplined job and whatever the reasons I should not have acted the way I did. To continue to maintain an attitude and keep up this resentment would destroy me, I had to let it go.

I also learnt something else that was to stand me in good stead. Later in my career I was an Inspector, Chief Inspector and Acting Superintendent in the complaints department where I was the one responsible for serving discipline notices on officers. The above experience provided me with great empathy about what it's like to be at the receiving end of a complaint and what a frustrating and worrying experience it can be. Although you may know you have done nothing wrong, during the course of the investigation other things completely unrelated to the complaint may turn up such as a breach of procedures that could still result in discipline. My advice to officers was always, never underestimate a complaint but if you have acted in good faith even if you made a mistake this will be recognised and taken into account.

Eventually promotion was to come some three and half years after I was initially selected but during the interim period whilst working in custody and patrol at Kidderminster and keeping my head down some interesting and entertaining things happened.

Once a week it was remand day at Kidderminster Magistrates Court where prisoners who were being kept in nearby prisons whilst pending a trial or court appearance would be brought back to the court by the prison service staff to have their remand in custody reviewed and to seek bail. The prison staff would drop them off at the police station and it was our job to book them in, put them in a cell, feed them and ensure they went to court as required. Following their appearance it was the responsibility of the Police to escort them back to the prison or ensure they were released on bail conditions as set by the court together with whatever possessions they had in custody. These days' private security companies are employed to do the job which relieves the police of being a taxi service for remanded prisoners.

During this time we had a group of several individuals who were all well known miscreants from the Kidderminster area and were on long-term remand for a variety of offences. They knew that eventually when convicted they were due to serve long custodial sentences and made it their business to be difficult and cause as much disruption as possible. Their aim was to wind up the police officers responsible for supervising and escorting them whilst in custody with the hope that they would assault them and then they could make a complaint. They would request a medical examination before they left the prison and then try and goad officers into hitting them so that when they went back to prison they would ask for a second medical examination and show how they had been assaulted.

Our officers were aware of this but because they were so difficult and obstructive it was sometimes necessary to use force to get them into a cell or a vehicle and then they would lie about the circumstances and claim they were assaulted for no reason. Because that did not work very successfully they started wrapping up and secreting small articles on themselves such as paper clips and small blades which they would then use to injure themselves in the cells and then claim they had been inflicted by the officers.

When young men or indeed women are totally bored out of their tree, have nothing to lose and loads of time to plan their next escapade there is no limit to what they will seek to do.

The situation was like working on a knife-edge where you never knew what was going to happen next from them fighting for no reason, abusing officers or throwing their food up the walls. It was a dangerous situation both physically and professionally and as the custody sergeant it was necessary to monitor and record everything in case of later comebacks. In addition you had to concentrate on other prisoners in custody and suppress any feelings of anger, being professional at all times.

I had not realised how much this was getting to me week after week until one afternoon after an early turn shift I went home and fell asleep on the settee in the lounge.

My youngest daughter Caroline who was a toddler at this time must have been annoyed by my snoring and the fact I was not playing because she suddenly came up and unintentionally thumped me in the privates. In a half sleep I suddenly woke up and grabbed her, imagining that I was still at work in the custody block fighting with prisoners. Jud suddenly rushed in from the kitchen and shouted at me to stop before I started to punch out.

I realised I was in a complete daze, but pent up emotion had taken over and thank goodness I realised in time what was happening. It also dawned on me that aggression has to be released somewhere and buying a punch bag for the garage would be more useful than allowing it to come out at home.

It was during custody duties though that one of the funniest things I ever saw happened.

On a fairly quiet weekday afternoon one of my officers, Brian Sanders called me up on the radio and said he was bringing in a man following a positive breathalyser test. Brian explained that he was giving me due notice because the bloke himself was covered in orange paint. I laid down some plastic bags in the charge room and awaited their arrival. Brian was not kidding. The bloke was covered head to toe in bright orange emulsion paint which stank like hell. The only thing that was visible was the prisoner's eyes like an orange panda. This was before the Orange tango advertisement became popular but he really looked the part.

There was no way we could proceed immediately to do anything except put the chap in the shower down the cell block and get him a change of clothes.

The problem was that he was still drunk as a skunk and Brian had to help him strip his clothes off and then scrub him down in the shower much to the amusement of everyone within 5 miles who came to watch! By this time Brian was covered as well and it seemed like a never ending cycle.

However, what topped it off was when we offered the prisoner one of our brand new boiler suits to wear which coincidentally was also bright orange. 'I think you are taking the piss Sarge,' the prisoner said looking at me quizzically.

I was intrigued by what had happened. Brian then explained to me that Mr. Orange was a painter and decorator who was well oiled on a few pints and had been driving his van along the Franche Road at Kidderminster when he collided into a line of parked cars. A load of cans of orange paint he was carrying in the back of the van then exploded all over him. He was forced to stop, got out of his car and then ran to his home which was nearby.

When Brian arrived he followed a trail of orange footprints which led to the driver's house where he had sought refuge and was hoping to keep his head down and avoid the breathalyser. After knocking the door for several minutes it was reluctantly answered by Mr. Orange whose initial reaction was to deny any knowledge of the accident. When Brian politely pointed out that it did not take Inspector Clouseau to work out that the driver of the car had left a trail of orange paint and here he was covered in orange paint he accepted the game was up and Brian duly arrested him.

Once we had cleaned him up a bit it was my job to put him on the Intoxiliser machine at the Police station in order to obtain a breath sample and see if he was over the drink drive limit. The problem we had was that the smell was still present and every time we tried the test the machine kept reading, 'Abort, abort!,' because the smell was interfering with the detection mechanism.

Eventually, we had to call a doctor and take a blood specimen which surprise, surprise came back positive.

As a custody sergeant the most common prisoners you deal with are drunk's day in day out and night after night. Most of them are regulars and some will be habitual alcoholics. Eventually you become so accustomed to dealing with drunks that if a drunk driver comes into custody you can actually estimate how much over the limit they will be depending on their demeanour.

Some of these drunks will be likeable rogues who provide good entertainment but are a persistent pain in the posterior and will never learn. Others, will be a danger to themselves and have hit the self destruct button. Two examples spring to mind.

The first was a man called 'Charlie' who I would put in the category of being the likeable rogue. Charlie by all accounts had been a bare-knuckle prize fighter in his younger days and a hard man. He walked with a very pronounced limp which rumour had it had been caused when he leapt out of an upstairs window of a house when the husband of the woman he had been in bed with came home unexpectedly and he had to leap to freedom.

Although he had broken his leg he declined to get any treatment and was left with a severely damaged leg.

Charlie was a persistent drunk who had spent a great amount of his life in custody following minor skirmishes with the law under the effects of booze.

He was a big man and when sober was extremely pleasant. When under the influence he usually became aggressive and he would take up the old fighting stance. Problem was as he went to draw a punch back, a combination of the beer and his bad leg meant he usually fell over backwards. Charlie was more awkward than violent but it would still take several officers to carry him to the station and put him in the cells.

On one occasion in a drunken haze he assaulted a policewoman and when he realised what he had done once sober he was devastated. The minute he was released he went and bought a bouquet of flowers for the policewoman which he brought into the station full of apologies, until the next time of course.

When off duty in Kidderminster I would very often see Charlie in the shopping centre who when sober always had a kind word. I was with one of my daughters one weekend when he came ambling over and pressed 10 pence in her hand to buy sweets. The sight of a big, gruff old man frightened the living daylights out of her but she accepted the 10 pence!

The last time I saw Charlie was in the Swan Centre at Kidderminster. He had recently come out of prison and was in a right state. He looked dishevelled and was shaking. He asked me if he could borrow a pound to get himself a sausage sandwich. I duly obliged and he told me he would pay me back when he next saw me in custody. Unfortunately, Charlie didn't get chance because not long afterwards he died and a little bit of Kidderminster character probably died at the same time.

The second example was a man called Kevin. I would put Kevin in the self-destruct category because not only was he an habitual drunk but he would continually make serious attempts at slashing his wrists and arms in an effort to either hurt or kill himself.

Kevin was ex-army and the minute he was brought in to the custody office he would stand to attention and shout out his full name, rank and number which he completed by shouting 'Sir,' and throwing a salute up.

I put him in a cell one night and was so concerned about his condition I kept paying 10 minute visits to the cell. Eventually, in the middle of the night he went quiet. When I looked through the cell hatch I saw one of the most horrendous sights I have ever seen of a drunken man which should have been videoed and shown to every teenager.

Here was Kevin, stripped of all his clothes except for the statutory orange boiler suit, lying on the floor of the cell crying to himself and quite obviously suffering delirium brought about by alcohol. He had excreted and peed himself and had rolled over into a pool of vomit. In circumstances like this, hospitals are reluctant to accept drunks unless completely unconscious and it was a case of keeping a regular eye on him and making sure he was safe until he had sobered up enough to clean himself up. There is nothing remotely funny about a drunk in this situation and it reflects the depravity that some people enter into.

Occasionally I got let out to do some patrol work. I worked closely with a fellow sergeant called Barry March and we took it in turns to do acting Inspector on the shift.

Barry was a positive character who originated from the North East and had a pragmatic, no nonsense approach to dealing with any situation. Barry was small and wiry but as hard as nails.

One evening whilst working a 2-10 shift we received a red call (urgent call) to assist a policewoman on the shift called Jo. Jo had spotted a well-known local villain called Slippery stealing some wooden pallets from a nearby factory whereupon he had assaulted her and then locked himself inside his own house which was nearby.

When we arrived we were joined by another officer called Tony Quinn. Barry was not impressed that Slippery had given Jo a hard time and was determined we should arrest him then and there. Barry hammered the side door and made it clear that unless Slippery opened up the door we would smash it down and come in to arrest him. Slippery eventually opened the door enough to tell Barry that if he came in he would set the dog on us and to bugger off.

Barry pushed the door hard, Slippery fell back against a wall and then we all filed in. It was then the problems started. The house was in complete darkness and the light switches did not work. Slippery struggled like a mad man. We all fell over on the floor and then the bloody dog got involved. At one point I thought I had Slippery round the neck and then realised it was the dog which from memory I think was a Doberman. I was then frightened to let the dog go but had to because Slippery's wife then joined in as well which led to even greater confusion.

Eventually, we managed to arrest and subdue Slippery where we placed him into the back of a panda car and took him to the police station. Slippery was a persistent complainer against Police and immediately we got to the Police station complained that we had assaulted him and cut his lip. Indeed, he had a split lip which had obviously occurred at some time during the struggle but it could have occurred at any point and was definitely not intentional.

What followed was another official complaint, a nasty not guilty trial in which we were all accused of assault under cross examination and an investigation by the complaints department in which eventually our actions were vindicated. Oh well. *C'est la Vie...*

It must be said that the way women were treated in the Police during the 70's and 80's sometimes left a lot to be desired. A largely macho and male-dominated organisation meant women were, as they are now very much in the minority but attitudes have now thankfully changed. In those days it really was a case of women had to gain respect and show they were as tough as men to be accepted otherwise they could find themselves quite isolated.

During the time that Barry March and I worked on the shift at Kidderminster we were joined by a policewoman called Annie Arthur and we had the job of mentoring Annie whilst she carried out the role of Acting Sergeant. Over the years Annie, along with many other policewomen had coped with considerable male banter and practical jokes which in retrospect by today's standards would be downright offensive. However, I suppose it reflected the way society's attitudes were at the time before the days of equal rights and diversity. Wrong now and wrong then but a completely different context existed.

Annie took most of this in her stride. She had principles, high standards both personally and professionally and was never about to compromise those or her femininity despite the ribbing she would get from colleagues. I admired her for that and both Barry and I supported Annie in her new role of Acting Sergeant. Annie developed confidence very quickly and the fact that she was dead straight and you knew where you stood made her popular with colleagues on the shift where she gained their respect and she grew into the role very quickly.

However, occasionally I cringe at some of things we did, sometimes with the best of intentions. Somebody reported that some stolen goods had been deposited down a deep hole in a wooded area on the outskirts of Kidderminster. What was needed was someone who was very slim who could be lowered into the hole on a rope to grab hold of the buried treasure and ensure it was recovered safely. Annie was volunteered for the job.

She donned a pair of blue plastic waterproof overalls and was then lowered into the hole attached to a rope. This was a recipe for disaster. So many things could go wrong. The rope could have become detached; Annie may have fallen or become trapped and even suffocated.

These days, a risk-assessment would be required and no doubt specialist teams and equipment would be used with permissions required from all and sundry. There was none of this. Annie remained calm but eventually she had to be withdrawn from the hole because it became too dangerous.

It's fair to say that most of us would not have been either eligible to have conducted the task (because of beer bellies) or indeed willing to undertake this task.

If ever anything major is going to happen in policing it usually happens at night. When it does happen it is never usually in isolation. Sometimes there is real pressure and the night is long. Sometimes, it is a night you will never forget.

On a weekday night shift during early autumn at around 10.30pm I was the patrol sergeant called to the scene of a serious road accident in a country lane on the outskirts of Kidderminster. When I arrived at the scene I could see there were two cars involved which had collided on a slight bend. The young male driver of the one car which was a small Peugeot was still in the car and I quickly established he was dead. The other car involved was a Daimler Jaguar. The male driver of this was alive and was walking-wounded with slight injuries. I also formed the impression from his demeanour that he had been drinking. An immediate inspection of the scene suggested that the Daimler had possibly been travelling in the centre of the road at the time of the collision.

The young male driver of the Peugeot was removed to an ambulance and I went in the back of the ambulance with him to the hospital morgue. This is necessary to prove continuity of the body from the scene to the point where the deceased can be identified by someone who knows them.

Whilst in the ambulance I was informed by the Police control that he was in fact the son of a civilian colleague I worked with. Although I did not know the young man who was dead I realised this was going to be a traumatic night for the family and all concerned.

When we arrived at the hospital it was necessary to make the arrangements for notifying the family and getting the deceased identified in the mortuary. At this point we were informed that the father would be attending the mortuary to undertake this because the mother (who was my work-colleague) was at that moment in time on a plane travelling abroad to visit family.

Eventually the father and brother of the deceased driver arrived at the mortuary and carried out the identification of the young man. I looked at the policewoman who was with me and could see that like me she was desperately trying to stop herself crying. There is nothing sadder than seeing closest family members identifying a loved one who has been killed in sudden and tragic circumstances. Suddenly lives have been destroyed, lives that a few hours earlier were normal, routine and dare I say it, sometimes, taken for granted are changed forever. A life has been extinguished; there will be no more future or dreams with that person, just memories. It is all so final.

I was then informed that the driver of the Daimler was also at the hospital receiving treatment and we needed to speak to him and breathalyse him, which is routine in these circumstances. When I saw him and spoke with him I confirmed my earlier suspicions about the fact he had been drinking but he refused to take a breath test and was most uncooperative. I was also aware that he had consumed drink immediately after the accident in a neighbour's house having left the scene of the accident which was nearby to where he lived. This was problematic and absolutely essential to bottom out immediately what he had consumed and how much because it would impact on any future breathalyser procedures.

I called a colleague who went to the neighbour's house and seized the bottle and glass and ascertained from the neighbour exactly what the driver had drunk.

I arranged for the driver to be arrested and taken to Kidderminster Police Station for further tests on the intoximeter machine once he had been discharged from the hospital.

I then went back to see the father and brother of the deceased boy and was in the middle of getting a statement in relation to the identification of the young man when I was called again on the radio.

The control centre informed me that another incident had taken place where a man had been hit over the head with an iron bar in his flat and was on his way into casualty but was in a serious condition and likely to die. They requested that I speak to him, seize all his clothing for forensic and then ask him to make a dying declaration about what happened. A dying declaration is where a police officer tells someone that they are likely to die and then asks them to explain what happened and tries to get them to sign it. In the event that they do die, providing it is taken in the correct way then it can be used as evidence in any future trial. I tried to explain to the radio controller that I was more than a little busy and could they get someone else to do it. They informed me that everyone was totally tied up and because I was at the hospital I was best placed to undertake it.

When the man was admitted I found he was completely unconscious so any dying declaration was not possible. I then gave the nurses a lesson in how to seize his clothing into separate bags, to label it and to keep it safe until I could take it with me. They duly stripped him off and did the task brilliantly. I told them to let me know if he regained consciousness and then went back to the family of the deceased young man.

I understand eventually, the man who had been hit with the iron bar did not die and I had no further dealings with this case.

When I managed to get back to the police station I found that the driver of the Daimler car had also refused to provide any form of breath sample and was not going to comply with the procedure. In these cases they can only be prosecuted for failing to comply – it is not possible to take any sample by force. We were suspicious that the driver would not provide a test because he was so far over the limit that he knew he would be well over and that he would rather take his chances for being prosecuted for refusal to supply a test rather than risk a heavier penalty and disqualification for a high reading.

As it happened subsequent events were to prove us correct but not without months of investigation.

I left the driver in the cells to be interviewed by officers in the morning once he was in a fit state to be interviewed so that we could obtain his first account of the accident and we knew what he was likely to being saying. I went home after a long and stressful night but knew that the responsibility for the investigation would rest with me when I returned to work and that it was likely to prove difficult without any independent witnesses to the accident itself.

I slept restlessly and when I returned to work I was assisted by a colleague on the shift, PC Brian Sanders to investigate the circumstances of the accident thoroughly. This involved full forensic analysis of the scene and reconstruction of scale plans by accident investigators, mechanical examination of both cars involved and efforts to trace the last movements of both drivers prior to the accident on that fateful night.

The deceased driver's actions prior to the collision did not seem to pose any problems. He had been returning from work. There was no suggestion of alcohol and the accident scene examination confirmed that the driver of the Daimler appeared to have been driving in the centre of the road when he collided head on with the Peugeot as they negotiated a bend. The road was more than wide enough for two cars.

As we delved deeper into the inquiry a picture started to emerge of the Daimler driver having a reputation for drinking and driving and inferences from local sources that on the fateful day in question he had been drinking throughout the day prior to the collision.

The worst-case scenario and the one that initial evidence suggested was that the Daimler driver had been drinking for most of the day, that he was well over the limit and whilst under the influence his driving judgement had been affected to the point where he had driven in the centre of the road around a bend and collided head on into the Peugeot car driving in the opposite direction. Also, that following the accident he had left the scene to consume alcohol in an effort to frustrate any subsequent breathalyser test and to top it all had refused to give a later sample because he feared that it would show a very high reading.

Proving these facts would be likely to result in a charge of causing death by reckless driving which is an extremely serious offence likely to result in imprisonment.

However, to do so we needed to prove firstly that the accident was caused by the Daimler driver, secondly that the actions of the young man driving the Peugeot were not contributory in any way by virtue of excessive speed or position of the car in the road, thirdly that the driver had been drinking excessively and fourthly, despite the fact he had refused samples that the Daimler driver would have been over the limit at the time of collision and that his actions were reckless.

If there was no evidence of the excessive drinking over the limit then we were left with the probability of just careless driving in the centre of the road. If we could not prove that the actions of the driver caused the collision but could prove the drinking aspects then we would probably be left with just refusing the breath samples.

Cases such as this merit considerable time and effort to investigate in detail. We were assisted by a very competent accident investigator who pieced together a reconstruction of the scene by way of scale plans, video analysis and aerial photographs. These facts showed that the Daimler driver had been in the centre of the road at the time of the collision and that the Peugeot had been travelling correctly within speed limits on its correct side of the road. It also refuted any suggestion of weather or road conditions as being contributory causes. Furthermore, vehicle examination of the Peugeot showed it was roadworthy and post mortem results on the deceased driver showed that there was no evidence of alcohol present in his body. By process of elimination it was possible to show that the actions by the Daimler driver rather than anything else had resulted in the collision and subsequent death of the young man concerned.

However, we were still left with the allegations regarding the Daimler driver drinking before the accident and how much he had actually drunk over a period of time and what would have been left in his body at the time of the incident.

Brian and I made inquiries of every pub in the vicinity of where we suspected the driver had been that day both near his place of work and his home address. We spoke to staff at the pubs and where these inquiries showed that he had been drinking we traced and interviewed every customer who had been there at the time.

Gradually, over a period of time we built up a picture that showed during the day of the collision the Daimler driver had been drinking over a period of time which amounted to about 7 hours and were able to estimate the amount he had consumed which consisted of lager, stout and wine.

The next stage once this had been compiled was to get a scientific opinion from an expert as to an estimation of how much alcohol would have been in the driver's body at the time he was involved in the crash. This of course would depend on the type of alcohol, the amount, over what period consumed, and the likely absorption rate into the body which amongst other factors would depend on the size and body weight of the driver.

We established all of these facts and then sent off the evidence to a forensic scientist for a conservative estimate as to what any alcohol reading in blood/breath would have been at the time of the incident. The result was that even taking the minimum estimation of intake and allowing for maximum absorption rate the driver would have had a very high reading of alcohol in his body if he had consented to having samples taken on the night in question.

It took several months to piece all this together in painstaking detail. Eventually, we re-interviewed the driver, who showed no remorse even when faced with all the evidence. We submitted a comprehensive file of evidence to the Crown Prosecution Service who had only recently been established as the independent prosecuting body in England and

Wales and they sanctioned a prosecution for death by reckless driving and refusing the breath samples.

At this point we felt we had overcome a massive hurdle. However, any experienced police officer knows that at the point where you submit a file the prosecution evidence is at its best. There was every indication by the defence that they would fight this case tooth and nail, had employed their own investigators to go over the evidence and that we that could expect a robust defence at Crown Court.

When the trial eventually came it was 16 months after the collision occurred. During the interim period the allegations/complaints that had prevented my promotion had been largely lifted and three and half years after being initially selected I was promoted to Inspector.

I had been promoted for about 9 months when the trial for death by reckless driving took place at Worcester Crown Court over six days.

Firstly the defence needed to refute the evidence we had accumulated regarding pre-collision drinking and then the evidence of the scientist regarding the fact that he would have still been over the limit at the time of the incident. When it was my turn in the witness box I was cross examined as anticipated on the basis that I was mistaken in believing the driver had been under the effects of alcohol when I had seen him at the scene of the accident and afterwards at the hospital. They alleged that my judgement was clouded because I knew the mother of the young man killed and therefore was making a biased judgement. I refuted this vigorously because I knew it was rubbish, but I was unsure what the jury or indeed the judge would make of it. This allegation was repeated at several junctures in the trial and remained a constant theme for the defence in an effort to discredit my evidence.

They produced their own expert, a very eminent pathologist (who also worked for the police as a Home Office pathologist) to dispute the evidence given by the forensic scientist as to the amount of alcohol that would have been present and the fact that the driver would have been under the drink drive limit.

When it came to the collision scene itself our evidence rested solely with accident investigation officer, PC Paul Fulbrook. Again the defence had employed their own expert. When an expert witness is used then unlike the police and other lay witnesses they have the opportunity of being in court whilst the other side give their evidence so they can feed questions to the prosecuting counsel to ask the witness on the stand. Then they give their own evidence, drawing out the contradictions in opinion.

Paul gave his evidence extremely well. However, he was cross examined over a period of two days in intimate detail regarding every possible aspect of the conclusions he had reached regarding the cause of the collision and position of the vehicles. He was even questioned about the very basis of triangulation of measurement and fixed points upon which accident investigators base their scaled measurements. At one point even the Judge became somewhat frustrated at the questioning of basic scientific theory and formula but Paul remained calm, answered every question with meticulous accuracy showing that he was a master of his subject and would not be moved from basic fundamental points. In addition, for the benefit of the jury the Judge asked him to translate all of his metric measurements into imperial.

I have to say that it was one of the most professional examples of a police officer giving evidence I have ever seen despite being under extreme pressure. After the trial I arranged for Paul to receive a personal commendation both because of his professional ability and the way in which he efficiently presented it at court.

However, when the defence expert gave his evidence he was also very confident and at a complete tangent to the conclusions that Paul had reached where he placed the blame for the collision on the deceased driver.

Inferences were made that the Peugeot driver must have been travelling faster than Paul estimated. Sometimes gamesmanship gets played in court and at one point the defence barrister slipped into his summing up that that the Peugeot car was a GTI which was completely untrue. This of course could leave an impression on any jury that the car was a faster version of saloon than it was and leave them to infer that maybe it was being driven faster than the prosecution evidence suggested.

Fortunately, our barrister was a mature sound counsel who immediately picked up on the point, admonished the defence and corrected the false inference.

On the sixth day the jury retired to consider their verdict. The family of the deceased driver were in the public gallery as they had been throughout the trial and I knew they were listening to every word. Also, I knew that a conviction would give them some comfort but that an acquittal would devastate them. As the officer in the case I felt responsible and accountable if the prosecution case was not proved. Had I missed something? Could I have done more? I was in trepidation as to the result.

I was also aware of certain facts in relation to the defendant that would only come out if he was convicted and which for professional reasons I had not disclosed to the family or anyone other than the prosecution. This was in relation to his previous driving history which I knew would shock both the court and the family of the deceased.

After what seemed an eternity the jury returned and said they could not reach a unanimous verdict. The judge allowed them to retire again and to reach a majority verdict.

Eventually they returned and found the defendant guilty of death by reckless driving.

I looked up at the family of the deceased boy and could see them emotional and relieved but treating the occasion with the respect it deserved.

I felt numb but did not have time to dwell on this because I was called into the witness box to give details of the defendant's previous convictions and driving history. The police court officer had volunteered to do this for me but I declined the offer because I wanted to deliver it as sensitively as possible. I knew what I was about to say would come as a shock to a number of people.

I outlined what I would describe as an extremely serious driving record which stretched back over 18 years.

From complete silence there were suddenly gasps of disbelief from around the court.

I was concerned about the effect on the family of the deceased. I could see they appeared shocked and bewildered but were calm. I felt guilty in not being able to forewarn them but if I had done so and he had not been convicted then I could have been in breach of disclosing confidential information. I could not have released the information to any other family and therefore could not release it to them until inevitably it became public information following conviction. Afterwards, when I explained, they graciously said they understood and I think they were just relieved it was over.

In passing sentence the Judge said to the defendant, 'You are a menace to public safety. Your driving record is probably the most appalling I have ever seen. I have been unable to detect any sign of remorse.' He sentenced him to 4 years imprisonment for death by reckless driving (at the time the maximum was 5 years) and gave an additional short imprisonment sentence for refusing to give the breath samples. He was disqualified from driving for 15 years.

The parents of the deceased driver told me that they received some comfort from knowing justice had been done but nothing would ever bring their young son back.

I took some consolation from the fact that we had achieved a result, in some ways against all odds. It had been a difficult and at times traumatic case and the anniversary of that collision and the memories of that night remain with me till now. The family will of course never forget. On that fateful night a number of people's lives would never be the same again and that is the nature of such sudden, tragic and unexpected events.

CHAPTER 19

CORNFLAKES WITH WHISKY

'Spec, Spec, there's a telex for your attention.' Denise brought me a telex and dropped it on my desk at the podium where I was sitting. Two things irritated me. The first was the expression 'Spec' which was short for 'Inspector' and which was used constantly by members of staff instead of Inspector, Sir, Mr. King or even just 'Les.'

The second thing that irritated me as I stared at the telex was that it appeared to be in a completely nonsensical language that I could not read.

'Denise, you had better check the telex machine, its churning out rubbish so I can't even read the message. It must be the print ribbon that's damaged.'

Denise came across and smiled at me with a look that I felt was more out of pity than friendliness. 'It's a coded message Spec from the Ministry of Defence. You need to decipher it – we don't have access to the codes but you do in your secret cabinet.'

I didn't have a clue where to start. Here I was a newly promoted Inspector sitting in the Force Operations room at West Mercia Police headquarters which is situated at Hindlip Hall in a beautiful old mansion house near Worcester.

If ever there was a fish out of water it was me. I had been in the Police at that time for 20 years. All my experience had been in either operational patrol or community policing. But, here I was in a completely fresh role as one of five Inspectors responsible 24/7 for the Force operations and control centre which forms the heart and the hub of policing across the three counties of Shropshire, Herefordshire and Worcestershire.

It was full of computers, radios, telex machines, faxes, switchboards, phones, tapes and just everything else electronic I had very little experience of operating. Everything was down to process, systems and secret codes where most things were confidential and some highly sensitive such as this telex which I could not decipher.

Policing the streets is always familiar. The town, the geography, the people might all be different but a fight is a fight and an arrest is an arrest. You can find your way around but the situation in the force control room was a new and specialised area that is a completely new discipline to most who went to work there.

Within my first week I was on nights when again one of the operators shouted, 'Spec, Spec, PNC is down.' The only bit of this I understood was that PNC is short for the Police National Computer system which basically both then and now is the lifeblood of policing and upon which police officers rely completely to check for people wanted, missing and their previous convictions supplemented by other local systems. I wasn't sure where it had gone down to or who it had gone down on but the problem was obviously mine!

'What do I do then?' I asked. The answer was to ring PNC headquarters in the Metropolitan Police and tell them. This I did, whereupon one very helpful gentlemen told me that what I needed to do was to refresh the red button energiser on the kilo-stream box and all would be fixed. This did not enlighten me....We had a brief conversation in which I asked him what he knew about the Police and Criminal Evidence Act Codes of Practice and the duties of a custody officer sergeant. He replied somewhat confused, 'Not a lot.'

I then proceeded to tell him that his knowledge of being a custody officer which is what I had been doing the week before was just about the limit of what I understood about computers and that what I knew about the subject I could write down on the perforations of a postage stamp or a gnat's private parts and that it would be ever so helpful if he explained to me in 'dummy' language what the hell he was on about.

Eventually, after negotiating several locked doors and alarms I found my way into the main computer room at Hindlip where I found a manual. I followed the instructions and inputted a number of codes into the central keyboard. I then looked around the room and saw a box marked 'Kilostream' which on the front had a red button. I pressed the red button and PNC immediately leapt into life, no longer a patient on intensive care.

Whilst I realised this did not actually qualify me as a computer programmer I was very proud and lost no time at all in telling all and sundry I was now a 'computer whizz kid.'

The job of duty Inspector in the Force Operations was complex and highly responsible. Not only were we responsible for keeping the technology rolling across the Force out of hours but it also involved supervision of the motorway network that went through the area including the M5, M50 and M54. This meant control of motorway signs, diversions, accidents and being the control centre for roadside assistance and monitoring of the CCTV system.

The job also involved taking control of all firearms incidents, police pursuits and all the routine, major and serious incidents that occurred across the three counties. It was also overseeing and planning for major events and operations including security of VIPs and liaison with military and other specialised units over terrorist incidents and exercises.

The operations room was the hub of contingency planning and control for all foreseeable and unforeseeable incidents and my particular specialism was keeping the highly confidential operational orders and plans up to date.

Out of hours the Inspector represented Chief Officers and had to report to them anything that required their consent or knowledge whatever the time of day or night.

I quickly developed considerable respect for both the staff that worked in the operations room sometimes under quite considerable pressure and also the specialised departments of the police I had not previously come into contact with such as traffic, firearms, helicopter unit and special branch.

I would describe the job as sometimes long periods of boredom when quiet, interspersed with short periods of mayhem when a job kicked off.

Most of the communications and conversations were taped and after an incident you became very accountable for every action you had carried out or authorised.

However, my early months in the operations room were somewhat diverted by having to give evidence in several not guilty trials that were left over from my previous two and a half years of operational policing at Kidderminster. Most of the defendants at the trials were those who had previously lodged complaints against me and colleagues so a lot rested on the results of the trials. Even though the complaints had reached a stage where the judgement of the Deputy Chief Constable was that I could be promoted I was aware that a lot of them were live and anything interpreted as untoward during the process of giving evidence by either the defence or the complaints department could easily result in additional complaints or aggravate the issues already outstanding.

The trials were in both Crown and Magistrates Courts and I approached them with some trepidation on the basis that although I knew I had done nothing wrong, when in court anything can happen and cross-examinations can be pretty fierce making it appear you have done something wrong even if you haven't!

I was not to be disappointed. At the conclusion of one trial at Hereford Crown Court during which there were considerable arguments about allowing a confession to stand the Judge summoned me back into the witness box and stated that although he was not alleging that I had broken the codes of practice under the Police and Criminal Evidence Act by no means did he think I had entered into 'the spirit' of them?

I interpreted this as his meaning that whilst I had done nothing wrong technically or legally he believed I had been responsible for some sharp practice as a result of which he did not feel the confession could be relied upon and hence the prosecution were obliged to offer no evidence and the case was dismissed.

I started to ask the Judge where the reference in law to the 'spirit of the codes of practice' was but was immediately interrupted by the prosecuting barrister who gave me a look that said, 'Stop there or else you will held in contempt.' I said no more.

On another occasion at Kidderminster Magistrate Court whilst giving evidence in a not guilty breathalyser case in which I had administered the intoximeter procedure in the station I got involved in an argument with the defence solicitor and magistrates to the point where the magistrates threatened me that if I didn't shut up and go to the back of the court they would hold me in contempt of court! As an Inspector in full uniform I felt like a scalded schoolboy and felt that this was completely over the top. Nevertheless, in court it is their jurisdiction and even though technically the points I was making were correct there has to be a time to be subservient to the court.

That was followed soon afterwards by another trial at Kidderminster Magistrates Court where both myself and a fellow Sergeant were accused of giving a prisoner we had arrested the 'short caution.' I hadn't got a clue what the defence solicitor was on about until he accused me of physically hitting the man which had not occurred and which we denied strenuously.

A lot of this is in the hustle and bustle of policing and which has to be expected. However, after three and half years of being on a promotion list and two and half years of complaints and allegations I had really had enough. Whenever, I left home to give evidence I knew that the dock was only ever a short distance from the witness box in policing terms when under pressure in court and Jud used to make a joke but seriously worry about whether or not I would lose it and not be home for tea!

When people think about the dangers of policing, they usually equate them with the physical dangers. Most cops know that the real dangers lie in vindictive complaints or misinterpreted actions that can be the real career stoppers. At higher ranks it is the politics now that get you.

However, we survived and won some cases, lost others.

In the September of 1990 I was sent on an Inspectors Development Course at the West Midlands Police Training centre which is situated at 'Tally Ho,'

Edgbaston in Birmingham. The course which was 6 weeks in duration was intensive and was designed to prepare officers for senior management in the police. Overall, it was excellent and provided time to refuel the batteries to the point that when I came back I really felt like an Inspector rather than a sergeant in an Inspector's uniform. It prepared me for the challenges that lay ahead and there were to be plenty of them.

One of those challenges was surviving six weeks of living away from home in Birmingham within the capital of Balti land at Balsall Heath combined with imbibing copious amounts of alcohol in the police club bar at Tally Ho and surrounding hostelries of which there were many.

The natural inclination is to try and do something to get fit and offset the effects of generous living. This is where a conflict lies and where I do have to smile. Time and time again I have seen officers try to do this and fail miserably. I will give an example of Bob.

Bob was one of the delegates on the course from one of the Midland forces. He had just been promoted uniformed inspector having spent about twenty years on CID. He was a big man, with a big appetite, a bigger thirst and a large belly that had been well-earned over the years. On the first night, knowing that he was away from home he decided that to get fit he would go out jogging with some rather younger, slimmer and fitter colleagues who were perhaps more accustomed to physical exercise that Bob had been for the past twenty or so years. I saw him leave his room wearing the regulatory shorts and a t-shirt that exposed a few inches of generous midriff. I gained the impression that the last time he had worn it he had probably been at school.

As he set off with the others with the best of intentions, his 6'2' bulky frame ambling towards the idealistic utopia of super fitness I did wonder when or indeed if he would ever come back and offered my advice to be realistic and play a game of cards instead. He dismissed my concerns and ran off bringing up the rear of his contemporaries.

I lay on the bed and had a doze. After about 40 minutes the runners returned but there was no sign of Bob. They had all showered, changed and were on their way to tea by the time Bob appeared an hour late stumbling up the corridor, colliding into the walls and collapsed onto his bed where he remained for 12 hours solid in a big heap unable to move.

The following day he was subject to some ridicule and taunts of: 'We told you so.' The following evening he was invited to join the crowd again and who asked if he was joining them for a jog. The reply was something like, 'No, thank you, piss off I am going for a Balti and a beer,' as he donned his whistle and flute (suit) for an evening's entertainment.

Now, based on Bob's experience you would think I would have known better.

However, determined that I must do something to keep my body beautiful I decided to be more subtle and join an aerobics induction class which consisted mainly of women but a few men. I tried to keep it quiet but some of the lads on the course found out and came to watch me from the gym windows.

I had never done aerobics before and didn't quite know what to expect. We started off being serenaded by tunes of Madonna which quickly picked up pace. I positioned myself behind a rather attractive policewoman and decided to try and concentrate upon the rhythmic motion of her very shapely bottom in an effort to divert the engulfing feelings of sickness and breathlessness which were quickly starting to make me feel distinctly unwell. However, not being one to give up easily I kept going but I realised something was wrong when I started to lose all means of co-ordination and that my movements of arms and legs were in direct contradiction to everyone else's in the class who seemed to be very familiar with the routine for an induction class. I could see the lads making gestures of fun at me and laughing their nuts off but no matter how hard I tried I could not regain the correct rhythm.

Suddenly, things started to go black, I felt dizzy and I knew something was wrong when I started being sick all over the floor and then collapsed.

The music stopped, the class dispersed due to lack of interest and the lads watching through the windows thought it was hilarious! The only person who was concerned was the very fit female instructor who was obviously not relishing the thought of being the first instructor at Tally Ho to have a corpse in her class. I was hoping for the kiss of life but even the thought of sudden death didn't seem to encourage her to embark down that road.

After a few sips of water and with my head stuck between my legs I started to recover.

I said to her that I was surprised with the pace of the class for an induction session whereupon she told me it was actually an advanced class and that obviously I had read the timetable wrong. A combination of that, skipping meals in order to make up for the evenings intake of food and beer and the fact that I hadn't exercised properly for about 20 years might have been the reason why I collapsed. That night I joined Bob for a beer and a Balti!

I have to say, although this sounds very macho there is nothing like great company on a course. After a few days you get to know each other extremely well and a strong bond develops because of the common denominator of being a cop. Most cops have a great sense of humour and one of my fondest memories was one evening being in Tally Ho police club drinking and swapping jokes and stories to the point where I was virtually ill through laughing. It was during this particular evening that I was told a joke about a donkey called 'Wanker' which I have recited thousands of times since but is not for the pages of this book! A fantastic time was had by all but this went alongside a lot of hard work which had to be followed up and assessed when we returned back to the work-place.

Back in the operations room it was business as usual. Once at work you were fully on call and had to be available to respond and take control of any serious incident. This meant that if you left the operations room even to go to the toilet you had to take a radio to maintain contact with the control. A couple of years later after I left this post and was working in a non-operational role I used to keep telling my secretary when I was going to the toilet who used to look at me quizzically and say, 'Too much information Les.'

Some shifts were full of endless pressure and stress and several examples spring to mind.

These are the shifts where when you finish duty after a hard night shift, (because most of the tough shifts always seem to be on nights), I used to indulge myself in a bowl of cornflakes and a glass of whisky. The cornflakes were because I usually felt hungry and wanted to stem any pangs of hunger before going to bed, the whisky because I always felt I needed a drink to celebrate getting through a tortuous night. Sometimes, as a time management exercise to prevent doing two things I would just chuck the whisky over the cornflakes and milk – heaven!

During a relatively calm night shift in charge of the force operations room on a balmy August evening in which I was relieved to be sitting in air-conditioned accommodation I received a telephone call to authorise armed officers to attend a suspicious incident at Telford where a man had been seen on foot at a service station carrying a gun and that he was being searched for by local officers.

I made an immediate appraisal of the information and decided it warranted armed officers attending. I immediately despatched a firearms response double crewed vehicle which was on the M5 motorway and instructed them to report immediately to the duty inspector at Telford. As they were making their way I rang the Assistant Chief Constable on call at his home and sought authority to back this up with further armed officers and formalise the firearms response calling on a fully trained firearms tactical advisor to attend the scene.

The ACC gave the authority but then I knew I had a problem. Our top firearms team was the force task force which consisted of officers who specialised in this area of work. However, they were unavailable being committed on a covert operation.

This meant that it was necessary to call out officers from each of the divisions who were trained and authorised to be issued firearms and get them on their way to Telford where they would be co-ordinated and come under the supervision of a firearms commander and the tactical advisor. I then called out the firearms commander on call who was a Superintendent. The tactical advisor I chose was a sergeant who was an authority on the use of firearms within the force.

After numerous telephone calls and a fairly frantic period of time by both me and my staff in Ops room we managed to get a firearms team together at Telford to supplement the initial firearms crew I had sent from the motorway who had held the fort in the interim period.

After a while I satisfied myself that we had done what we could at that stage and feedback from the division was that they thought the man concerned was in a certain area and had been contained by putting an outer cordon of firearms officers around that area.

As is always the case in these situations information is confusing and often not complete.

I settled back with a cup of tea to nurse a dry mouth and was about to take the second swig when I received an urgent call from the Duty Inspector, Colin West at Redditch.

Colin informed me that they had received reports of a man going berserk with a firearm in the centre of one of the villages on the outskirts of Bromsgrove who it was believed had fired the gun in the street and was causing some commotion in the middle of the night!

My immediate reaction was that Colin had heard the situation going on at Telford, knew the limited resources we were working with and decided to wind me up. However, the tone and urgency of his voice very quickly convinced me this was a genuine request.

Once again it was a case of ringing the Assistant Chief Constable and getting permission to arm officers. Then, arranging for some further authorised shots to be got out of bed (we were now struggling for available officers and had already exhausted those that were on call) plus I needed another firearms tactical advisor. I immediately diverted the tactical advisor who had only just started on his way to Telford to go to Bromsgrove and then arranged for another officer who was available even though he was not on call and who lived in Shropshire to undertake the same tactical advisor role in Telford.

An unarmed crew were available on the outskirts of the village area pending the arrival of the armed response officers to maintain a discreet low profile, make no approaches but try to maintain a watching brief and contact with the control to keep everyone up to speed with what was happening because in circumstances like this things change every few seconds. It was at this point that things changed dramatically. These two officers were parked in what they considered to be a safe location according to the last reports from the public. Anecdotal information given to me afterwards was that they were therefore somewhat surprised to be disturbed by a man knocking on the side window of the car with a weapon slung over his shoulder who said: 'Are you looking for me?' This was the man they were looking for but I think my response might have been, 'No, not at all mate!'

Fortunately, he was compliant and handed himself in. I believe from later reports that he was ex military who had retained a number of weapons and ammunition, (a large quantity was recovered from his home address) who lived locally and had just gone off on one but fortunately non-one had been injured and no serious damage caused. This was a very fortunate event that could have turned out completely differently. It wound down quite quickly, local officers were left to deal with the offender and I resumed my attention to monitoring the Telford incident.

After what seemed a prolonged period of time as I settled back down to the second cup of cold tea things started to erupt at Telford.

We suddenly started receiving reports from the scene that the man with the gun had either broken out of the firearms cordon or had never been in it in the first place because he was now believed to be heading towards a nearby railway station in the town of Wellington which is part of the Telford conurbation. At the scene of a firearms incident the officers actually in the operation have their own radio communication which in those days we could not monitor. We were therefore relying on relayed reports via telephone or VHF force radio to keep updated with events.

After a few minutes a call came in to say that the man with the gun had been shot by police officers and that he was on his way to the local hospital.

My heart sunk because I realised what the implications for this would be not only to the individual involved and their family but also the Police officers involved and those responsible for making the operational and management decisions both at the scene and for us in the operations room.

We waited anxiously for news as to the man's condition. We did not have to wait long before it was confirmed that he was dead. I immediately rang the ACC for the umpteenth time that night to update him. He had long since given up trying to sleep and was waiting for my call. When I told him the news he said, 'Right Inspector, you've got a murder on your hands.'

My immediate reaction was to say, 'Can we be a little more inclusive sir, WE have a murder on our hands.' At that moment in time I was feeling rather isolated and sat on a podium in the force operations room seemed to be a very lonely place even though I was over 50 miles away from where the shooting had actually taken place.

However, I knew exactly what he meant. Although this was an authorised police operation the scene and everything that followed had to be treated as we would treat a murder scene with the added complications that this was the Police responsible for the death and nothing could be assumed as lawful until full inquiries had taken place which would take months. In the interim period the priority was the preservation of the evidence and ensuring that technical resilience and resources were available combined with ensuring someone independent was appointed to lead the inquiry.

What followed over the next few hours was an intense period of activity in ensuring all aspects were covered including dealing with the media and the immediate aftermath of questions that were likely, quite rightly, to be asked.

What transpired was that the man who had been shot was a 24-year old man who was local to the area and suffered from mental health issues.

Subsequently, it came to light that the man killed had been in possession an air pistol which was incapable of being fired. However, of course the officers could not be aware of this at the time and defended their actions on the basis that they had been threatened by the man with the weapon and had to take the action they did. That decision and the events surrounding it were subject to extensive independent examination by Merseyside Police who carried out the inquiry on behalf of the Police Complaints Authority (the independent body at the time responsible for overseeing complaints against Police or incidents referred for supervision to the Authority by Police).

This referral was done before I left duty that morning before I got home for the cornflakes and whisky.

The following evening I was on nights again and was praying for a quiet night. However, before mid-night I received a call from Wellington Police Station to say that the station was under siege and they were being forced to take refuge from youths who had gathered outside and were stoning the station demanding justice for the shot man and making physical threats against the police in retaliation for the shooting.

This necessitated calling together local PSU's (Police Support Units) of police officers with the resources to quell what was turning into a riot.

This continued throughout that night and the following days with considerable impact for the local community in Telford and policing resources throughout West Mercia. In addition there were personal threats being made in some quarters against the two officers who had carried out the shooting which raised security problems for them and their families resulting in contingency plans to protect them. The whole thing seemed to escalate with a different tangent each day. This was a distressing time for all involved especially the family of the deceased, the local community and those officers directly involved in the incident.

The inquiry from my perspective was intensive and thorough. I was personally interviewed by Merseyside senior officers as to my actions and decision-making that night as well as checking a transcript of several hours of long telephone conversations which had been taken from my phone extension and radio transmissions.

This must have been an extremely worrying time for the two officers involved who were also subject to an internal disciplinary investigation. Few people will ever find themselves having to make instant life and death decisions with limited information and then have to justify those actions knowing that their own liberty and career may be at risk. There have been many other examples since and all I can say is, it is very easy in these situations and with hindsight to be an arm-chair commentator.

In February of 1992 an inquest was held with a jury in which over a period of three weeks, 57 witnesses were called to give evidence. The jury reached a majority verdict that the killing had been lawful.

This verdict was not accepted by the family of the man shot who called for a public inquiry and voiced their frustrations as to how the whole inquiry had been conducted.

Following such a traumatic event I guess there will always be irreconcilable differences of opinion and perspectives from those involved with no one conclusion that will satisfy all those involved. Overall, this was a sad and tragic event for the family and all concerned and one in which all those closely involved will continue to remember.

Twenty years later I bumped into one of the officers involved in the shooting in a police canteen having lunch. We reflected on the events of that night and he said, 'Yeah, thanks for the call out that night Les - not!'

Alongside the events I have just described the death of a police officer on duty will usually rank as one of the most emotional events.

It was another night shift in Ops room and it was April. The Ops room shifts were generally coterminous with the shifts of officers who worked the motorway and hence we all knew each other extremely well. Very often traffic officers would come into Ops room to use the kitchen facilities during their breaks and radio transmissions with them were constant in dealing with incidents on the motorway.

I got to learn a lot about the specialism of motorway patrol work whilst working in ops room and held a healthy respect for the officers who patrolled. When things happen on the motorway it is sudden, at fast speed and highly dangerous, requiring officers to drive at fast speeds and react quickly to changing events. However, not only did they patrol the motorway they would also patrol the areas surrounding the motorway services and junctions in order to vary their routine and very often catch offenders up to no good.

The common perception is that traffic officers just deal with traffic and only deal with motoring offences. In fact most officers are heavily involved in detecting quite serious crime because most criminals are either on their way to commit crime or on their way back using vehicles that merit being stopped. I have never failed to be amazed at the aptitude that some officers have for developing a nose for a dodgy vehicle or a criminal driving it. If they stop 10 cars, 8 of them will either have offences on the vehicle or the driver will be disqualified, drunk or the vehicle stolen with drugs or something stolen on board.

On this particular April night the shifts had only just booked on the radio to commence their patrols.

There were two crews in the vicinity of the M5 motorway. Not long after the shift had commenced the one crew shouted up on the radio for assistance because the crew in the other car had come off the road and crashed. From word go it sounded serious. The accident was on a road in south Worcestershire and one of the feeder routes surrounding the M5. Immediate feedback was that the driver's condition was not too bad but that the passenger who was a male officer was seriously injured.

An ambulance was sent and I arranged for the motorway sergeant covering the unit that night to attend the scene and investigate the circumstances.

Whilst I had been in Ops room for about 12 months at that stage I was not as familiar as perhaps I should have been with regard to all the radio codes used as shorthand to prevent long conversations. After what felt like an eternity I asked one of the operators to contact the sergeant at the scene and ascertain what was happening. The response came back, 'It's five one over, repeat five one.' I could tell from the operators face this was serious but was not familiar with the code. I screamed at him, 'What the hell is five one?' The reply came, 'It's a fatal boss, the officer is dead.'

In those split seconds as the mind registers what has been said there are a mixture of emotions and concerns combined with the full realisation of what these mean to so many people, primarily the officer's family and colleagues. Some staff in the Ops room immediately burst into tears and I could feel myself frozen with concern on a number of fronts.

The priority was to get the scene under control, to preserve the evidence, to get the driver treated and to inform the officer's family.

I called senior officers responsible for the traffic department out of bed and we made a log of all actions as well as providing the mechanism to get things under-way.

Immediately I knew there were serious questions to be considered that would require a full and extensive investigation as to how the accident had occurred and why.

Those investigations took months. Everyone was devastated by what had happened and I can only begin to imagine the pain the family went through in losing someone at the young age of 32 years when just doing his job.

This was an extremely sad and tragic incident and for me personally and many others, losing a colleague on duty was a night we will never forget

Pursuits: When a police car is following a specific vehicle usually at speed and usually with a view to stopping the vehicle and apprehending the occupants it is called a 'pursuit.'

The term 'pursuit' is important because it brings into being certain protocols and procedures that make the police very accountable for the safe conduct of the pursuit to try and ensure no-one is injured. This is a fine line and requires instant assimilation of facts, decision-making, risk-assessment and keen judgement based on sometimes very limited information.

In the protocols at that time there were three key decision-makers who at any time could make the decision to call off the pursuit based on the dangers it presented when balanced against the merits of apprehending the offenders. Those three key people were a) the crew of the police car in pursuit b) the controller of the incident in the operations room and c) the duty inspector/supervisor in the control room. That decision was then final.

What does that mean in practice? Well, it means that as duty inspector one night I was on the toilet but monitoring what was happening by carrying a personal radio when I was called and told a pursuit was underway. When I entered the Ops room everything was a flurry of activity. It took a few seconds for me to work out what was going on but eventually I realised that a Police fast response car consisting of highly trained drivers was in pursuit of a car travelling extremely fast in the area of south Worcestershire.

There appeared to be at least two people in the car being pursued by Police but it was unclear why they were trying to evade being stopped by Police for a routine check.

Herein of course lies the question? Despite no record on the police computer was the car stolen? Have the occupants committed a robbery or burglary and have stolen property on board? Have they kidnapped someone? Are they wanted by the Police? Or, are they just playing games have no driving documents, disqualified from driving, drunk or have no tax?

Balanced against that of course there needs to be an immediate assessment of what are the speed and driving conditions. Is it a built of area? How busy are the roads? What is the weather and visibility and how competent are the crew of the Police car to maintain the pursuit? Are there other Police patrols, dog handlers or a Force helicopter available to assist? Then the controller needs to assess where the vehicle might be heading and think ahead as to mobilising support ahead of the immediate incident in case they suddenly abandon the car and run off on foot.

All of this then is information that has to be digested in a few seconds as an immediate risk-assessment and decision-making in circumstances which are changing constantly.

Should it be obvious that the vehicle is wanted in connection with a serious crime and it is travelling late at night in a quiet rural area where there is minimal chance of danger the decision to maintain the pursuit becomes easy. Suppose though as in this case, there was no clear reason why they wanted to evade the police and we reach a point where it is obvious that to continue the pursuit could be dangerous because the roads are busy and there is obvious danger. This was the example I faced and at the point where I could see it was speeding through built up areas and there was no chance of getting the Force helicopter to monitor I made a decision to call off the pursuit and much to the disgust of the Police crew told them to back off and follow at a safe distance.

The exasperation in their voices over the radio was obvious. Then after approximately a couple of miles they came across the car which had left the road, collided into a tree and it looked as if the car was about to catch fire. The officers then did as Police officers naturally do, they put their own lives at risk to drag the two occupants out of the car until they were safe. They survived, were treated and eventually prosecuted for offences in relation to dangerous driving. I was never made aware of the reason for them trying to drive away because the inquiries were concluded well after I finished duty.

What I do know though is this. If I had not called off the pursuit and those two young men had died or been seriously injured whilst being actively pursued by the Police the people answering the questions would have been the Police whatever misdemeanours may have been committed. Tough decisions have to be made, sometimes with limited information. Is it right that the Police must always err on the side of safety? Is it right that every car thief knows that if you are caught by the Police, just drive off like a maniac and you will always get off? On the other hand suppose someone innocent gets killed? These are close calls of judgement made sometimes under extreme pressure but heaven help you if you get it wrong.

Another example was a motorway patrol car containing two officers being driven through Ross-on-Wye, Herefordshire late at night having just left the M50. Suddenly, on the radio came a call to say that they were in pursuit of a stolen car which had just been used in a ram-raid in Gloucestershire the same night. This was part of a series of ram-raids that was taking place along the southern boundary areas of West Mercia adjoining Gloucestershire.

It was late at night, not a lot of traffic, in a rural area and we knew that the vehicle was stolen and had been used in serious crime. It was an easy decision to allow the pursuit to take place.

The radio transmissions were monitored and it became apparent that the car was being chased into the rural lanes on the outskirts of Ross. The Police car was able to keep up quite easily and the observer was giving an excellent update on progress. However, there was a point where the radio airwaves burst into life something like this commentary.

Police observer in car: 'The car in front is slowing down, slowing down over. The car in front is stopping. They have stopped. Crikey, they have just kicked out the rear screen. Bloody hell they are pointing a gun at us.'

The next sound was a continual stream of anxious comments from the Police officers and the sound of the Police car being reversed backwards in a hurry! This was a pursuit in reverse.

As the engine revs accelerated suddenly there was the sound of a thud, then a crash, and then a deathly hush.

The operator tried calling the patrol for several seconds and someone arranged for other patrols to attend the scene.

It was a relief when a few seconds later the radio blasted into life again and the crew stated that they were both safe and explained what had happened.

At the point where they thought that a gun had been pointed at them they reversed like hell but the car in front also reversed backwards. The police driver then misjudged the road and drove into a wide ditch where the police car toppled over onto its side. Both officers were then trapped, had no time to get out and were convinced they would just be killed.

The stolen car then just stopped in the road adjacent to where they were lying in the ditch.

Convinced they were done-for the police driver turned off the headlights of the car and they just waited. Suddenly there was the sound of laughter and the car drove off. Phew!

Eventually the occupants of the stolen car were arrested and charged with a number of smash-and-grab burglaries across the south Herefordshire Gloucestershire borders.

Another not so favourite duty in the Ops room for the duty inspector was going out live on local radio. This usually occurred at least twice a day to do routine traffic broadcasts and at other ad hoc times whenever there was a serious incident that required broadcasting to inform the public.

On an early turn shift just after breakfast motorway patrols were at the scene of a lorry which had overturned where the M5 motorway joins the M50 at a place known as Trumpet bend. Police patrols had cordoned off the nearside land and hard shoulder and put out Police warning signs. Unfortunately, one unsuspecting motorist whilst driving a very nice BMW car down the motorway at a fast rate of knots, failed to observe the signs in time whilst negotiating onto the M50 and clipped one of the Police warning signs. This sent the sign winging straight over the roof of one of the nearby Police cars which hit the blue light and then catapulted straight into the chest of a very large Police officer who was at the scene supervising the recovery of the lorry. The car stopped momentarily, the driver got out and then leapt back into the car and drove off in a puff of smoke.

The first we knew of the incident in Ops room was when an extremely breathless officer crawled to the patrol car and put out an emergency red call on the radio for assistance.

He sounded dreadful and our first impression was that he was seriously injured or dying and that potentially we had a non-stop fatal Police road death on our hands and that unless we acted quickly the offending driver and car would never be traced.

We had a method of immediately transmitting urgent traffic information to all radio media via a network known as RoadTraf. This meant sending an urgent telex to a central media location number who would then send it out over the airwaves to radio stations if necessary nationwide in order to warn motorists of traffic crises.

We had sufficient information from officers at the scene to describe the vehicle, the driver and the direction of travel. So, rightly or wrongly I decide to use the RoadTraf message to appeal for the driver to give himself up and go to the nearest Police station or for other motorists to ring in with information.

By now other officers at the scene were able to tell us that the officer was not seriously injured just very winded, in pain and angry. However, the broadcast worked wonders. Within a few minutes the driver heard the broadcast and even though we had no registration number he decided to go into Malvern Police Station and give himself up.

When he was asked why he didn't stop at the scene he said something like, 'I did stop, I got out of the car and walked back to where I could see a Police officer lying on the floor who I realised was injured. I started to go towards him, whereupon he started lumbering towards me. He was a big man and I could see he was very angry and red faced. I thought, Christ I'd better get of here because I feared for the consequences if he got hold of me, so, I jumped in my car and made off. I heard the appeal on radio and decided I'd better give myself up.'

The officer confirmed a part version of that story but at the point the motorist drove off adrenalin failed and the most he could do then was to crawl to the patrol car!

All's well that ends well. Discretion is sometimes better than valour.

During the winter of 1990 to 1991 it snowed very heavily one Saturday morning. My shift was on early turn. It started to snow soon after we arrived at work in Ops room at 6am and by breakfast time the whole of the counties of Shropshire, Herefordshire and Worcestershire were gridlocked.

The usual crises occurred. Accidents by galore, people stranded, roads blocked and no bugger able to get anywhere. The red 999 lights on the switchboard were constantly blocked and flashing until the point where the Perspex covers on the key pads were hot to touch. Police were struggling to respond and in those days we had limited numbers of mobile phones and 4x4 vehicles to mobilise.

Our main mechanism in order to keep the public up-to-date across West Mercia was via the local radios of BBC Hereford and Worcester and Shropshire and of course some of the small commercial stations such as Wyvern. This meant I was constantly, every few minutes going on air to do a broadcast about roads blocked and to warn motorists.

In situations like this I have to say the Police have a tendency to come out with worn-out hackneyed phrases and clichés such as, 'Please be prepared for your journey and do not travel unless it is absolutely essential, etc etc.' Even I was getting tired of repeating myself but I was not as pissed off as one poor motorist, who like me had started travelling out even before it started snowing, was on an essential errand and unfortunately was now stranded, cold and thoroughly annoyed. He managed to phone into BBC Hereford and Worcester where he suggested that the 'tosser' from West Mercia Police who keeps giving obvious but useless bloody advice ought to get off his fat arse from the warm centrally heated Force Operations room and into the real world where he could see what the hell what was going on. Fair advice in the circumstances, I think.

On my very last day working in the force Operations room I was in the middle of the live traffic radio broadcast when one of my civilian staff, Stuart suddenly flashed up a glove puppet over the top of the podium just at the point when I started reading the news. I couldn't stop laughing and had to admit to the presenter what had happened who joined in the merriment because he had been forewarned that it was my last broadcast which he announced to the public at large.

Once the broadcast had finished, Thelma who was another staff member on the shift said to me, 'Spec, I have just had a call from a lady who said she is a great admirer of you and your sexy voice, she wishes she could meet you and is devastated you will no longer be serenading her whilst reading the traffic bulletins.' Well, I can tell you the words sexy and Les King have never been on the same page let alone in the same sentence so I was naturally intrigued. I got the tape played back and kept listening to the dulcet tones of what sounded like a very lovely lady, also with a sexy voice and what appeared to me be a local accent. I played it again and again but was convinced it was no-one I knew and could only hope she would ring in again to satisfy my intrigue. She didn't so I was left wondering.

When I got home Jud told me she had listened to the debacle of the radio broadcast and asked if anything else interesting had happened. Well, I wasn't going to tell her that some woman had phoned in with the 'hots' for me was I so I said, 'No, nothing.'

At this point she said, 'No women commenting on what a sexy voice you had then?'

I am not sure whether I was more embarrassed that I had not said anything or that after 20 years of being together I had failed to recognise her voice. Either way she let me off the hook and another era came to an end.

CHAPTER 20

REDDITCH – BACK TO COMMUNITY POLICING ROOTS

I looked at the commemorative plaque on the mantelpiece which was inscribed to the 'Peacemakers.' The message passed me by until Madge returned with a cup of tea and explained the significance of being a full-time 'peacemaker' in mediating disputes and reconciling differences between neighbours and communities.

Madge Tillesley was the Chair and general co-ordinator of Redditch Smallwood's Residents Association and a legend around Redditch as a local councillor, ex-Mayor and founder and supporter of many community organisations including the Smallwood Association. Madge who was of Afro-Caribbean descent and born in Jamaica married a British serviceman, Jim and came to Redditch in 1957 where she dedicated her life to ensuring that good community spirit ties existed between all the various community groups and was eventually awarded the MBE for her services.

Madge was a big lady in every way. In stature she towered over most people but with an even bigger heart and personality and a booming voice and laugh that would dominate most conversations and meetings. I was present at a leaving function once at Redditch Police club where someone made the mistake of giving Madge a microphone to make an impromptu farewell speech. The one thing Madge did not need was a microphone. She bellowed out her speech till the walls reverberated and residents came out of the nearby houses around Grove Street to see what all the commotion was about. By the time she had finished everyone who lived in half a mile of Redditch nick knew that Chief Inspector Phil Purslow was leaving town and not only that he was as Madge quoted, 'A damn good cop!'

But Madge was not just affable, she was also assertive. In the summer she was always in possession of a fan to cool herself down. If a meeting was not going her way Madge would gradually get hot under the collar and out would come the fan. Quick as lightening like Billy the Kid's six-gun, in one movement she would pick it up, open it, fan herself several times at the same time remonstrating with someone to make a point. The speed of the fan in split second timing was always an indication of how passionate Madge felt about the subject under discussion.

Her husband Jim as an ex soldier was equally a great character. Despite his elderly years when I knew him he was bolt upright and always by Madge's side. They were a devoted couple. Jim loved having a drink and was a regular at the Queens pub opposite the Police station and on a Sunday lunchtime after leaving the pub he would wander across to the Police canteen where he had a Sunday lunch booked whilst Madge was engaged either attending church or on a community errand.

Madge told me a lovely story about Jim who incidentally was a little hard of hearing.

They were lying in bed one night when Madge heard noises and was sure they had an intruder. She shouted to Jim that they had a burglar but being partly asleep and hard of hearing he did not really catch on. In desperation Madge shouted, 'Jim, get the gun we've got intruders.' Jim then roused enough to say, 'What gun, we haven't got a gun.'

Madge gave up and decided to investigate herself but fortunately there was no intruder.

However, if there had been I do wonder if the burglar may have been more frightened by the towering stature of Madge and a booming voice than he would have been of Jim, gun or no gun.

It was late autumn in 1991 and I had escaped the Operations Room. A vacancy had arisen for an Inspector in charge of a community safety department at Redditch which I had applied for and got more or less immediately based partly on my previous experience of community policing but mainly on the basis that no-one else applied for it.

I was over the moon. Back to my policing roots and a town that I was familiar with, and had so many fond memories of. A town that encompassed all the best of a Worcestershire county town but was a busy microcosm of cosmopolitan life that existed a few miles away in the city of the Birmingham which is just over the boundary and from which much its overspill of population is derived. Exciting because there was always something going on and in which there were many energetic people like Madge to keep you on your toes and a lot of keen people in agencies to develop initiatives. But, it was also like a worn old pair of slippers. I knew it; I loved the town and felt great affection for it. Although much had changed over the previous 20 years since I had left such as the sprawling Kingfisher Centre shopping Centre it was great to deal with the sons and daughters of some of the characters I had worked with, fought with and sometimes shared a drink with in the town. Every estate, every road and every street held a memory.

The job was simply about keeping the public happy and maintaining a professional police high profile for public confidence via the media, schools, community groups, neighbourhood watch, victim support, crime prevention and every other possible consultation and meetings. It was a hectic role and with my small team I embarked upon six years of some of the most satisfying and productive work in my career.

There was one thing I felt I needed to do as a priority. That was to build confidence and relations with minority groups in the town. Redditch has a significant Asian and black population largely situated within the town centre. Whilst relations were good with most of the prominent ethnic leaders the odd incidents of racial tensions that kicked off from time to time tested this and take my word for it that racist incidents and prejudice do occur even within the best of communities and can easily spark off into something more serious. There was also little informal networking between Police and the youth population which is where a lot of tension occurred, particularly between white and Asian youths. Also, the majority of the taxi drivers in the town were Asian and again suffered racial abuse and problems from a small minority of white youths. Taxi drivers of whatever descent suffer abuse, particularly late at night. It's almost like policing, it comes with the territory but should not and does not have to be tolerated. That abuse is particularly insidious when it is made personal by making obscene racist remarks. For anyone that ever doubts this happens then let me tell you of a covert tape I once heard of Asian taxi drivers in a Midlands town being routinely and systematically abused by white men under the influence of drink late at night in a town centre. It is difficult to believe how low some of our fellow citizens will stoop and how much prejudice and hate is directed towards people who are just trying to do a job. The problem is that sometimes this results in the victims taking the law into their own hands, particularly where they feel they are not being supported or listened to by those who should be protecting them like the Police. The result can be serious incidents of racial tension and public disorder with faults on all sides.

I knew the Police needed to ensure that good communication existed between all sectors of the white and ethnic communities and set about with colleagues and people like Madge and other community leaders to continually monitor and work towards solving problems as quickly as possible when they occurred. This meant regular contact with the Mosques, community groups and the youth centres.

Another prominent person in the community at Redditch was a man I also developed enormous respect for and became good friends with. Arthur Price was like Madge a well respected ex councillor and dignitary in the town who spent most of his life supporting good causes and acting as the chair or trustee of a number of groups. Arthur worked harder in his retired volunteer capacity than most of us who work full time. Arthur chaired both the Police Consultative Group and Victim Support so we shared many platforms together. Arthur was like a wise old owl, always ready to listen, with time for everyone and a large dose of interpersonal skills and charisma that would calm down the most difficult of meeting audiences and usually calming them down to the point where he would eventually win them over and recruit them as a volunteer for Victim Support.

Unfortunately, Arthur was not with me one night when I went to what I thought was a routine meeting of the residents of Lakeside estate at Redditch who had asked to meet with Police and Council officials. I was with a council executive officer and a local councillor called Richard Timney (husband of Jackie Smith who at the time was prospective Labour party parliamentary candidate for Redditch and was eventually promoted to Home Secretary under the future Labour Government led by Gordon Brown).

The residents were angry, really angry with a number of genuine grievances about how their area had been run down and where crime and drug dealing incidents appeared to be neglected by the police despite constant complaints. This was not whingeing, it was genuine frustration felt by a number of the local community who felt let down by the Council and Police. There was no formal chair appointed for the meeting and all we could do was listen, make notes, and give assurances we would sort things out. However, promises were not what they wanted; it was action then and there. Things were not helped when Richard Timney had to leave the meeting early and the council officer and I were left to face the flack. I had a free meal and drink lined up at an open Police Federation meeting but knew if I dared leave until they had exhausted their venom then there would be anarchy and I feared chairs would fly. It was not helped by virtue of the fact that we were in a local working men's club where they were able to avail themselves of some fuel from the bar. After about three hours things reached a natural conclusion but even after the meeting had ended it took me another 30 minutes to get out of the room without being stopped by individual residents who wanted to speak personally.

But, they hadn't finished there, next day they went to the press and vented spleen to make their grievances public. In addition a number of them were Neighbourhood Watch co-ordinators who resigned from their voluntary posts which added to the embarrassment.

In these situations there is nothing to do but react, firmly fairly and be seen to do something. I catalogued the complaints and passed them to the local Chief Inspector and Beat Officer's team to flood the area with Police and take some positive action. We worked closely with the council to ensure the area was tidied up and between us after a number of weeks I do believe we started to regain some trust by the community. However, it is difficult to keep all balls up in the air at any one time and no doubt as we were concentrating on Lakeside other areas suffered because there are not limitless resources.

There were many lighter moments. I had a good team of people to work with including two sergeants, Ron Lewis and Dick Jones who were so laid back they were horizontal. Dick was responsible for crime prevention and Ron for schools liaison and talks to the community. Ron had developed an annual fishing competition for youngsters which took place each school summer holidays at Arrow Valley Lake and a mini Olympics event for kids which was held at the Abbey Stadium.

When I first arrived at Redditch we had a secretary in the department who was called Carol. After 18 months of working in the Force Operations Room I could not get used to the fact that I could actually go to the toilet without telling everyone where I was going! Carol was bemused the first time I told her and inferred I was a big boy now and did she really need to know that?

After Carol left I appointed a lady called Shirley Wiltshire. Shirley was almost overlooked during the recruitment phase because of a bit of a cock up. Thank goodness we never missed recruiting her because Shirley became a loyal and trusted friend and colleague who worked alongside me in two major roles for several years.

Shirley was very bubbly with a fantastic sense of humour and got on well with everyone at the Police station. Most people hide their birthdays. Not Shirl, she would write it in my diary 12 months in advance and when it came round everyone knew it was Shirl's birthday. In fact, even the first day of spring would be a reason for celebration in Shirl's world.

When she passed her driving test this was a call for major celebration. She asked me if she could have some time off in the afternoon – no, not to practice her new found skills of driving but so that she could go round the offices and boast she had passed first time!

One of Shirl's other claims to fame was that being a party animal not only did she enjoy her own birthday but she was more than happy to share other people's. At Redditch we had a lovely young woman called Bev who worked on the switchboard. Bev was extremely alert, very efficient and totally on top of her job. She knew everything and everybody and was full of fun. Bev was confined to a wheelchair but this did not inhibit her one little bit.

When it came to Bev's birthday Shirley arranged for a crowd of them to go across to the Queens Head pub and have a lunchtime drink.

Now Bev, although very sociable was not accustomed to drinking so being introduced by Shirl to a few snifters of 'White Lightening' cider this had a dramatic effect on Bev.

Upon their return to the station Bev proceeded to carry out a number of wheelies in her wheelchair around the corridors at a fast rate of knots. When eventually she was corralled and persuaded back to the switchboard she confused a number of callers by putting them through to the first extension number she could recall which bore absolutely no resemblance to who they wanted to speak to. Bev was warned to never again go drinking with Shirl!

After being at Redditch in Community Relations for about 2 years I was offered the opportunity to serve as Acting Chief Inspector for about 3 months whilst the incumbent post-holder went to Bramshill Police College for 3 months.

This proved to be a very busy period for a number of reasons but two incidents have remained in my mind ever since for completely different reasons.

The first was a pub in Redditch that at that time had a problem with drug dealers congregating on the car park despite the best efforts of the management. Over the years we had raided them several times but after a lull they kept returning. It was just a focal point and it became difficult to keep on top of. The owner of the pub made a very useful suggestion of turning the ground floor into a Balti house and retaining the top of the premises as a member's bar. We supported him fully in his change of use planning application but I must admit I had my doubts over whether it would work. However, the effect was dramatic. It completely changed the clientele. Not only were the customers different, the previous ones who had resorted there purely for the opportunity of scoring drugs did not wish to indulge in an expensive meal and were put off completely. The dealers not only had a dwindling trade but found themselves in a distinct minority amongst the diners arriving for a meal and stood out like a sore thumb.

Eventually they went away over the border and off our patch which was good news for us.

I learnt two things by that experience. Firstly, there is more than one way of skinning a cat and that changing the environment of an area can have a more dramatic effect on reducing crime than any heavy-handed police presence. Secondly, that I have a low threshold of metabolism to Asian food. I along with a number of others was invited to the official launch and opening of the Balti house and I rather eagerly over indulged myself in scoffing large amounts of a banquet of wonderful curries and savouries.

The following day we were hosting a visit from Sir Geoffrey Dear who at that time had just retired as Chief Constable of West Midlands Police and had become Her Majesty's Inspector of Constabulary. He was at Redditch nick to inspect us and had been invited to a buffet lunch. During the morning I had developed an extremely bad headache and started to feel queasy.

Madge Tillesley was present as a local dignitary and was insistent she wanted to introduce Sir Geoffrey to me. Geoffrey Dear is a very, very tall man who you definitely have to look up to. Madge introduced me to him and we commenced small talk. At this point I was trying to be polite and attempting to eat a sausage roll. Suddenly, the combination of a throbbing headache, the sausage roll and looking up with a crick in my neck at Sir Geoffrey made me feel sick and I could feel myself going faint and starting to sweat. Sir Geoffrey looked at me and said, 'Are you feeling alright young man?..........'

At that point I decided I had a decision to make. Either exit sharply and rudely or be the first copper that has ever spewed over Her Majesty's Inspector of Constabulary. I rushed out to the nearest toilet and was violently sick. Later I realised that I was obviously allergic to something in the array of Asian food I had consumed the previous day and have always had to be wary ever since.

The second incident involved the drowning of a man whose body was recovered from a pool outside of the town in a park where he was found by the local park-keeper. Initially we had to treat the death as suspicious and that meant dealing with it as a Coroner's case and employing a Home

Office pathologist to carry out a post mortem. Eventually, it was established to be an accident but we did not know that at the time. Ray Humphreys was the Detective Sergeant at the scene when I arrived and it is fair to say we had a certain rapport between us. We had both been custody sergeants at Kidderminster together in the 1980's and were accustomed to playing practical jokes on each other. I usually followed Ray when he was on nights and I was on early turn. His usual prank was to write up a load of false names on the custody whiteboard and tell me we had about a dozen in the cells and that he had had a hell of a night. He would spend time outlining a load of serious complex false stories about those that were in cells. It was only after he had left that I would wander down the cells to check and find that it was complete rubbish and the cells were empty.

Even worse, on one occasion he wiped the whiteboard clean and told me the cells were empty when in fact they bloody full!

So, when I attended the scene of this death I did not expect to have much sense out of Ray but I did note that he seemed somewhat perplexed. I asked why and he informed me that we may get a complaint from the Coroner. He took some time to convince me that he was not joking and this is what happened.

In those days mobile phones were at a premium. Ray was not allocated one so he used the mobile owned by the park-keeper. One of the things you had to do with any sudden death in those days was to get permission from HM Coroner to remove the body from the scene. Ray had used the park-keeper's phone to put a call through to the Coroner and left a message for him to phone back on the mobile. Ray then without thinking gave the phone back to the park-keeper. Eventually the Coroner rang, spoke to the park-keeper and thinking it was the police told him he had permission to remove the body.

The park-keeper being rather bemused by this spent no time in telling the Coroner he didn't know what the hell he was on about because he only managed the park and removing dead bodies was beyond his pay grade. The Coroner rang off rather confused. Ray feared the consequences in having to ring him back. I thought it was payback time and told him so!

Playing with the Media: After the above interlude I returned to my Community Relations Department where one of the main roles was keeping the press updated and attending any major incidents as the police spokesman. I have to say that I thoroughly enjoyed this role and in the department we had it off pat.

We worked closely with the Force press office at Police HQ which was headed up by one of the most skilled men I have ever worked with. The late Allen Peach was an experienced journalist who was quite simply a 'wordsmith.' Whatever the situation Allen would find the words to euphemistically describe sometimes the direst of situations in way that would never lie to the media but would feed them a story without giving the main game away or destroying the confidence of the public. He was a corporate man who would do everything he was paid to do to protect the integrity of the police and comply with the legal requirements placed upon us but at the same time had the confidence of all who came into contact with him. A master of words, a superb strategist and excellent consultant, woe betide any senior detective who did not heed his advice because they would almost certainly come unstuck. However, on top of that he was unassuming, never basked in the glory and always allowed others to take the credit.

I have always had respect for any professional who was at the top of their game and Allen most certainly was. It was a tragedy that shortly after retirement and having lived through the sharp end of most of West Mercia Police's major incidents and controversial inquiries he died in 2004 aged just 60 years.

Whenever we had a major job that involved the immediate need to engage the media we would inform the Force press office who would devise the messages and the strategy and field the national inquiries. I would go to the scene and deal with the press where the incident was and my deputy Sergeant Ron Lewis would field local inquiries back at Redditch office. That way we had it covered and it worked a treat.

Friday 14th January 1994 was to be a fateful day for Captain Brenden Hearney of the US Marine Corps who was on secondment to RAF Wittering. Captain Hearney was flying a Harrier GR7 plane when it crashed approximately 5 miles south east of Evesham just missing the village of Aston Somerville. The pilot did not eject and was killed instantly.

I was in the operations room at Redditch shortly after the call came in and it was pandemonium. Initial reports suggested that the plane had collided into a local school but there was little in the way of any credible information. I decided to drive straight to the scene to deal with the press and liaise with the Force Press Office.

I took a police radio to monitor what was going on but again all I got was conflicting reports of what had happened because police were only just arriving on the ground.

I was driving my own car so I put the radio on and listened to BBC Hereford and Worcester. They summed it up as saying that a RAF Harrier plane had crash landed just outside Aston Somerville and that the pilot had been killed and it was believed no-one else was injured. Also, that the police were now in attendance, they had thrown up a cordon around the area and were notifying military authorities to attend. The most essential thing they said was that the plane had been reported to have crashed into a school but that appeared to be completely untrue. It was brief but it told me a lot more than I was getting over the police radio.

When I arrived I parked away from the main area and walked to the scene. Bits of the aircraft fuselage were strewn across a field and nearby lay the body of the pilot. There was a horrible smoke and a stench I was unfamiliar with.

Vehicles had started blocking the only small access road leading to the site and a lot of people were milling around including a press pack who were baying to get pictures of the scene but were being kept back by a small number of police.

In the centre of the field was a colleague of mine Inspector Brian Smith who was acting as incident commander and he was up to his eyes in it. I tried to ascertain from Brian what was happening but he told me more or less to just bugger off and keep the press off his back because they were becoming impatient and he feared they would trespass across the field.

At that stage we were fearful about what chemicals or arsenal might be on the plane so it was unsafe. Also, we did not want the press taking photographs of the pilot or the scene that may prove insensitive.

When we were in training I recall somebody telling us to stick your wet finger in the air and then only approach the plane crash in the direction of the wind that was on the back of your finger. I didn't understand at the time whether that was upwind or downwind – I was now wishing I had listened more closely to this lecture because the dangers of inhaling noxious gases were becoming very prevalent in my mind.

I decided to approach the media pack of assembled hacks and take the bull by the horns.

If I could ask them for an informal word then maybe I could explain the situation off the record and play for time until I had more verified information and could give a formal press release.

As I approached them I realised this was not going to work. I could hear the camera motors whirring and a voice saying, 'A police spokesman is just approaching and we are now going live with the officer at the scene.' I realised this was live TV and radio and also present was a number of local journalists. The fact that I was wearing a sash which said 'Police Press' also rather gave the game away!

I realised that the best strategy was to say what I had heard on BBC Hereford and Worcester. It was repeating the same information but the press don't care as long as someone official is saying it. So, I ad-libbed as follows, 'Good afternoon, Inspector Les King Police spokesman for West Mercia Police. Our update is that we understand a Harrier Jet plane has crashed and the pilot has tragically been killed. We have thrown a cordon of officers around the area in order to protect the scene whilst awaiting military authorities who are on their way to investigate the cause of the incident. We appeal to anyone to come forward who may have witnessed the crash and ask that everyone keep away from the scene so as not to hamper our inquiries. Meanwhile, I would like to reassure the public that although initial reports suggested the plane had hit a school that is untrue. Tragically, the pilot has been killed but we believe there are no other injuries and no damage to any property other than the plane itself.

That really is all I can tell you at the moment. We will of course continue to keep you updated.'

I paused and inwardly congratulated myself on splendid bit of ad-libbing and my ability to articulate under pressure.

My relief was short lived when one of the reporters asked me, 'Did you say no damage to any other property officer?' I immediately smelt a rat, so, I looked round and realised that we were standing outside a bungalow and that in my haste I had failed to notice that a corner of the bungalow had been demolished by the plane as it landed. In fact, I was later told that parts off the plane had landed in the kitchen. Now, in shock I said something daft like: 'Except for that bungalow.' I then made a sharp exit and made immediate inquiries. It was not beyond the realms of possibility that no-one was aware what had happened and someone might be dead or injured in the bungalow. Fortunately, we established no-one was in the house at the time and all was well. Well, except for having part of your house demolished by a bleeding plane of course.

I have always expected that to appear as an outtake on TV but so far so good!

The press were still baying to get across the field where the plane had landed and to take some pictures of the fuselage close up. The problem was that the remains of the pilot were also nearby and the area had to be reserved for the military authorities who would make a painstaking search of the vicinity. I had great difficulty persuading the press to keep away and eventually some of them did enter the field and had to be threatened with arrest and warned off.

One reporter who was present but behaved impeccably was Julie Etchingham. At the time of writing Julie is the ITV News at Ten anchor woman having had a distinguished career in journalism. On that day in 1994 she was a young reporter for BBC Midlands News and complied with all requests from the police to stay behind the cordon, waiting patiently. As it was drawing dusk and most of the media had long disappeared back to their warm offices Julie stayed on and asked if she could possibly have an interview in the field where the plane had landed as a backdrop but without any quest to publish graphic pictures or detail.

Well, I have to say when someone as attractive as Julie Etchingham in a smart pair of wellies asks you for an assignation in a field, how could one ever refuse. I dutifully complied and sincerely believe that it set her on the road to fame and fortune! It was definitely my only claim to fame.

It was a freezing cold evening and in the half light the military authorities attended and examined the scene including the recovery of the pilot's body. His next of kin were informed in the United States and made arrangements to fly over immediately. A full inquiry into the circumstances commenced. I liaised with my media equivalent in the military and we worked out a strategy for dealing with further inquiries.

It was at this point that we received a warning that the dust and particles coming from the air craft, in which we were covered, could be noxious and that our clothes must be destroyed or sent for special cleaning.

On the way home I stopped and rang Jud from a kiosk and told her to put a load of plastic bags and change of clothing in the garage for when I got home to prevent further contamination. My uniform, shirt and underwear and boots were disposed of, and yes I lived to see another day.

Many years on I have revisited the scene of the crash where there is a touching memorial stone laid in tribute to Captain Hearney who came from a very distinguished military family. I was never made aware of the official reason for the crash but many certainly believe that Captain Hearney did not eject from the plane so that he could steer it away from the main part of the village of Aston Sommerville which is what happened otherwise total devastation would have occurred.

Local residents still talk about the moment the cows in the fields froze completely several seconds before the plane landed as if anticipating something dreadful was going to happen. Sixth sense is not therefore not just confined to humans!

CHAPTER 21

'THIS IS MURDER – NOT ROAD RAGE!

When the phone goes in the early hours of the morning you just know its trouble. It's not likely to be somebody inviting you out for a beer is it?

In the middle of a deep sleep during the early morning of Monday 2nd December 1996 my home phone rang. On the other end was a colleague, Detective Chief Inspector Steve Walters. Steve told me that a young man named Lee Harvey had been stabbed to death near Alvechurch and he wanted me in immediately to deal with the press which was likely to go ballistic at breakfast time onwards.

When I arrived at Redditch nick it was still early but buzzing with cops, forensic officers and the general frenzy that follows any major incident. Controlled chaos is the best way to describe it until order descends. Every major incident is going to be chaos at the beginning with thousands of things to do. The knack is getting the chaos into order at the shortest possible time.

It's the best bit of policing, it's what we all joined for and it's what the police are best at and what the public expect. I have never failed to be both amazed and proud at what cops can pull together when the shots are called. Murder is sad, it's tragic, it's challenging but it is always fascinating.

The Detective Superintendent in charge of the case was Ian Johnston. Ian provided a briefing to the officers drafted in to make early morning inquiries and to me as to what had happened and you could hear a pin drop.

Ian was one of the force's most experienced detectives. A big man of enormous stature with a bull like neck and shoulders. He held a presence not only because of his size but because of a charismatic personality and the respect gained from colleagues following years of dealing with challenging and difficult investigations. He was every inch a cop with an incisive intelligence and a nose for taking any major crime inquiry in the right direction. Ian was usually very affable but he was not one to suffer fools lightly and would soon let you know if he was unhappy, hence there was intense concentration on every word he spoke.

We were shown some photographs of the scene that had been taken only hours earlier.

The emerging story was that Lee Harvey had been driving down a country lane near Alvechurch which is on the outskirts of Birmingham but in Worcestershire. He was driving a white Ford Escort car with his girlfriend Tracie Andrews sitting in the front passenger seat. Tracie and Lee had been out to the Marlbrook pub on the outskirts of Bromsgrove for a drink and were on their way back home to Alvechurch.

On that journey they had been chased by the driver of a dark coloured Ford Sierra car also containing a passenger following a driving incident. The Sierra had apparently followed them along the country lanes to an isolated area called Coopers Hill where the Sierra had overtaken the Escort and then stopped. Both Lee Harvey and the driver of the Sierra got out of their cars and remonstrated with each other. The driver of the Sierra got back into the car but his passenger got out and what followed was a violent altercation in which Lee was stabbed numerous times and died at the scene. The story continued that Tracie had tried to intervene and had been punched in the head.

The Sierra and occupants disappeared and had not been traced. What appeared on face value to be road rage had turned into murder. We were now desperate to make public appeals for the dark coloured Ford Sierra car and details of who the occupants were.

The usual intense investigation at the scene and inquiries to inform next of kin and trace witnesses had already been underway for several hours and Ian was in the process of setting up a murder incident room at Redditch police station. My job was to liaise with headquarters press office, draft press releases for approval and together with Ian Johnston and the police press office at Hindlip provide a media presence for interviews at the police station and scene.

What followed were hours and hours of frenzied media activity which captured the nation's press. We were desperate to put out appeals and they were desperate to get information. A similar incident had occurred on the M25 in May 1996 in which a man had been stabbed to death following an alleged road rage incident and of course links were being made.

The famous quote of Ian Johnston in one of the early press interviews on that Monday morning was, 'You might call this road rage. To us it is murder.'

I drove out to the scene where the press were gathered outside a house where the stabbing had occurred. I gave a series of interviews to television, radio and press reiterating the information we had. They wanted photographs of Lee Harvey's car which we were not prepared to have photographed until all forensics had been completed. They were keen to establish where it was which unbeknown to them was in the garage of one of the nearby houses literally yards from where they were standing.

Eventually, they were satisfied with the interviews and photographs of the police searching the roads and I went back to Redditch nick.

Later that day we held a meeting with Allen Peach from the Force press office and discussed a media strategy for the following day and thereafter. The detectives present were keen to release as much information as possible so as to gain maximum publicity. The media were keen to get photographs of the victims. Allen, as wily as ever was adamant that we were to drip feed information to keep it as headlines in the national press for as long as possible.

We decided to hold a press conference with the family the following day, Tuesday 3rd December at Redditch Police station. I was given responsibility for setting it up with assistance of Allen and the Force press office.

What followed that day was one of the most infamous press conferences ever to take place in this country.

In a room at the back of the club room at Redditch Police Station we assembled with the nation's press crowded into the room hanging on every word spoken. Present was Ian Johnston, the parents of the murder victim Lee Harvey, Maureen and Ray Harvey and Tracie Andrews herself.

Maureen sat holding Tracie's hand throughout the conference and was flanked by her husband Ray on the one side and Ian Johnston on the other. Allen Peach and I remained at the side of the room to monitor proceedings, record tapes of the conference and to provide post conference interviews and information.

Tracie was visibly upset and shaking with a number of bruises to her face. Tracie was invited to speak and gave a description of the assailant as: 'A fat man with staring eyes.'

At one point in the conference Tracie appeared to become confused over the time she and Lee had left the Marlbrook Pub and the subsequent time of the actual murder in the lane. There were awkward pauses in that the times did not seem to match up but most present probably accepted that Tracie would be easily confused after such a traumatic incident. Shortly afterwards Ian Johnston terminated the conference and Allen and I were left to debrief the reporters present who always want that little bit more information, even if it's a snippet that their competitors will have missed.

At that juncture, Tracie was definitely being treated as a witness. Whilst Police always maintain an open mind there was nothing at that stage to make Tracie a suspect.

However, subsequent events were to prove that Tracie was indeed Lee's killer and that following an argument she had stabbed him with a knife 42 times in the neck in that lane leading to Alvechurch. There never was another car that was chasing them nor any road rage incident. There never was a fat man with staring eyes and her press appeal and explanation to the Police was all complete lies.

Tracie had secreted the knife into the top of her boot and it was believed she subsequently discarded it when she was being treated at Redditch Alexandra Hospital that same night.

However, it took several days for facts to emerge that cast doubt on Tracie's story. Most significantly witnesses came forward to say that they had seen Lee's car being driven towards Alvechurch and that it was not being followed or chased by another car.

In the interim period before the real story started to emerge the media frenzy continued. This was a massive story. Tracie had at one time carried out some brief modelling work and we released what was a very pleasant photo of Tracie which was published extensively by the media alongside the story of a young man savagely killed in a road rage incident with his attractive young fiancée also savagely beaten.

The story ran and ran with headlines every day. My office and mobile phone was in meltdown along with headquarters press office. There was no satisfying the media appetite for this story including requests from reporters for inside information and briefings and from programmes such as GMTV breakfast-time for Tracie to appear on the settee and to be interviewed.

We carried out an anniversary traffic stop-check the following Sunday night along the route Lee and Tracey had travelled hoping to speak to anyone who had been in the vicinity the previous Sunday night and had not previously come forward.

But, in the interim period several things started to happen. Tracie took an overdose in what was regarded as a serious attempt on her life. She was admitted to hospital. The witnesses also came forward to say that the Ford Escort car driven by Lee was definitely not being followed that night. Also, facts were emerging as to a stormy on/off relationship that had existed between Tracie and Lee as a couple who were consumed by jealously but also by passion and lust who would break up frequently but then get back together again and then repeat the cycle.

The role of the media liaison officer and relationship with the senior investigating officer and team is sometimes difficult. The media spokesperson must never mislead the press. However, there are certain things that cannot be released to the press and it is a decision of the major investigation team as to what the media liaison officer is briefed on and the timing of that information so that nothing is released by mistake whilst under pressure. Also, it means that if the media officer is asked a question about a sensitive topic they have not been briefed on they can honestly say at that point that they are not aware or have not been briefed.

At a point around the time Tracie had taken an overdose I was preparing to do a live interview outside the front of the police station to one of the major news channels.

I checked with the incident room to see if there was anything topical I either should or should not say as to latest developments. Ian Johnston made it clear to me that the course of the investigation was changing but he could not disclose why. What he did say was that he did not want any more appeals for dark coloured Ford Sierra cars. I gathered that was fast becoming irrelevant but asked him what I should say instead when asked about it, which inevitably would occur.

His response was blunt and to the effect that it was for me to decide but no more appeals for dark coloured Ford Sierra cars.

The cameras were lined up outside. I sat in one of the interview rooms at the police station pondering what words to say. Nothing came to me so I decided to do the only thing you can do which is ad-lib and hope the words just flow under pressure.

I reiterated the latest police release but omitted to say anything about appealing for sightings of a Ford Sierra. The interviewer did not pick me up on it and I really thought I had got away with it until right at the end he said to me, 'Inspector, I note you have not made any appeal for sightings of the black Ford Sierra, does this still feature in your inquiries?'

I paused momentarily, but which felt like an age, searching for something to say or wondering whether I could just collapse and pretend to be ill! Suddenly, it came to me, I said something like, 'We are asking for sightings of any car or activity that was witnessed along the lanes that evening and would ask for anyone with information to come forward.' Simple.

When I got home that night Jud had video-taped the interview and said to me casually, 'I think you were struggling in the interview to find the right words.'

I explained it had been necessary to be evasive and provide a politicians answer for reasons I could not disclose! Jud said, 'Oh well, let me tell you this. I will always know now when you are 'prevaricating' or whatever you may call it because you roll your eyes round to the right several times and avoid looking at the interviewer, so be warned if you ever try that one with me!'

I looked at the video - she was dead right and I was warned!

The saga continued, and I have to say got more complicated and had more twists and turns than a game of snakes and ladders.

After being hospitalised for a few days Tracie was formally arrested on suspicion of the murder of Lee Harvey.

This caused immense problems from a press perspective. Firstly, the press were aware that Tracie had taken an overdose. Secondly, they were also aware that a young woman had been arrested on suspicion of murder. However, at that time national guidance was that details of someone arrested should never be released to the press until they are charged or about to appear in court. The reason is obvious, they may be released from custody without charge and if their name is released then this could seriously impugn their character with subsequent claims being made against the Force.

What this meant in practice was that the media suspected Tracie was the murder suspect but we could not state that directly so we played games whereupon they would ask firstly how Tracie was and secondly how was the woman in custody. We had to continually refer to them as different people for the reasons as outlined.

Eventually, it was formally released on the basis that it could no longer be kept a secret. Tracey was eventually placed in custody at Redditch police station, charged with Lee's murder and placed before the Magistrate's Court.

However, the story was only just beginning. What followed were some of the most unorthodox tactics most of us had ever seen in a murder case.

Tracie was represented by a defence solicitor called Tim Robinson from Gloucestershire. Robinson was a dapper man with white hair and small round framed spectacles. It quickly became apparent that Tracie was denying the murder. Robinson asked for reporting restrictions to be lifted at court and his tactics became apparent. He wanted maximum publicity to make a public appeal for witnesses to come forward to again appeal for the alleged assailant involved in the road rage incident with the Ford Sierra.

He took the unusual step of arranging a press conference which he attended with Tracie (who had been released on bail pending trial) to make the above appeal and in which the police attended as bystanders, bemused by the whole scenario of events that was unfolding.

This appeal resulted in one person referred to as a local business man coming forward and reporting that he had been threatened in a road rage incident by a similarly described man, driving a Ford car near to the same location.

The police were therefore placed in the unenviable position where they were being requested to pursue a line of inquiry that they had already eliminated and were satisfied was not true.

In July 1997 Tracie Andrews came to trial at Birmingham Crown Court and pleaded not guilty. Evidence in her defence was discredited and she was convicted of the murder of Lee Harvey and sentenced to life imprisonment where a tariff was set of 14 years. She appealed against her conviction but this was not upheld.

Eventually from her prison cell Tracie made a confession that she had killed Lee Harvey following a violent argument.

Maureen Harvey, Lee's mother published a book in 2007 called 'Pure Evil' which is her account of the pain and suffering caused as a result of this murder involving her whole family including her daughter Michelle, husband Ray and Lee's daughter Danielle who was five at the time of her Dad's death.

If anyone should seek to try and understand the depth of despair caused by losing a child in circumstances such as this then they should read Maureen's vivid description of what took place not only at the time but years after Tracie had been convicted and was in prison. It touches upon every aspect of Maureen's personal and working life as well as her marriage and relationships with family and friends.

Immediately after the murder although some of her family had their suspicions that Tracey could be responsible, Maureen acknowledged this but held on to the hope that she was not and held Tracie's hand in that infamous press conference to support her.

Can there ever be any greater deception?

There are two ironies to conclude this story, which I feel are worthy of mention.

The first is that the media never realised that approximately ten years earlier in February 1986 in exactly the same room at Redditch Police Station a 19 year old man called Stuart Hopkins sat in a press conference holding his mother's hand having reported finding the body of a woman called Carol Martin who had been stabbed to death on a multi-storey car park in Redditch town centre.

Stuart Hopkins was eventually convicted of her murder.

The second irony is the way in which the media portray the circumstances of a crime and how quickly this can change. The initial photograph used of Tracie was that of an attractive blonde model posing in a photograph and that of an innocent victim.

Immediately the circumstances changed and Tracie was charged then the photo changed to the one taken at the press conference where her face was battered and her eyes were staring. This is the photograph that is synonymous with what the world would associate with Tracie Andrews and which will no doubt continue to haunt the real victims of this awful incident.

As I said, a case with numerous twists and turns and as I write Tracie Andrews is now released from custody and attempting to start a new life in another part of the country.

CHAPTER 22

DARK DAYS

Every career has its ups and downs, good times and bad times. When I look back over 33 years most of those years were good. Some were bad and one or two were just horrid.

In career terms, 1997 was to be my *annus horribilis* – the Queen had one in 1992 and made a speech about it. Following the tragic death of Princess Diana in 1997 the Royal Family may have felt they had another year of great unhappiness and misfortune.

For me the year started off well. I had been at Redditch as the Inspector responsible for all things 'community' for 6 years. We were heavily into preventing crime and working on some major projects with the Council to tackle those estate areas where crime and problems with youth anti-social behaviour were at their highest.

Our architectural liaison officers were busy working with the council planning department on initiatives to reduce crime spots where estate areas such as Woodrow centre were being refurbished. Together with the Probation Service we had set up a scheme whereby offenders who were low risk carrying out community service were fitting locks and security devices to houses that had been burgled.

Again with probation and the council we had set up a group known as Redditch Anti Harassment Partnership (RAHP) where we would case conference those most vulnerable victims who being harassed by neighbours or others in the community. We had a network of Police Local

Beat Officers across Redditch who were piloting a new initiative as Beat Managers where their job was not only responding to incidents but also working on the long-term problem-solving so that they did not become repeat incidents. These officers were the identified high profile officers for the public and other agencies and had considerable discretion in how they policed their own areas.

We had excellent relations with the public and ensured that we took full advantage of attending local neighbourhood meetings across Redditch where we had a joint presence with council officers and local councillors.

Our relationship and procedures for dealing with the press was well honed and we had carried out a number of high profile campaigns resulting in good publicity such as Operation Bumblebee where press reporters and TV cameras accompanied us on early morning raids to arrest burglars.

The jewel in the crown for me was working with a number of local partners on a successful bid led by Redditch Borough Council which resulted in a total of £11 million being provided to Redditch to provide facilities for young people.

Redditch at that time as a New Town had one of the highest pro rata youth populations in the country. With that comes a number of issues requiring initiatives such as outreach youth work and support to keep young people out of trouble and improve their education, leisure and future employment opportunities.

The money was provided from a Government fund called the Single Regeneration Budget and required a lot of hard work from many people. The success was largely down to the bid writers in the council but my team provided a number of ideas and as part of the match funding required I placed a full time police officer to work within the council who jointly worked with young people and other agencies on preventing youth crime.

Much of this was ground breaking stuff and Redditch Police developed a reputation within the force as being innovative in working at a strategic level in tackling some thorny and deep rooted problems.

Up until then I had worked at Redditch under four different Divisional commanders (Superintendents) and I felt that both my department and myself personally had sustained credibility and I was particularly proud of those achievements which were largely because we had been allowed to innovate under supportive leadership.

As I reflected at the beginning of 1997 I did think things don't get much better than this but it may be time for a break and do something different for a while.

An opportunity came to carry out an Inspector aide to the Complaints and Discipline Department which was based in an office at Droitwich which dealt with complaints from the public and internal misconduct.

Between March and June I went on the aide-ship which made a refreshing change. The job was all about interviewing people, taking statements and investigating cases.

One of the first jobs I did was to investigate a complaint of assault made by a prisoner who alleged he had been beaten up by the police whilst arrested at the back of a pub. I took a statement from a witness in his house.

The fire was raging away to the point I felt like I was in a sauna. The telly was blaring, the kids were crying and wiping chocolate over my nice new suit, the room was full of cigarette smoke and the Jack Russell dog was jumping up and trying to snatch my clip board off my lap.

It took me right back to when I was a PC, it was familiar, it was great, it is what policing is all about and I loved it.

I learnt a lot of new things and refreshed a lot of old skills that had lain dormant for a few years.

After 3 months I was ready to go back to Redditch and late June I returned to find the entire Command team of senior management had changed and things were different.

The Division was in the middle of a murder inquiry. Two children aged 10 and 14 had been tragically burned to death in a house because one of them had allegedly 'grassed' someone up for stealing a bike to someone other than the police.

I knew the family well. We had case conferenced the family at Redditch Anti- Harassment Partnership because they had been suffering extreme harassment such as windows broken and name calling for years on the estate where they had been living and eventually got them moved to the new estate where the fire had occurred.

They needed a five bed roomed council house so it took some time to arrange and there was not a lot of options. At the time they were eventually moved we put in a lot of support from the agencies such as social services, council and victim support and monitored the situation for some time. Everything went quiet, they suffered no further harassment at the new address and the family kept a low profile.

The incident that had occurred at their new address was in total isolation. However, questions were raised about why the family were moved to the particular estate where the tragic incidents occurred and the whole concept of what RAHP was about was queried on the basis that if that was the best that could be done why bother? As the chair and one of the founding members of the group I took these inferences personally and reflected seriously on what had occurred.

I responded that as far as I could see the incident had nothing to do with the previous problems; that there were severe limitations in placing the family; that we had done everything we could but that if the deaths had occurred where they previously lived and nothing had been done we could have been severely criticised for not taking actions to protect the family.

Eventually two men were convicted of the deaths and RAHP continued to operate for many years after.

Not long after returning to Redditch I detected a distinct cooling of enthusiasm from the new senior management for the work we were doing in the Community Safety Department and this was evidenced by both me and one of my sergeants being moved to other duties with much of the work of the department being diluted.

In my case I was moved to the job of Geographic Inspector responsible for local policing at Redditch. This meant a combination of covering the operational shifts and responsibility for policing Redditch. I actually did not mind too much. I needed a change and the job covered much of what I had been doing at Redditch anyway in terms of community work and contacts. However, I decided that if I had to work shifts again and having been at Redditch for 6 years and travelled 50 miles a day during that time I may as well do it locally so made it known I would prefer to be posted nearer home.

Then two things happened. The Deputy Chief Constable visited and made it clear that 'community/crime prevention work' was to be integral within every Police Division with major focus being placed upon it. For Redditch this would have been easy because we were already doing just that.

Secondly, the role of Geographic Inspector was to be absolute key within the local management structure. So, this meant far from feeling marginalised I was now to be the central focus of this 'new' approach.

I decided to get stuck in to the role and started to really enjoy it. Things were busy. We were the focus of a number of animal rights demonstrations due to certain farms that existed on the division who were responsible either for exporting livestock abroad or breeding of battery chickens.

Policing these demonstrations proved difficult. They were usually spontaneous and very disruptive. They were also full of conflict, providing a constant stream of arrests and subsequent complaints. This lasted for weeks and meant a distraction from dealing with other issues. However, we coped but it meant continually drawing up plans, operational orders and arranging the resources required.

Earlier in this book, whilst writing about my time as a young constable at Redditch I described attending a domestic violence incident on the Batchley estate in which a man had ripped a lump of hair out of a woman's head and we fought with him to arrest him with the kids cowering behind the settee crying.

Twenty four years later and I am duty Inspector at Redditch when I hear one of our fast response drivers shout out 'red call, red call' whilst attending a domestic dispute on one of the estates. When cops call red call it means only one thing, they need urgent help and everyone needs to respond. I jumped into a police vehicle and drove straight to the scene. By the time I got there most of the shift officers had attended and things were relatively under control – in a manner of speaking.

Whilst at the domestic incident in a ground floor maisonette the man present had turned his attention from beating his wife to pulling a knife on the two constables that had attended as first response and threatening them with it. At that point they had shouted out the red call for urgent assistance. The two officers who had attended were typical of most front line officers who drove fast response cars. They were young, they were fit, they were not easily frightened and were in possession of casco batons and CS which they had used to good effect and gained control of the situation.

As I arrived though there was still an element of chaos. The male protagonist was being led away to a police van still struggling and being verbally abusive. Both he and the officers were covered in CS with tears rolling down their faces and shirts soaked.

I then saw the woman victim being wheeled in a chair by two paramedics towards an ambulance. Again she had caught the effects of the CS which had brought on a bout of asthma and she was struggling to breathe.

Somebody said there was still a child in the house and they were concerned. I walked into the living room and surveyed the scene. Furniture was tipped over, ornaments were lying broken on the floor and as I stared my eyes started to tingle and burn from what must have been the remnants of the CS.

Sat in the middle of this chaos on the one remaining chair that was upright was a young lad about 10 years of age eating a plate of beans on toast off his lap and watching the telly.

'Hey young man, I think we had better get you out of here and lock the place up hadn't we?' I said putting my avuncular voice on.

'Not till I finished watching Neighbours and ate me beans mate' he said!

Many years later I gave a speech to a conference on Domestic Abuse. I reflected on that story as I did at the time and I do now. Firstly, was that young boy so conditioned by seeing violence as part of his routine life that it had not impression on him? Or, was that his strategy for coping with it?

Secondly, since my first experience of witnessing violence in the home in 1972, in twenty four years we hadn't come very far had we? It was a problem then – it was a problem in 1997 and it is a problem now.

Thirdly, what about those children who witnessed it? Did those little girls cowering behind the settee in 1972 on Batchley estate grow up accepting that this was true love, the natural way for relationships to exist and become the victims of today? Many do.

Did that little boy on Woodrow grow up to become tomorrow's perpetrator having learnt that control and dominance through violence usually wins in the home and gets you what you want or did he grow up as a well rounded partner or father? Who knows? When does the victim suddenly change and become the perpetrator?

I ponder these things and it worries me sometimes.

If there was any comfort from this it was that the demands of operational policing do not change much over the years and that overall this was a familiar place to be where knowledge, policing skills, brave actions, sound judgement and swift decision-making will always be the main attributes in protecting the public and covering your own back.

Between the period of July and November that year I started to feel under considerable pressure. For me personally a number of things happened that resulted in a deteriorating relationship with some senior managers on the division. Over a period of four months it is fair to say that this relationship deteriorated to the point where my own health started to suffer and I felt under considerable stress at work which resulted in tension at home and concern by Jud and my daughters for my welfare.

I lost my confidence and my self-esteem. I became insular and felt continually sad and upset. I had constant butterflies in my stomach and felt sick each time I arrived at work.

I had difficulty eating and felt sick. I started working excess hours to ensure I completed everything properly and the harder I seemed to work the more tired I became and the slower I worked so I had to work longer...... it was a vicious circle.

I had difficulty concentrating and things reached a peak when I got home one night and could not even count out the kid's pocket money. At that point I took one day sick leave and went to see my Doctor but refused to go on extended sick leave.

The purpose of writing this is not to outline what happened or why – those memories are personal and painful and there will be many different perspectives on the causes and that is in the past. The purpose is not to apportion blame or point fingers, just to outline the personal emotions and turmoil that I like many other professionals go through in a long career when they hit a sticky patch and that this story of my career would not be complete if I did not allude to it.

Eventually, I went to Police headquarters and requested a move which fortunately was granted before I reached the point of breaking down completely.

That short period of four months was the toughest in my career and reached a peak on the 6th November 1997 where I made an entry in my diary 'Worst Day in Police Service.'

It was the end of an era for me. I was sad but also relieved to leave Redditch in those circumstances.

However, through it all I never once considered for one moment that I should leave the force. That was never ever going to be an option. Nothing would ever make me leave the police service other than retirement and at 44 years of age I was too young for that.

There was little time for formal goodbyes and my public contacts were only made aware that this was a career move. My own officers were supportive and understanding and I retained their confidence for which I was eternally grateful.

I went back to the complaints and discipline department as an Inspector investigator where there was a short term vacancy. I was determined to regain my old confidence and credibility.

What followed was a fascinating further 6 years in the eventide of my career that opened up opportunities and a promotion.

Every cloud has a silver lining..........

CHAPTER 23

NEW BEGINNINGS IN RUBBER HEELING

I left Redditch Police Station with a cardboard box of personal belongings but a mountain of memories on a wintry November Sunday afternoon.

Emotionally, I was on my knees as I metaphorically crawled to my car and looked back at the Grove Street police station building with mixed feelings.

The day after on the Monday morning I reported to the Complaints and Discipline Department at Droitwich. The office was in a leased building opposite a pub and above a public relations marketing office. It was basic in its provision but functional with its own in-built security.

From here we covered the southern area of West Mercia including the whole of Worcestershire and Herefordshire in so far as complaints against the police and internal discipline were concerned.

The gaffer was Superintendent Pete Herbert. Pete was a career detective who had been the Force in-house expert on utilising the Holmes incident system to co-ordinate major crime inquiries. In the twilight of his career he was now in charge of this department. Pete was affable, shrewd, extremely clever with a wise head and enigmatic smile and a charismatic personality that made him the ideal person to lead a department that basically dealt with the Force's alleged dirty laundry.

A number of other colleagues in the unit were old associates of mine whom I had worked with on and off over a number of years. One of those was Phil Purslow. Phil had been my Chief Inspector when I had been based at Redditch in 1991 and a fine fellow he was too. I had great respect for Phil and when I was carrying out Acting Chief Inspector duties at Redditch in 1993 after Phil had left there were many occasions when I would sit at my desk with a difficult situation to deal with and think, how would Phil deal with this? I can tell you that I would count on one hand how many people I could name who I would put into that league.

Phil had eventually ended up in Complaints and Discipline Department as Chief Inspector but had since retired where he was now a civilian case-worker who assisted the Chief Inspectors, Inspectors and Sergeants to investigate cases and pulled together the admin but much more. I quickly learnt that Phil had virtually a photographic memory and an amazing ability to assimilate masses of information. This combined with sharp intelligence and vast knowledge of the department and procedures meant he was an invaluable asset to the department. His only problem was his handwriting. You could leave a tome of a file on his desk to summarise the salient points and précis and within a few hours it would return with a scribbled but illegible note drawing out all the key information except it needed Phil to decipher it! However, the information he provided, his judgement and advice was always spot on. A consummate professional in every sense and a very hard man to follow.

Jeanne was the office manager who had been in the department for years and prided herself on providing first class admin support to the investigators. Jeanne was a lovely person and nothing was ever too much trouble. She headed up the admin department which consisted of Liz and Pauline who had also been there for years and again were always helpful and supportive with fountains of knowledge as to what was expected as well as turning out some excellent typing and files from some pretty scrappy handwritten notes and statements.

Then there was Vicky. Vicky also worked in the admin department and was largely responsible for the case recording and monitoring of records going in and out of the department. Young, vivacious and very attractive, Vicky combined her talents with a wicked sense of humour, a beautiful smile and was an absolute pleasure to work with.

This then was the team I joined after leaving Redditch on my knees. At first the kind words and sincerity of help and support choked me but I quickly regained my old confidence and once again started to enjoy the job, albeit this was a different job and despite the earlier aide-ship I had carried out I knew I had a lot to learn.

When I first went on to the complaints department one of the Chief Inspectors there was Bob Bray. Bob was quiet, unassuming but with a very dry sense of humour. One of the first things he taught me was this. When a complaint against the police comes in from the public it is at its worst. They don't hold back. It is worst case scenario and sometimes even exaggerated even if there is some foundation to it. However, when internal misconduct comes to notice it is at its best. It isn't until you lift up the carpet or open the locker that you realise it's a mountain not a molehill. He was absolutely right.

The other Chief Inspector in the Unit was Dave Hemming. Dave and I knew each other well and had a healthy respect for each other. Again a career detective, Dave was a Black Country lad and had a fantastic sense of humour. He had a huge repertoire of jokes and stories which he would regale us with until we were aching with laughter. Also he was huge fan of West Bromwich Albion and Monday mornings usually consisted of a post mortem on the weekend's football.

Whilst I worked with Dave he achieved a Masters Degree on top of the Bachelor of Arts Honours degree he already possessed. One morning he announced he announced he had passed the Masters after several years of hard work and said he was going to have a plaque put on his office door to read, Dave Hemming, Chief Inspector, MA, BA (Hons.), WBA, SC, BRE. I asked him what the bit meant after BA Hons., and he said with a wicked smile, 'It will read, David Bryn Hemming, Master of Arts, Bachelor of Arts Honour Degree and West Bromwich Albion Supporters Club, Brummie Road End!!

Another piece of advice Bob Bray gave me was this. No matter how good an investigator you were the essential quality required on the department was your interpersonal skills in dealing both with the public making complaints and the police officers who were subject of them. Also, the ability to write comprehensive reports consisting of complex information both for the Crown Prosecution Service and Independent Police Complaints Authority who oversaw all our work.

Every report went via the Deputy Chief Constable and had to be written to a very high standard.

After the pressure of Redditch I was lost for a while but basked under the calm of it all whilst refuelling my batteries.

It wasn't long before I developed a caseload and after shadowing people like Bob and Dave I quickly picked up the on the work and really enjoyed it.

Complaints fall into three different categories. Those that are false and malicious, usually made by criminals who are well-accustomed to using the system for their own ends to deflect from their own actions. Those that are genuinely made but for which there are usually explanations to be made and where officers have acted within their authority but not to the liking of the individuals concerned. Thirdly are those complaints where there may be merit to the complaint made which may or may not be possible to prove.

The complaints will vary from those that are minor about a breach of procedure or unfairness to those which allege serious assault, or accusations that officers have perverted the course of justice or lied on oath.

Sometimes, if the complaint is relatively straightforward and not serious it is possible to deal with it informally by giving an explanation and an apology. However, the more serious and complex the issues are they usually require full investigation which can take several months or years until completed. The system has now changed and complaints are now overseen by the Independent Police Complaints Commission.

Complainants also vary from those who at the one end who will be difficult, vindictive and manipulative to deal with. At the other end are those who are genuine and have been aggrieved and just want to see justice done. Somewhere in between are those who develop a neurosis about an issue usually driven because of personal circumstances which may have started over a neighbour dispute, breakdown in marriage or relationships with a partner, disputes over children or because the Chief Constable has taken away their firearms or shotgun licence. Yes really!

These types of complainant are sometimes using the police to get at another third party and because police have failed to respond to their demands or done as the complainant requested they become obsessive on getting things changed. These types of complainant are highly unlikely to let go of the issue, will take it to its highest level and very often become the most demanding and difficult to deal with taking up a disproportionate amount of time and effort. I believe it is a common phenomenon and a known trait capable of diagnosis. I am not saying all suffer this but I am sure I met my fair share of those complainants who did because they would never let go, sometimes to the detriment of their own health and personal circumstances.

Bob was absolutely right about needing good interpersonal skills combined with a massive amount of patience. As the investigator you have to be impartial and you have to give the complainant the confidence that you will deal with the matter fairly. The same applies to the officers being investigated. They will often be upset and worried over allegations which they see as false and could be detrimental to their career, causing them months of worry or anguish even if they feel they have done nothing wrong. The complaints investigator is stuck squarely in the middle and needs great sensitivity, tact and diplomacy in dealing with difficult and emotional situations around which there is very often considerable legacy. Determining the real agenda is sometimes crucial.

The northern part of the force area in Shropshire and Telford was covered by an office at Bridgnorth with a similar but smaller unit. The Chief Inspector was Bernie McDermott and the Inspector was Jess Shore. They made a formidable team. Both were extremely genuine and personable characters who usually had complainants eating out of their hands, even the type that are not easy to deal with. They would very quickly get to the heart of the matter and resolve a complaint leaving all parties satisfied.

They gave me a number of hints as to how to deal with difficult people and over the next 6 years I was to draw on their advice daily. How to take the heat out of an emotionally charged personal situation was their forte.

Not long after I joined the department I was offered the job of introducing new legislation and national changes to the disciplinary code across the entire force area. Major changes were to take place in procedures which meant designing new processes and forms as well training 2,000 officers from constable to Deputy Chief Constable.

I relished the opportunity which proved to be one of the most satisfying episodes of my career. One of the major challenges was designing training for Superintendents and Chief Officers on chairing and holding a disciplinary tribunal. Historically this had only ever been done by Chief Constables who were now only to be used at the point of appeal along with members of the police authority who also had to be trained. This involved not only training them on the new amendments and codes but also on how to chair and officiate over a hearing dealing with legal and technical decisions including changes of proof from beyond reasonable doubt to one of balance of probabilities.

The aim was to bring what was regarded as archaic police disciplinary regulations more in line with those in other organisations and to make it easier to get rid of bad apples.

I made up a case scenario based on a real case which was regarded as 'cusp' – in other words it could have gone either way depending on how you viewed the evidence from giving officers the benefit of the doubt to sacking them for gross misconduct. The case scenario involved a serious breach of discipline around defrauding an elderly neighbour whilst off duty and bringing the service into disrepute. I wrote a script and later we made it into a video. I worked with David Twigg who was the senior representative for Russell Jones and Walker solicitors who represented officers on behalf of the Police Federation when serious allegations were made against them. We put in a load of procedural anomalies and legal aspects and then used the audience of trainee senior officers to act out the role of being a presiding officer at a hearing so that they could play it for real.

To say it went down a storm was an understatement. Not only did we train our own officers but David and I were called to several other forces across the country to train their senior officers and we received rave reviews. Eventually, we had to start making charges for the training in order to reduce demand and provide recompense for our time.

It took several months but eventually we had trained every officer in the Force and procedures were embedded.

During the interim period we had moved to Police Headquarters at Hindlip Hall near Worcester and I was given a substantive Inspector's position on the department.

Under the new regulations Inspectors were given the powers of Chief Inspectors to act as the main Investigating Officer. We therefore moved to a position where the department reduced to one Chief Inspector and teams were built around Inspectors sergeants and civilian case workers. Eventually, I became the Inspector responsible for Worcestershire and Herefordshire.

During the whole of this time I worked with some fantastic people and far too many to mention, with one exception. I recruited a sergeant called Nick Leith from the traffic department who worked to me for several years as one of the deputy investigators. This story illustrates the loyalty of a man who is typical of many unsung heroes in policing.

Nick was on call one weekend when he called me on the mobile whilst I was in the middle of purchasing a new car. We had an incident running which I was monitoring involving an off-duty senior officer and a non-stop accident.

Nick proceeded to saliently outline the latest situation and together we discussed and arrived at a decision over what to do next. He then told me that his sister had died suddenly from a heart attack and that he needed to go and deal with the family situation but that he would remain on call and ensure he was contactable. I immediately told him he had enough on his plate, that I would take over his on call and for him to go and do whatever was necessary. He was apologetic and took some persuading but eventually agreed to do just that.

This came as no surprise to me. Nick was a truly dedicated professional officer. His integrity and industry was beyond reproach and this story illustrates his total loyalty to a job that he loved doing. I could always depend on Nick for sound judgement and to come up with the goods. There are many who achieve high rank and high plaudits including honours but Nick is typical of many who exemplify these attributes quietly and without asking for anything in return other than for the force to take care of them and their families.

Shortly after I retired from the Police I was astounded and saddened to be rung on a Boxing Day from the then head of the Department Chief Superintendent Julie Harries who told me tragically Nick had died on Christmas Eve whilst preparing for Christmas with his wife and children. It was suspected that he had suffered from a genetic heart condition. Nick was just approaching retirement from the police but was still a relatively young man and about to take up a civilian investigator post in the department.

This hit many of us very hard and our hearts went out to his family. What a terrible and sudden tragedy to happen to such a loyal dedicated officer and family man. I have reflected many times on the work we did, the miles we travelled together and the laughs we shared but most of all on that afternoon when he exemplified for me the very best attributes of love for family and loyalty for job.

During the time I worked in Complaints and Discipline over a period of 6 years I must have carried out or supervised hundreds of investigations. Most of them fade in the memory and some of those that don't relate to people and situations that are best left in the pages of a confidential report where they belong. The vast majority related to routine complaints about excessive force or officers being rude or aggressive whilst carrying out arrests. A lot of the internal misconduct could be avoided if some male officers didn't do what the wife of one officer told me one day. I knew her husband who was a constable in another force quite well and after I inquired about his health she said to me, 'Oh Les, I'm sorry he's got a bit of a hormone problem at the moment.' Naively, I responded in a sympathetic voice, 'Oh dear sorry to hear that, how is it affecting him?'

In a spiteful and resentful tone she spat out, 'He would be OK if he could keep it in his bloody trousers!'

OK, you probably get the picture. Over 30 years I found out that sex is OK but the force does not like paying for the privilege if officers are on duty or when it blows up if it brings the force into disrepute. Scorned partners would very often make numerous complaints about officers' conduct and soured relationships make for vengeful retribution and sorting out the wheat from the chaff can take up a lot of time.

On the other end of the scale we were occasionally dealing with serious allegations made against officers arising from serious crime inquiries such as murder, kidnap or serious assault alleging a variety of misdemeanours carried out by the police.

One of those inquiries I found particularly challenging which required a complete reinvestigation of the original case.

Two men had been convicted of kidnapping and malicious wounding and sentenced to several years in prison.

They had forced their way into a house on a typical council estate and kidnapped a bloke inside who they thought was a police informant. They took him struggling violently into a car nearby and then drove him to an isolated piece of ground on the outskirts of the town where they slashed his throat with a knife and then left him. Fortunately he managed to crawl to a nearby house and summon help.

The original charges had included attempted murder but had been dropped to wounding.

Both men made numerous complaints about the investigation via their solicitors alleging breach of the codes of practice under the Police and Criminal Evidence Act when they were detained in the police station to allegations that officers had planted the victim's blood on their clothes and then lied on oath at their trial committing perjury and perverting the course of justice.

The complaints were numerous as were the officers who had been involved in the case.

It took myself and a colleague several days to just record the statements of complaint from the two men who were both in prison pending an Appeal to the Court of Appeal following conviction at Crown Court.

We seized all of the video tapes when they were in custody and every one of the original exhibits and statements. We read and went through everything with a fine toothcomb.

Both men were well-known to the police but that made no difference. Each complaint has to be looked at on its own merits and the Police Complaints Authority (later replaced by the Independent Police Complaints Commission) maintained a close watching brief over the case.

When we viewed the custody videos and then reviewed some of the logistics about how the victim and then the prisoners had been transported on the night of the incident we were dismayed. It appeared that some officers had made some mistakes in the custody unit and indeed in transporting the victim and offenders in the same car to the point where the prisoners could claim that blood or forensics from clothing could have been transferred.

I decided that the only option was not only to investigate the complaints but also to reinvestigate the entire case around the areas where doubt had been raised due to the impending appeal case. We re-interviewed the vast majority of witnesses including all of the officers and forensic staff involved in the case and the original victim. We had all of the forensic material re-examined by the forensic science service with the hypothesis in mind that the blood specimens on clothing may have been deliberately planted or could have been accidentally transferred.

Following this I drew a complete schedule of events that happened on the night showing timescales and overlap of staff and movements of the prisoners and their personal belongings.

The case took months to review. Every officer over which there was any allegation made was interviewed under caution including members of support staff who had been involved.

Eventually I shut myself away for the best part of one month and wrote a 20,000 word cover report and 1000 page file outlining every significant detail with my conclusions.

The conclusions were that some officers had been responsible for unprofessional conduct and there had been minor breaches of the codes of practice whilst the prisoners were detained. Those matters should result in advice or discipline. However, the independent scientific advice was that there was absolutely no way the blood found on the two prisoners could have been planted or even accidentally transferred due to the nature of the staining and the way it was contained on clothing. There was no evidence to suggest officers had lied on oath or had in any way attempted to pervert the course of justice.

That file went both to the Crown Prosecution Service at Gloucester to review the criminal allegations against staff and then to the Police Complaints Authority who agreed with my conclusions and congratulated us upon the standard of the report and file.

That file then went to the Court of Appeal and the prisoners' solicitors but they remained in custody for the remainder of their sentence. The public do not realise the lengths that the police go to when investigating complaints against the police over serious matters and these days those complaints are scrutinised, supervised or indeed personally investigated by the Independent Police Complaints Commission. No stone is left unturned.

Despite all the rhetoric that is heard about the police investigating themselves, there is no-one who can investigate like the police.

Another example was a series of complaints around the circumstances of a murder. It involved the murder of a man beaten to death in his home with the body then removed to an isolated country area which was linked to another murder which had occurred a year earlier. Both murders were under investigation by West Midlands and West Mercia Police and the circumstances of both murders were brutal with a man charged and in custody.

The family of the victim made a number of complaints about the way in which both cases had been dealt with and over lack of communication and failings by officers.

From the outset it became apparent that the complaints could fall into four categories where firstly, there was no complaint because it was down to process and procedure. Secondly, there may be a justifiable complaint but they were minor issues that required explanation and apology. Thirdly, the scenario may be where further inquiries would be needed to establish whether or not a complaint was justified. Fourthly there may appear to be grounds for a complaint but the extent needed to be determined and indeed the need to establish who may be responsible.

There were a number of aggravating features around the issues which I will not go into but what I needed to do was find a way of dividing out the various stands as above so we could separate out the main issues that needed to be addressed and deal with them immediately. The problem was they were all intertwined and on paper this was proving difficult to disentangle them.

I had just been trained as a facilitator in restorative justice. What's that? Well, restorative justice or RJ as it is known in abbreviated format is a method like mediation that allows for parties to repair harm that may have been done by the process of coming together to hear each other's perspective and where the alleged person at fault is obliged to consider the impact of their actions on the victim and is given the opportunity to make amends. Sometimes this may be done via letters or third parties and sometimes it involves getting together in what is termed an RJ Conference where all interested parties come together in a meeting to discuss the issue.

I decided to use the conference technique and bring together the family of the murder victim who were making the complaints with relevant members of the investigating teams from West Midlands and West Mercia Forces.

We met on a lovely summer's evening at a hotel situated in one of the most beautiful parts of the West Mercia countryside. I chaired the meeting according to a strict protocol and agenda laid down for this type of intervention.

The family very clearly and emotively outlined their concerns. The police then responded point by point, apologising or explaining where necessary or agreeing to undertake further inquiries or actions. At times the meeting was emotionally charged with some forthright views being expressed by the family leaving the police in no doubt as to how they felt and what they expected. However, the police officers present responded delicately, maintaining respect and dignity for the family and never losing their cool.

At times I thought it was going to get out of control and facilitating it so that everyone had measured time to speak was a challenge, so much so that at several points on this warm summer's evening I could feel sweat pouring down my neck and my shirt stuck to my back.

Eventually, after about 3 hours we reached a point where all aspects had at least been discussed and everyone had had their say. Some of the complaints had been answered to the point where either an explanation had been given and accepted or the family felt there was no merit in pursuing it and agreed to disagree.

It was not possible to resolve a small number of complaints and it was agreed that these needed to be looked at again and further work done to bottom them out.

After the meeting we all shared a buffet meal and the family were able to engage in less formal conversation with the investigating officers.

What the meeting achieved was to allow the family dedicated time with senior police officers to express themselves personally and to raise any issues they felt they needed to either complain about or needed answers to.

Eventually we were able to sort out the wheat from the chaff in terms of what we needed to formally look at in respect of complaints and work from that basis. People may not always agree with the other party's point of view but if they have had the opportunity to be heard and express themselves and how they feel then this goes a long way to enabling them to come to terms with matters that quite frankly they may never find answers to.

A more amicable approach to resolving some of the outstanding issues was reached and I think the family at least felt that they had been treated with dignity, albeit that it would never make up completely for the way in which at times they felt unfairly treated and some matters still required further investigation and were beyond the scope of being resolved that evening.

I retired before the matters were finally resolved.

Presenting cases against officers accused of misconduct at disciplinary hearings was another part of the job and not one that I ever relished. Occasionally, you get an officer who has done something so serious and acted in such a way that they do deserve to lose their job and it is a relief to know that when they are sacked they will no longer carry the warrant of a police officer. One example was an officer who whilst off duty had been ejected from a nightclub drunk and then tried to barge his way in again past the bouncers using his warrant card forcing them to call the police. This caused embarrassment to all concerned but fortunately was caught on CCTV. I have never had much time for officers who behave as yobs out of uniform and cause embarrassment for their colleagues and bring the force into disrepute. There are enough problems to deal with without police officers adding to them. I was not sorry when the Assistant Chief Constable sacked him but I have always regretted the fact that people sometimes throw their careers down the drain on a whim.

On another occasion I presented a case relating to an officer who had made some serious errors in both recording evidence in his pocket book and in giving evidence in court together with a colleague. This had resulted in the trial at court being halted and the case thrown out with severe criticism being directed at the officers.

What transpired was that mistakes had been made but this was not a case of deliberate fabrication or false evidence. However, the one officer faced formal discipline for his mistakes and this was the case I had to present with the officer likely to face some serious sanctions.

What I had found out during the investigation was that this officer was extremely hard working and loved getting out doing the job. He was the first one to volunteer and help a colleague on an investigation; he had a high arrest record and never turned work down no matter how busy he was. He was the type who would be the first to rush to the scene of something and get stuck in. The sort of bobby every Sergeant would want on their unit. Unfortunately, he was not so diligent with his paper work and very quickly got buried. That was how the mistakes leading to this came about.

After outlining the facts of the case to the Assistant Chief Constable I then felt I must say something about his industry and why the errors had occurred, largely because this was an officer who always responded and does the job rather than making excuses for why he couldn't do it like some others. The ACC looked taken aback and said that was the first time she had ever heard a presenting officer give credence to an officer accused and because of that she instituted only a minor penalty. Sometimes people need a leg-up and officers who do the job should always be supported alongside making sure the mistakes do not occur again.

I had not entered the department to achieve promotion but it was always hovering. In the year 2000 I had been an Inspector for 10 years, I was a couple of years away from retirement and was somewhat ambivalent about getting another rank. On the one hand it would go towards the pension but on the other hand I did not particularly want to go back out on a division into operational policing for the last couple of years because I enjoyed what I was doing. Fate is a strange thing and was to play a part in making my mind up.

Around this time a new Superintendent came into the department and one who went right back to my roots and schooldays. Roger Griffiths originated from the Bromyard area and we had loosely gone to school together. I say loosely because I went to the secondary modern and Roger (who always was a clever bugger) went to the grammar school. A couple of years before I left they amalgamated into a comprehensive and I used to go to the grammar school for some lessons which is where I first met Roger. Our parents knew each other and we both joined the force and were stationed at Redditch together for the first couple of years.

I had not worked closely with Roger since so it was a pleasure to work with him in the eventide of both of our careers.

Roger had two characters. Extremely intelligent and very shrewd he had been very ambitious and flown up through the ranks having undertaken a variety of roles. Alongside this he was also a pragmatic individual who believed in basic coppering and had no illusions about what the priorities were and believed in leading from the front. He also had some comical traits.

For example, Roger had moved around quite a lot and following a second marriage had settled down to live in Suffolk. He used to commute weekly. When it was time to go, Roger would just decide to get up and go. I would go into his office and there was his pen lying on his blotter in mid sentence of a piece of work, the light still on and lying in the middle of the floor would be a pair of trousers over a pair of formal shoes. Never sure whether Roger had packed up and gone home for the weekend and changed before he left, or just been whisked off the planet I would go and ask in the Admin office as to where he was and when we could expect him back. Usually, they were as mystified as me.

However, they were good days which unfortunately were to end prematurely.

Dave Hemming who was our Chief Inspector was moved sideways into CID. I was offered the chance to do temporary Chief Inspector which was good because this counted towards pension, albeit the difference in pay was not a lot.

After a short period of doing this Roger went on holiday to Tobago and I was left holding the fort. Tragically for Roger whilst relaxing on a lido in the sea he was bitten on the hand by a stonefish. Although he received some initial minor treatment in Tobago by the time he arrived back home his hand had become badly infected necessitating immediate surgery and a partial amputation. This meant Roger was going to be off work for some time.

Instead of backfilling his post the Deputy Chief Constable decided that I would carry out the job of Acting Superintendent on top of my temporary promotion to Chief Inspector. Two roles but in addition I was still holding a number of cases I was investigating from my substantial post of Inspector.

This was unprecedented. I was now acting up two ranks above my own rank – one might have thought that this was because they had confidence in my abilities but mainly I think it was because they could not find anyone to undertake the role and did not want to spend additional money! I realised I could not do everything. Strategically the department was about to undertake a number of new activities and a massive business plan needed to be written. However, we also had to keep the day job moving in investigating a number of sensitive cases and my workload in this respect had doubled overnight.

I went to see the Deputy Chief Constable and told him there was a straight choice to make but I could not undertake both roles to the same standard he expected. He was receptive and told me first and foremost to keep the wheel on and leave some the strategic planning until things had sorted themselves out.

For three months I carried out what was equivalent to two and a half jobs. It was hectic. It meant 12 hour days and intense pressure but in a masochistic way I actually enjoyed it. I felt I had the respect of my peers and the bosses were supportive. I found out that as a department head you had great autonomy and I was allowed to get on with the job.

After three months Jud noticed I was beginning to wane and was concerned about the amount I was working. I felt OK because I think I was just running on adrenalin. I had complete charge of everything and was able to carry out all decisions without much recourse. However, it became plain that Roger was not going to return to work, that he would retire and therefore a new Superintendent would need to be appointed.

That replacement came very quickly afterwards in the shape of Superintendent Julie Harries. I was relieved – it was like the cavalry had arrived. Soon after the Chief Inspector post was filled and I resumed back to my role of Inspector and one job. I could not apply for the Chief Inspector post because I had not qualified via a promotion board which had been held prior to my undertaking the promotions.

Julie was great. Totally professional, extremely sharp and a brilliant strategist she immediately got stuck into reforming the department. Julie and I developed an excellent working relationship. She was serious, straight and demanded excellent standards. If you upset Julie then she would shoot you a death stare that could stop enemy aircraft two miles away.

However, she also had a brilliant sense of humour and at times amongst the seriousness of it with the door closed we would share a laugh until the tears rolled down her cheeks. We went through some tough times and made some tough decisions, sometimes we would disagree but through it all I had the ultimate respect for Julie in carrying out a role I knew was thankless, extremely tough and in which confidences cannot be shared.

Julie carried on with some work I had started in setting up an integrity unit within the department which was to deal with those sensitive internal investigations which require covert inquiries around officers believed to be dishonest but where the information is based purely on intelligence.

We recruited a very able Detective Inspector, Bob Evans who set up the unit which was both complex and took some time both to recruit officers who were strongly vetted and to put in place procedures. There are not many officers who would fall into the category of being corrupt but when they are then special procedures are needed to deal with it. Sometimes there will be nothing to it but sometimes it requires long, detailed and extremely sensitive inquiries in investigating officers who have very good detective ability. Not a popular role and one that is surrounded in mystery must operate purely on a need-to-know basis but nonetheless is essential.

I carried on with the reactive overt work of dealing with complaints and misconduct and when the next promotion boards came along I applied and was selected for promotion to Chief Inspector. Eventually, I was offered a post in the same department now referred to as Professional Standards and that is where I remained until I retired.

I was grateful for the promotion – I carried on acting up in Julie's absence as Superintendent and I worked with some great colleagues. However, I did miss a lot of the direct contact with the public complainers because some were great personalities. The job was mainly reading and vetting massive reports and dealing with all the operational running of the department. During this time some serious inquiries came along which involved colleagues I had worked with over a number of years. They were internally very political and caused us considerable angst involving inquiries by other forces. It is not appropriate here to detail those matters – all I will say is they were difficult and on occasions I found my loyalties very torn. Unfortunately, it went with the territory.

After two years I had reached the point where it really was either retirement or move out of the department back to operations on a division with only a faint prospect of further promotion which I was not sure I wanted anyway.

I did not want to leave the job I had loved for so long but I was also intrigued as to what the future might hold outside of the police where I could retire at 49 years of age and start another career.

I decided to retire and in doing so made one of the most difficult choices of my life.

CHAPTER 24

THE FINAL LAP

I was sitting in a room in a police station on what was one of those beautiful balmy days of summer. The sun was streaming through the window, the room was warm and the walls were littered those familiar notices which contained the latest instructions to officers, photographs of local miscreants believed up to no good and the odd advert for a social event. The table was full of large cups of tea with a tea-urn babbling away on a stained table in the background.

Casco batons, handcuffs and police officers utility belts were spread across the floor and approximately eight officers and members of civilian staff including phone and radio operators and forensic officers were sitting around a large conference table which was completely clear of papers except for my prompt cards.

Some were sitting formally with their arms folded and bolt upright. Others were sitting back relaxed into their seats but all of them were focussing and listening intently to a male police-dog-handler who was describing the search for a dismembered leg in long grass and debris adjacent to the side of a busy main road where the remains of a torso had been recovered.

I was chairing this meeting in order to de-brief the officers after the incident. The dog-handler's attention was focused on me as he said something like, 'Problem I had boss was fearing I was going to find it (he was referring to the leg).' Naively, I said, 'Why was that?' In all seriousness he replied, 'Well if my dog had found the leg then it would have been the biggest juiciest bone he had ever seen and I just didn't fancy a game of tug of war on the side of the road.'

There was a ripple of laughter, the tension was lightened and the images of what could have occurred were played out in every-ones head sat round the table. Macabre? Yes. Black humour? Yes. Inappropriate? No, not in the circumstances I am about to describe.

I was conducting what is known as a critical incident de-brief: a model of debriefing teams of staff to alleviate the later effects of post traumatic stress disorder following a traumatic incident.

I had been trained by a psychologist along with other officers to conduct these debriefings in 1994. The rationale for holding them is perhaps best described in the following example.

A young woman was passing through a chemist's shop in Bromsgrove when she suddenly felt weak, started a wild panic attack and collapsed shaking and crying into a heap on the floor.

Was she frightened by someone, was she unwell, did she normally suffer from panic or anxiety attacks? No, it was none of those things.

It took some time to determine that along with a number of other women, some years before she had been attacked viciously by a man with a knife whilst in the cosmetics section of a department store in a major city.

Whilst walking through the chemists in Bromsgrove years later she had smelled scent which completely unbeknown to her must have been the same scent she had smelled during the previous stabbing incident. Her senses had associated the smell but she herself didn't. All she felt was mad panic and sickness but could not establish why. This was an extreme symptom of post traumatic stress disorder.

The intention of critical incident debriefing is within a short period of time to debrief anyone who have been subject to a traumatic incident in order to stimulate their recollection of the events in intimate detail including what they saw, said, touched, tasted, smelt and heard prior, during and after the incident they were involved in.

This then means that if months or years later they are confronted by the same stimuli they will recognise why it may be having an effect on them and they can understand it, place it in context and deal with it without it making them ill.

Police officers and staff see and deal with some horrendous incidents. We were trained to debrief them as a shift or team and include as many of them who attended or were involved in the incident as possible. This is important because in rebuilding what took place it is like piecing together a jigsaw where those present need to understand not only what they did but what others did. During any crisis incident there will be cock-ups, misunderstanding, miscommunication and sometimes even resentment about what other colleagues did or didn't do. Understanding what others did and why and having knowledge of what others were having to cope with helps everyone come to terms with what took place and to build up a picture. In putting together the facts, recalling the stimuli and then talking through the symptoms of post traumatic stress disorder and how to deal with it plus what help and support was available would usually enable staff to cope much better with any future events than if they had not been debriefed. At least that was the rationale that existed at that time.

Over almost 10 years I conducted dozens of these sessions in accordance with a very tight model that we were given.

These took place after a range of incidents where staff had attended the scenes of murder, child deaths, road collisions, suicides or industrial or domestic accidents in which people had been horrifically injured or killed.

I never failed to be surprised at what staff had to see or had to deal with. This includes not only witnessing terrible scenes but coping with the emotions of dealing with the families and those involved and the overall sadness of it all. This would include not only the officers at the sharp end of the scene but the operators in the control room and the forensic examiners as well as those involved later in supporting families or victims.

In every one of those sessions they would usually start off with some defensiveness. Usually it was a macho culture of not needing this. However, as it progressed and the facts started to be laid out everyone would realise they were there not just for themselves but for everyone else as well. Some may not have needed it but the one common denominator was building the team.

In most sessions there would be elements of the black humour I referred to above. However, this was sometimes a mask or a diversion for other feelings or emotions that would later feature where there would be tears, exasperation and sheer frustration surfacing.

Occasionally, there would be feelings of guilt where officers believed they could or should have done more and had to reconcile their actions.

The rules were that nothing was recorded other than the fact that the debriefing had taken place. What was said in the room remained in the room and was confidential. The only exceptions would be where staff realised that what they had said previously in an evidential statement may be mistaken because of what they had heard in the debriefing meant it now needed correcting via the investigating officer and CPS as per evidential rules.

I found that conducting these sessions was a privilege.

As de-briefers we always explained that they had witnessed exceptional events and did an exceptional job that few other people would ever be able to either experience or endure. If they suffered reactions then this would be a perfectly normal reaction to abnormal events and that they could be helped by further support.

However, the greatest support they usually receive is via their colleagues. By the end of the session there would usually be a feeling of a good job well done in exceptional circumstances and a feeling of pride. Few people outside those who have experienced this first-hand will ever understand what this means.

Fire crews, doctors, nurses, paramedics, yes they all see horrendous things and have to cope with the emotions and stress of it. However, the cop has to deal not only with the scene when it is at its worse but sometimes for weeks and months after they will be in contact with the families and perpetrators of the incident.

They will have to investigate what took place, piece it together and then be accountable at an inquest or court case for their actions at a time when they were dealing with some of the most difficult, traumatic and emotional events anyone will ever have to experience.

To me, the debriefings and the incidents that resulted in them being convened epitomised the very best of what policing was all about and what the public expect. I have seen a lot of things in the police but these were surpassed by some of my colleagues when they described the horrors they had seen and how they had dealt with it in showing compassion but at the same time having to remain clinical, objective and detached with a 'can do' attitude.

Some of that is why I was proud to be a police officer for over 30 years and why it was so difficult to make the decision to leave behind the career I loved so much. Just like leaving a lover when there are still legs left in the relationship but you know you must move on.

I had another career lined up but it took me days to have the courage to put in my resignation – I typed it but kept putting it back in my drawer. Eventually, it came time to submit it and it was one of the hardest things I have ever done. The second hardest was handing in my warrant card and the point where my warrant expired at midnight on a Saturday night.

As I left on the final day one of receptionists called Jill said to me, 'Any regrets Les?' Without hesitation I replied, 'No Jill, not one.' I can't ever imagine having done anything else in life.'

I drove down the long drive from Hindlip Hall, Police headquarters with tears in my eyes and 33 years of memories of incidents, of trauma, of characters, especially the characters imprinted in my mind.

What followed was a disco and party at Hindlip Hall in which Jud and my two daughters Mandy and Caroline were present with their partners.

I acknowledged my thanks to Jud for her love, loyalty and support because this was one marriage, two lives but only ever one way of life in which very often the job had to come first because in my time it was expected.

I was always able to balance the bad times with the good. Unfortunately, Jud did not always see those good times and has less fond memories of policing than I do.

Twelve months later I deeply regretted having left when I did and mourned for the force. It felt like bereavement and I was not prepared for the emotions I would go through or how much I would miss the camaraderie of colleagues and 'the craic.' However, twelve years on I think I am finally cured but 'the job' still fascinates me and yes I probably would do it all again despite the modern challenges and changes to conditions of service, austerity cuts and the politics.

The basic needs of what the public want and what they need has not changed since the first day I went on patrol in the early 1970's. There is some comfort in that.

END

Printed in Great Britain
by Amazon

84052014R00192